√3o7

DATE DUE   JUN 04

DEC 0 9 '04			
GAYLORD			PRINTED IN U.S.A

*f*P

ALSO BY JUDITH LEVINE

Harmful to Minors:
The Perils of Protecting Children from Sex

My Enemy, My Love:
Women, Masculinity, and the Dilemmas of Gender

Do You Remember Me?

―――――∽◦∿―――――

A Father, A Daughter, and
a Search for the Self

JUDITII LEVINE

FREE PRESS
New York · London · Toronto · Sydney

Note: All names have been changed, except those of scholars and writers.

ƒP

FREE PRESS
A Division of Simon & Schuster, Inc.
1230 Avenue of the Americas
New York, NY 10020

For information about special discounts for bulk purchases,
please contact Simon & Schuster Special Sales:
1-800-456-6798 or business@simonandschuster.com

Designed by Dana Sloan

Manufactured in the United States of America

1   3   5   7   9   10   8   6   4   2

Library of Congress Cataloging-in-Publication Data
Levine, Judith.
Do you remember me?: a father, a daughter, and a search for the
self/Judith Levine.
p. cm.
Includes bibliographical references.
1. Levine, Judith, 1952- —Family. 2. Fathers and
daughters—Biography. 3. Alzheimer's disease—Patients—
Family relationships—Case studies. 4. Self, the. I. Title.
HQ755.86 .L48   2004
306.874'2'092—dc22   2004040467
ISBN 0-7432-2230-X

To my parents

Contents

Do You Remember Me?

Prelude

MY UNCLE SHOT THE VIDEOTAPE. Its light is yellow, its sound track an uninflected human rumble. I now see it as a crude anthropological document of one couple's *rite de passage*, hailed and hallowed by family and tribe.

Or, sometimes, I look at it another way. Its light is jaundiced, its sound track a persistent gravelly cough. The tape is a diagnostic scan of my father's health, and my family's.

November 1992

My parents are celebrating their fiftieth wedding anniversary at their Brooklyn Heights apartment. The camera pushes through the crowd like a waiter making his way to the kitchen. Passing without particular interest over this face or that embrace, it slows only once, to survey the collective anniversary gift, a homemade collage. Here, among political slogans and pictures and phrases clipped from magazines, is a snapshot of my brother, James, at ten, with a boxy camera and front teeth too big for his face; me as a distant-eyed teenager; the luscious grandchildren. From the center of the frame smile Stan and Lillian, their tan, handsome middle-aged faces cheek to cheek before an impossibly blue sea. Beneath the picture the collagists have pasted, "The love never goes out of some marriages."

I am at the party with Paul, my boyfriend of about a year, who is being presented for the first time to the *ganseh meshpuchah*, the entire family. We look dowdy—I've got a bad haircut, he's wearing a baggy shirt of a murky shade—as if trying to persuade the assembled seventy-somethings of a coupled domesticity we do not yet feel. James has flown in from California along with his kids, Jessie, a perky eight, and Ben, who at thirteen is trying not too successfully to disguise his shyness as adolescent cool. James leans against a wall cradling a glass of white wine, chatting up the Goldsteins, Millers, Jacobsons, and our parents' other kin-by-choice, keeping a distance from the immediate family.

Mom bustles on slender legs from friend to friend, talking intimately with each. Wearing a harlequin-patchwork vest of purple, yellow, green, and hot pink and a large gold amulet around her neck, with a missing tooth awaiting a new dental bridge, she resembles a good witch casting an animated spell over the room. Noticing the camera, she pulls her lip over the gap in her smile, then lets it creep up again. Vanity is not her habit.

Dad is separately, heartily working the room, spreading his arms in welcome, back-slapping the men, sidling close to the women. With his aviator glasses, woven tie, and sweater vest, bushy mustache and lubricious saunter, he is the 1960s hipster suburbanite shrink of Woody Allen routines and John Updike stories.

Only occasionally is the honored couple seen standing together or even looking at each other. They turn outward, toward their guests, whom they have loved as long as they've loved each other.

These people met in the alcoves of the City College cafeteria, on union picket lines, and at antifascist rallies. They wheeled strollers in the ratty playgrounds (all nicknamed "Piss Park") of New York's left-wing enclaves and bonded through the lost jobs and jail sentences of the McCarthy Era. A few became professional do-gooders; many got rich peddling dishtowels or advertising. And all floated on the benevolent postwar economy, moving to suburban houses with oak-shaded backyards, sending their kids to well-funded, all-white public schools and in the summers to camps where we threw pots and sang "We Shall Overcome." They took the train to Washington to march for civil rights and against the war and the next war, and when they got too old to march against the war after that, they continued to glean their outrage from *The Nation* and send money to the ACLU. Only several, including Mom and Dad, never stopped marching.

Mostly, they talk. Their talk is a perpetual motor of pitch and polemic, of shtick, kibitz, kvell, and kvetch—and laughter.

"How are you, Mike?"

"Oy, with this president?"

"So, Bella, what's happening with Emily?"

"Emmy! She's marvelous! Still living in Minneapolis with her girlfriend, playing the viola. They just started a—Joey, what is it? A bluegrass? A what? *New-grass?* You know, with the banjos . . . Thank god, she still plays Brahms."

I know these conversations by heart. Tribal chants amended year by year, they are always essentially the same.

Amid much noisy stage direction I call the room to order. "To us members of the rapidly aging younger generation . . . and the even younger generation"—I touch the shoulders of Jessie and Ben, flanking me—"Lillian and Stan's enduring marriage is a mind-boggling accomplishment." When everyone laughs at this little dig, I feel a twinge of guilt. "It's also a very inspiring one," I say, as if to cross out the word *mind-boggling.* "It's an inspiring one." The room quiets. I look over at Mom, who is listening as if to a poem. "It's inspiring how they have remained alive to each other, alive to all of you, alive to the world, to the beauty of music and the outdoors. Inspiring how they've continued to work to change the world and, with you all, to keep your community together. So maybe fifty years is a short time." I raise my plastic glass. "Here's to fifty more. The best is yet to be." Warm applause.

I introduce Leo Goldstein, who steps to the front of the room with the authority of universal affection.

"You make the collection speech!" shouts Shirley, veteran of a thousand fund-raisers.

Leo adjusts his glasses and pulls out a small packet of perforated computer paper. "It's not easy to talk about a half century of people's experience," he begins. "But I shall try." Deadpan amid hilarity, he lets the sheaf unfurl until it hits the floor. He and Gloria have had "the extraordinary luck" to have known Stan and Lillian for "the entire span of their marriage," he says, a marriage of "tenderness, caring, commitment, and love, all enveloped in the wrappings of the trials and tribulations of a lifetime." A pause. "And from the inside of this wrapping"—another pause—"comes a querulous call, a kind of leitmotif of this marriage: *Liiihhhll?*"

Sustained laughter as everyone in the room recognizes my father's perennial entreaty for my mother's attention.

Leo continues: "*Sta-aan?*" More guffawing at my mother's collaboration in this folie à deux of need and withholding, distancing and embrace. "When we hear this, we know everything is normal," says Leo. "May we continue to hear it for a long time to come."

Other friends speak of my parents' mutual love and respect, their work in worthy occupations, he as a teacher and school psychologist, she as the administrator of birth control clinics and union programs; their devotion to their friends and to "the movement," to hiking and biking and fixing up one country house after another. They speak of my brother and me, who have turned out (in spite of everything, it is implied) pretty well, and of my brother's children, who have turned out brilliantly.

I take the floor. "And now, Lillian will rebut. You have three minutes."

Mom kisses me and moves to the center of the room. Known in this crowd for riveting speeches delivered from stepladders on Manhattan street corners, she commands respect in inverse proportion to her diminutive stature. Everyone waits as she unfolds her notes, typed on yellow legal paper. "When my first boyfriend left for college, I cried and cried. My mother said, 'Ah, stop crying. He was no good anyway.' She was right. When my mother came to her daughter's wedding to a penniless soldier about to go off to war, she said it again. 'Stop crying. He's no good anyway.' This time, she was wrong."

Mom goes on. "There are many things that keep a long marriage together. Inertia, dependency." A beat. "Total insanity." Laughter. "No doubt, we've got plenty of these. But our relationship has also been held together by some other very powerful forces." The experienced rhetorician enumerates the positives: politics, children, grandchildren, meaningful work, respect for each other's accomplishments, "our mutual delight in moving around on legs and wheels in the great outdoors," music, "and our dear friends—including those who are no longer here with us.

"But there's another thing too. The love and caring that Stan and I have always shared." The room sighs in unison. "The sheer number of toilets outside of which Stan has waited for me are proof of his never-failing caring and support for me in any and all circumstances." Again, laughter. Everyone knows that since adolescence Mom has suffered the chronic diarrhea, constipation, and cramps of Crohn's disease. These days, Mom admits, "we laugh a lot less. Impatience, irritation, and annoyance have crept in," along with the sadness of loss at the death of friends. "But our togetherness makes everything better." *Ah* from the crowd.

"What sums it up for me is this: when I'm at home waiting and the doorbell rings, my first reaction is enormous relief: *He survived the IRT!* (to say nothing of what happens if he's five minutes late). As well, still, and every time, there is that wonderful feeling of joy and delight in seeing his face." She turns to Dad, who is standing close behind her, takes his face in her hands, and kisses him drily on the mouth. Dad is like a big old dog, at once protective and submissive.

Now it is Dad's turn. He begins in medias res, like a stand-up comedian sprinting up the stage steps and grasping the mike on the run. "So I met her in the evening college. I needed four more credits, so I was in evening college. And all of a sudden here was this young woman, and she was president of the ASU"—the American Student Union, the student branch of the Communist Party—"and she entered my life—I was in the evening college—and they made her the president of the ASU. The decision came from way, way, *way* up here." He reaches his arm ceilingward, his voice inflecting simultaneous esteem and scorn for anyone with authority or influence, to whom he always refers as "the powers that be." "So I fell in love with her, and, well, who knows—it really cannot be understood, because these things are not cognitive." His psychologist joke gets a few chuckles. "It's not cognitive, it's really subconscious, and of course it's hormonal too . . . So she got to be the president, and there was a professor, from the far left wing, a great, high-cocked historian, and by the way, later on he worked with the ACLU and—" He goes on. And on.

Shirley Miller shouts, "They're only up to 1929!"

Dad barrels on. "And then he was in the movement, and we were against the war in Vietnam, and they charged us with having an active hatred of our parents—and particularly of our fathers." A meaningful arch of the eyebrow. Is he talking about his father or himself? Never mind. He's got the timing, the inflection, the self-deprecating upward-looking glance, the okay-you're-right-I'm-funny shrug, the loopy logic of a Borscht Belt tummler. If you couldn't hear the words, you'd think he was hilarious. But there are too many loops in the logic, the transitions are disjointed, the jokes odd. "So finally, we did find each other, but there were other people who were chasing after her, and I can't tell you how many because we—" He loses his way, turns up on another path. "So it's this hatred against our fathers. I was in therapy for months and years to try to—months! Years!"

The Goldsteins' grandson Jake pipes, "Okay! We're finished!" Dad takes the audience's uncomfortable laughter as encouragement.

"We knew very little about the sexual life whatsoever. So we had

to get married and all these things we didn't know about—" Cries of
No, no! Don't tell us! "I don't want to go into our marriage" (he probably does) "and as a result of this we had to go downstairs to this old
synagogue, way up in the Bronx." In a Yiddish accent he segues to
their Jewish wedding, a concession to Dad's atheist mother, who at
the news of her son's engagement turned inexplicably, and fleet-
ingly, religious. The handful of guests comprised an insufficient
number of Jewish men to make a *minyan,* so Dad went out to the
street and conscripted a gaggle of beards to serve as witnesses before
the god that no one in the party had had any use for before that
moment. "And I told the rabbi, I said to him, 'Please don't talk too
much. I'll give you two dollars, I'll give you two dollars if you make
it short.' "

From Leo: "Stan, I'll give you two dollars!"

Ten minutes on: "And she's a very extraordinary person and
really a brilliant woman and her competency on every side, as far as
I'm concerned—" The audience visibly relaxes with each pause,
groans with the start of each new sentence. Some are glancing at
one another in perplexity or alarm; a few are visibly pained. Finally,
he seems to be summing up. "We look forward to all of us living
together in the kind of world that all of us would want together."

Desperate applause. "Stan, are you finished? Stan?" calls Hilda.

For those who do not know what is happening to him, the party
is Dad's coming out as a dement. Still, his behavior is only a few
degrees off the already off-center position it has always occupied.
He is as usual verbose, as usual mildly profane. As usual, he is
employing every trick in his bag to please, at the same time sprinting away from the encroaching displeasure of others. As always, he
is both exquisitely attuned to their opinions of him and resolutely
unaware of their desires or needs, since they might desire or need
him to shut up and go away. He dances onstage with the footlights
in his eyes, the music rising from the pit. He listens to the audience,
but can't tell the difference between applause and jeers. Basically,
Dad is being himself.

As his speech devolves to a dither, other conversations grow louder. A smattering of the guests are attempting to remain polite, but their attention turns to embarrassment, embarrassment to compassion, and compassion finally to exasperation. He keeps talking.

Finally, as if to gavel the meeting to adjournment, Mom calls out, "There's coffee and dessert!" As everyone claps and laughs in relief, Dad trails off almost nonchalantly. Forget the middle twenty minutes and his performance seems a perfectly crafted arc. The group moves toward the percolator and pies, pushing the keynote speaker gently out of the way.

After the party, while the caterers maneuver around each other in the narrow kitchen, James and I sit at the table and finish the last of the apple pie. As usual, my brother is barely suppressing his anger at Dad, if not specifically for getting senile, then for everything that preceded it. Senility is just the final straw. Indeed, James's theory seems to be that Dad has managed to mangle his brain cells just to bug his son. Although I concede that Dad might yet deploy his dementia in some nefarious way, I tell James that Dad can't help what's happening to him.

As kids we fought all the time, each vying to win our parents to his or her side. It is only belatedly that we have learned to commune, often by allying ourselves against them. Usually, I'm as dismissive of Dad as James is. But like a court-appointed public defender, I also tend to take the tough case. Now I'm employing the insanity defense. If I can't summon James's sympathy for Dad, at least I can instill reasonable doubt of his guilt. My own sympathy for Dad is still tentative. I have hovered over him today. As the guests started piling curried chicken, rice, and salad onto their heavy black plastic plates, the tape shows me directing and correcting Dad, limiting the amount he takes, herding him to a seat. There is condescension in my gestures, but a measure of tenderness too. If I am embarrassed by him, I also am trying to guard him from embarrassment.

He, on the other hand, is unembarrassed and uninterested in being guarded. He smiles at me sarcastically, then swats me away.

The next month Mom and Dad make an appointment with a psychiatrist to test him for Alzheimer's disease. When the diagnosis comes two years after that, it will hand Dad a sentence: he will lose his self. What he may not know is that he is already losing his wife. Mom now says their fiftieth anniversary marked the beginning of the end of their marriage.

For me, the diagnosis is not about endings. Instead, it is an invitation, maybe a dare—anyway, a deadline. I have spent a lifetime fighting my father. Now as he slips from me, I will try to find him. In the process I will discover something about this multifarious, elusive thing, the self. I will learn that like my father, the self is by nature gregarious. It cannot exist but in relationship. The self's demise cannot be accomplished by a brain disease alone. I will learn that like a father, a self is a hard thing to lose.

1. *Anger*

"I DON'T HAVE ANY MORE," says Dad, his whole body a shrug of resignation.

We are eating supper on a small white round Melamite table shoved into the corner of Mom and Dad's blue and white, barely "eat-in" kitchen. Mom and I occupy two straight-backed white Melamite chairs, a punitive imitation of modernism, on either side of the table. Dad sits between us on an antique pine ladderback, carried in from the living room.

At Walden Pond, Thoreau had three chairs: one for solitude, two for company, three for society. Tonight, here on West Twenty-fourth Street in Manhattan, it's one for loneliness, two for conspiracy, three for exclusion.

The pine chair is Dad's last repair job, monument to his Alzheimer's disease. A few years ago, when he refitted a loose rung in its back, he glued the shaped wood upside down with its garlanded edge drooping toward the floor like a fruited vine. Mom couldn't bear to correct him, he'd wanted so badly to be useful. Now, the chair and its formerly identical twin flank the upright piano. Among the first purchases of their marriage, the chairs are a pair like them: one "normal," straight, sturdy, and modestly festooned, the other a clownish imitation of normalcy, permanently out of whack.

Alone in the kitchen, the chair seems forlorn, though not so much as its occupant. "I have no boat. I don't have any money!" Dad rummages in his shirt pocket. "I don't have."

Mom answers: "You don't need money, dear."

"My boat, do you remember, Jude? I had in that, that—" He waves his arm outward and upward, compassing what I understand to be the coast of Maine. "A beautiful piece, handsome." The land-locked sailor smiles distantly.

"It was handsome," I say.

"But we had, we had to—we had to."

A familiar lament, the lost boat. Twenty-five years ago it was Dad who tired of sailing, biking, and blueberry-picking and insti-gated the sale of the steep-roofed little house on the ocean that Mom and I still mourn like a deceased member of the family. These points are no longer debated. "Maine" has become symbolic, its truth bigger than the details.

That truth resides in every photograph of Dad on the boat, face tilted back to gauge the luff of the sail, pipe in teeth, wind in hair, forearm relaxed on the tiller. The boat was pleasure, status, mastery, masculinity. "No boat," he mutters, pushing rice onto his spoon with his index finger. He glowers at Mom. "You have money." Turns to me with a disgusted sigh. "She's always making money."

"Dad, she doesn't make any money either," I say, insisting futilely on reason. "She's retired, like you."

"You have money!" he snaps at me. I don't reply. He heckles. "Don't you have money? Don't you have money?"

I confess. "Yes, I have money."

A nod of finality—*I rest my case.*

"Not much," I appeal.

He has returned to mashing hacked chicken flesh into the heap of rice soaking in the slick of salad oil he has poured over the whole mess. "She always has money," he says to his plate.

We sit in silence for a long minute.

"You have your things, too," I say, hearing condescension in my voice as I enumerate the items he carries each time he leaves the house. "You have your Metrocard, your senior citizen card, your keys." I leave out the plastic forks, magazine subscription cards, combs, and pencils and pens in a white pocket protector he also totes, a few of which he loses each week. "Everything you need."

"Myuh-myuh-myuh-myuh-myuh-MYA," he mimics the cadence of my sentence and chuckles mordantly. "I need, I need." His hand goes out for yet another chicken breast.

Mom and I lean forward, like two flanks of a defensive army, thwarting him. "Dad, you already—" "Stan, look at—"

With a dangerously large gesture, Dad shoos us both away but forgoes the second helping. Returning to work on his meal, he anchors a half-eaten piece of chicken with a spoon and forefinger and saws at it with an upside-down butter knife. I reach to flip the knife over.

"You!" he barks, pushing my hand away. "I'll!!"

Unfettered, Dad would eat the whole chicken. Assurances that he's already had a meal, as little as ten minutes earlier, are met with skepticism, sometimes outrage. Even hunger, it seems, is a function of memory.

"I am aware that I am no longer able to do the things I used to do," he pronounces after a while, almost calmly. It is 2001 and my father was diagnosed with Alzheimer's six years ago. He is most cogent when expressing his disintegration.

We eat in near silence, Mom and I exchanging a few words while Dad maneuvers chicken on spoon or knife or (once in a while) fork to his mouth, dripping juice onto his chin, which is wrinkled in disgruntlement.

Mom appears to be mentally thumbing through tactics: blandish, distract, ignore, commiserate. Sympathize, as in, *Yes, you are right. You are not what you used to be. That must be hard for you.* This last comes rarely. Sympathy stripped of judgment or advice is not big in our family's repertoire. Perhaps she thinks it will only reaffirm his despair. Or her own. "I can't save him," she has told me more than once, "but I am determined not to go down with him." She feels him like a drowning swimmer with his arms locked round her neck.

Tonight, she chooses commiseration. *Co-miseration:* a few comradely yards' swim alongside him in the drowning pool. "You know, Stanley, you're not the only one," she says. "We're all getting older. Every day. I'm getting older too. None of our friends are what they used to be." She ticks off the casualty list: Ruth's eyes, Sonje's paralyzed left side, Helen's cancer. "We're all losing something. We're all in the same boat."

"*You're* losing?" Dad snorts. Meaning, I infer, *You're not losing your mind.* And to what boat is she referring? Didn't he just point out that he doesn't *have* a goddamn boat.

"I've lost too," Mom says. *I have lost my husband.* A thin shell of anger closes around the pain in her voice. In our battle-ready family, the wounded are wary of resting undefended.

Dad reaches back and perches a water glass on the edge of the cabinet behind him. Mom and I simultaneously lunge at it. Amusement animates his face as he watches the hysterical pair he can so easily provoke. In this moment of disorder, he makes a final point: "I don't have." And then, "I don't want to talk about it anymore."

"Okay," I say.

"I don't want to talk about it anymore!"

"I said okay."

"Okay," says Mom, whether in relief or surrender I cannot tell.

Daddy is too big. I am small. His head is huge, his hair so thick it has muscles of its own. He loves to tickle me, but refuses to stop when my pleasure turns to desperation. He calls me "Little Jood," rhymes with "good." But his voice is loud, as if he were addressing a large audience, not one little girl.

His power is always poised to explode through his large body. Fear robs him of grace; he lugs his temper around like a tank of volatile gas, its incendiary potential seeming to scare him almost as much as it does the rest of us. Our tiny Queens apartment compresses him. We kids are told to be quiet, Dad is in his room with "a splitting headache." I imagine his head breaking in half with a loud crack, like a huge walnut. Once, in a rage, he slams a fist through the wall.

Dad is jubilantly silly. A summer camp director, he dances before all the campers with a fake plastic knife on a headband that look as if it's stabbed through his head. "Hotchky potky!" he shouts with joy, usually in public places and always to his children's mortification. He surges through the waves at Jones Beach with me on his salty-slick back. I feel both secure and unsafe, wondering if he just might (jokingly) flip his passenger off into the bottomless ocean.

He has funny names for things. A fart is a "poopel," and poopels are funny. "Poopel" is also pseudo-Yiddish, because it is related to a gastrointestinal function, and all things gastrointestinal are Jewish. Jewish is funny. Our family adopts a dog from friends. His name is Lox, his sister's name is Bagels. People find this cute. The Jewish things that are funniest are those that are in some way distasteful or painful, or at least inspire ambivalence—organ meats, poopels, mothers. Dad tells James and me the endless, directionless saga of Seymour Lipschitz, a runny-nosed, violin-playing skinny melink from the East Bronx, and Herman Schullenklopper, the strapping, daring diver from railway bridges and stealer of nickel pickles who is Seymour's idol and tormentor. In this more or less autobiographical story, Seymour is (of course) Jewish, Herman is probably German. One of Dad's remaining "jokes," since Alzheimer's, is to call out playfully and plaintively, for no particular reason, "Seymour! Sey-mour!," a "Jewish" name. He laughs, mystifying everyone with his painfully unfunny humor.

As I grow up I learn to joke with, or at, Dad. I become cockier, but I'm still scared of him. When I am nine, shortly after we move to the suburbs, I leave my bike unlocked at school and it is stolen. Fearing punishment, I run away. Two hours later, when I return, Mom is weeping, Dad apoplectic.

"How many times have I told you not to leave the bike?" he bellows. "How many times have I told you to chain it up?" His rage ratchets up and up, he can't seem to stop. *How many times, how many times, how many times!*

I duck past him, run to the bathroom, and lock myself in. He is yelling from the other side of the door. "I TOLD YOU NOT TO LEAVE IT! I'm not buying you another bike!"

"Okay, don't. I'll buy another one with my allowance."

"*How many times have I told you?* You're not getting another bike!"

"I said I'd buy my own."

As usual when Dad and I fight, Mom interjects only occasional pleas for us both to stop. Now, though, she needs to use the bathroom. Her Crohn's is exacerbated by stress. I agree to come out if Dad won't hit me.

"All right, I promise! I *said*, I promise!" he shouts the second time I insist he promise. But when I push the door and peer around it like I've seen the cops do on TV, it is suddenly yanked open. From my left side I see a hand swoop in like the wing of landing bird. It thuds flat and thick from my forehead to my jawbone.

I duck past him and around the corner to my room, where I slam the door and push a chair against it. I lie back on my orange corduroy bedspread, nursing the betrayal, which stings more than the blow. After a while, though, my dizziness and tears subside into a sort of epiphany. Striking me, Dad has displayed not authority but weakness in the face of his own impulses, not control but frustration at the limits of his authority. His palm is huge, but using it makes him puny. My hurt turns to dispassion. My eyes dry.

I address my threadbare Teddy bear: *Do I love Dad?* In my family, this is a legitimate question. Mom and Dad both felt they had been forced to love undeserving parents, and they did not want to burden their own children with what they saw as an emotionally confusing hypocrisy. To them, a child's unconditional love is compulsory love, so it was not required of James and me. For their part, my parents may have loved us, but we did not assume they did.

Do I love Dad? Beary stares in solemn witness, one button eye hanging by a black thread. The answer is no.

When I am a teenager, Dad and I fight over the usual things: chores, my clothes, the music I like, and because it is the sixties, sex and drugs. We make a misery of what ought to be fun. He takes me to the tennis court but instructs me so sternly that I throw the racket to the ground in tears. He takes me sailing, but corrects me so relentlessly that we are not speaking by the time we pick up the mooring. I don't learn either to play tennis or to sail. When I am an adult, I watch him avidly trounce my six-year-old niece, Jessie, at checkers, picking the red disks off the board as a brave tear rolls down her cheek.

It almost seems that we fight *for* fun. We fight about things that concern or interest neither of us, like cars or opera, or arcane subjects, like the temperature inside caves, about which neither of us knows anything. We goad each other, skirmish over politics, even when we agree. For instance, we fight about feminism. I know he supports women's rights; his marriage has been remarkably egalitarian. But I also think he can't stand it that I know more than he does about the subject. This may or may not be because I am a woman.

We know each other through our fights. I believe this means I know him well. Anger limits him; besides depression, it is his chief emotion. This makes him efficiently knowable. At the same time, he is large in his anger, a maestro of anger. He can be artfully angry, sensuously angry, wittily angry, coolly and warmly angry; he even can seem contentedly angry.

I begin to chart our relationship as a series of jagged spikes connected by flat lines: arguments interspersed with absences. I ask myself again and again in different situations whether I love him. The answer is always the same: *No, I do not love my father.*

Toward James, three and a half years my senior, Dad is dismissive at best, violent at worst. If you have to deserve the love you get at the Levines, James keeps coming up short. Dad takes his son to Washington for his thirteenth birthday. At the Lincoln Memorial, he suggests they "race" to read the Gettysburg Address. Although the reading is silent, Dad claims victory. In high school, every report card brings a conflagration. A German tutor is enlisted, whom James resists with aloof humor and persistently low grades. Dad seems to pay no attention to James's competence in all things mechanical, his charm and wit and good looks. He flirts with James's girlfriend, Leila. When she does not respond, he takes another tack. "We were in Jamie's room making out," Leila recalls. "Your father just barged in without knocking. He looked at us, half-dressed on the bed, and he just laughed. This supercilious laugh, as if we were cute."

All Dad's friends tell me he boasted about James and me.

James leaves home at eighteen without a word. Dad is shocked. "He was totally devastated by it. I think he was looking for reasons," says a colleague of Dad's at the school where he worked as a psychologist. "Such a bright man, with so much compassion for and perception of others that he met or counseled. It's a shame he couldn't use any of that for himself and his son." To me, Dad's surprise that his son ran off is evidence of the reason his son ran off.

During this time, James becomes a carpenter. Some years later, Dad and Mom visit him and his wife and first child in Montana. My brother takes my parents to see a house he is building. He does not remember a single positive remark from Dad. But when Dad returns to New York he tells a friend that his son is "the Michelangelo of carpentry."

Home from college at Christmas freshman year, girded by feminism and my first round of psychotherapy, I decide to tell Dad what a terrible father he was. I march into his bedroom, where he is reading. He puts down his book and looks up. I launch into my *J'accuse*. He was self-involved, volatile, unjust, overbearing, cruel to James, and negligent of me. He was not there to protect me; he was hardly there at all. "All you ever did," I tell him with nineteen-year-old certitude, "was criticize." I add that he's an asshole if he doesn't know why James left. I look not at him, but at his mother's Mexican hand-blown cobalt-blue glass jar, my favorite heirloom, spilling dim blue light onto the battered pine dresser.

I expect a fight, so I am thrown off when instead of roaring, he grovels. He did not have a father, he explains, so he didn't know how to father. He pleads for understanding. It is the first and last time I see him in tears. I remain impassive, unforgiving. But when I leave my parents' bedroom, I feel hurt, unheard and—though no voices were raised—fought with.

The next day, Mom comes into my room and sits on the bed. She asks me to go easy on Dad. "He's always been threatened by strong women, like his mother," she says. "And like you." I'm flattered but also disgusted. Why does Mom, a strong woman herself, play Dad's toady?

"He's fifty-two years old. He can grow up already," I mutter. I am like that blue glass jar: fire-made, a container of cold light.

·   ·   ·

"Water?" Mom asks, taking a carafe from the refrigerator and carrying it to the table.

"No thanks." The water is a little beige and tastes a little sweet. Dad sometimes pours undrunk soda back into it.

"I don't want to go there," Dad says. Mom and I look at each other. We surmise he's talking about his "program," the day care for adults with memory loss that is held in a community room of their apartment complex.

"You need to go," Mom replies. "Everyone depends on you. They miss you when you're not there."

It's another old discussion, a script Dad has memorized. He knows Mom's part too: a monologue of affirmation that he can reliably prompt. For Mom, who no longer has the energy to make him feel virile, it's a vehicle of unambiguous praise.

Usually her cheerleading works. And in fact, he likes the program. But lately, her exhortations are less honest, and he seems to know it. For the first few years the staff pretended Dad was the program's consulting psychologist. He attended meetings, took "notes." He even adopted a fractured version of the workplace plaint—too many clients, short funds, disorganized administration, etc. In the apartment, he erected a version of a busy home office on the radiator cover under the south-facing window in their bedroom, collecting, sorting, stacking, and restacking the postcards and circulars, magazines, and envelopes he finds around the house.

But as his dementia advances, his temper and rambling monologues make him unwelcome at the staff meetings; his anxiety about moving from one activity to another turns him from a help to a hindrance in organizing meals or cleanup. The workers have ceased to "consult" him. Superfluous in the last place he felt crucial, Dad is frustrated and angry, and expressing these feelings has only pushed him further to the margin. Without articulate language, he resorts to a more direct means of expression. Once, when the music instructor declines to take one of his suggestions, Dad slugs him.

"I can't go to that now," he says between spoonfuls of chicken-rice porridge. "It's anymore."

"They miss you when you aren't there," Mom repeats.

"You're not me!"

Mom, who has learned to let most things drop, is not dropping this. She reprises the earlier theme of loss. Because of his program, she seems to be telling Dad, he is actually better off than she. She volunteers at a public garden and a pacifist organization, yes. But volunteers are a dime a dozen. She comes and goes at these places; they could live without her, she says. Whereas Dad's daily connection with the people in the group gives him continuity and purpose.

She reminds him of the praise and affection he gets there. "You are really needed," she says. "At this point in our lives, that is a very lucky thing."

Dad's lucky? When his slack face arranges itself into an approximation of understanding, he also looks incredulous. I share the sentiment. I am beginning to feel as I often do in their altercations, exasperated by both of them.

Why is she persevering? Maybe it's nostalgia. This exchange, rare for its length and relative coherence, almost resembles a normal dinner table conversation. Or maybe she has seized this occasion to tell him, with me as witness, how she feels about her life. No longer running a large nonprofit agency, she is bereft of worldly responsibility and recognition, which is now supplanted by the private drudgery of responsibility for home and husband. The fate she escaped, uncommonly, in the prefeminist 1950s and '60s has finally caught up with her. She is needed, but only by Dad. And rather than recognize her for the competence with which she looks after all his needs, he resents her for the competence he's lost. Rather than show gratitude for the minor independence she arranges for him, he blames her for his dependence. Rather than loving her for caring, he hates her for taking care of him.

A lull in food consumption cues Mom to clear the table. It's all the same to Dad, just another arbitrary change of activity, though he has only half finished the vast quantity before him. He gets up to "help," moving the dirty dishes from the table straight to the cupboard. I tensely hold my tongue.

Back in his seat, Dad sets about tidying the environs within his reach. He picks up the spoon, turning and contemplating it, waiting for its message to rise to the shiny surface, wipes the spoon with the paper napkin, folds the napkin into a small square, lays the spoon on the napkin. Then, moving the spoon neatly to the right of the napkin, he fashions a scraper of the tiny paper square and proceeds to steer each crumb on his place mat toward a central pile, transfers the crumbs to a larger pile near the table's edge, and finally negotiates a swift drop of collected crumbs over the side and into his hand, dropping about half onto the floor. Looking around for a place to empty his palm, he shakes the crumbs out beside the mat, then scrapes that pile again into his left hand. Holding the crumbs in his half-cupped hand, he licks the napkin and rubs at each grease spot on the mat. Then he smacks his hands briskly together, scattering the crumbs onto the floor.

Mom, readying dessert, ignores him. When she sits down with a bundt cake and coffee, he grasps her arm, repeats her name, and repeats it again and again—"Lil, Lil, Lil"—until she doles out acknowledgment for his housekeeping, a coin in his palm. His eyes turn to me, asking for more.

But I look away, silent. After just an afternoon and evening with him, I am emptied of affirmation, and what spills into its place is my reflexive resistance to his lifelong demand for it. More than the extra chores he has created, what is irritating me is the unspoken requirement that I collaborate in the charade that he's taking care of everything. It is the same illusion my mother has perpetuated all her married life, and now the day care staff has joined in too. The first time it was farce. Now, it's tragedy.

At the moment, for Mom's sake, it seems easiest to collaborate. "It's true, Dad. You're a leader at your program." That's not saying much, considering the competition, but I am not exactly lying either. Despite the staff's efforts at industry and jollity, the esprit in that cinderblock room is vegetal at best. Dad is the life of the party. When he's not pissed off at someone, he is a singer and dancer, lady's man, and all-around happy camper. I tell him now, "You're definitely the most fun guy in that room."

He looks skeptically from Mom to me and back. Are we ganging up? Although he angles for flattery outside, in this kitchen nothing inflames him more than phony compliments. And more often than not, he wagers that Mom's and my compliments are phony. If he doesn't want to go to his program, why are we insisting? He knows why: because it lets Mom *get rid of him*. He tries expressing this complicated idea. "She's always going," he says to me, his hands fluttering up and out like quails flushed from a forest floor. "There here and there and there and there." Mom and I look at one another—conspiratorially?

"Dad, why can't you hear what Mom and I are saying? People like you in the group. That's all."

His face darkens. "Like me?"

"They like you."

He laughs, the parody of a villain—Boris Badenov. "They like me."

"Yes, the people in your group like you."

A pause, while he regroups. "What are you talking about?"

"You understand," I say. "We're saying people need you."

"What?"

"People need you."

Angrier: "I need you?"

He's a man who can't take yes for an answer, Mom always says. But his refusal is more selective than that. He pulls desperately for yeses most anywhere he can get them, but when one comes from a person close to him, like Mom or me, he can't stop himself from rebuffing it. "Dad," I hiss. "Listen. To. What. We. Are. Saying."

"They need me?" His voice rises, then steadies. "You need me?" Upheaval, his most familiar emotion, seems to stabilize him.

"Mom and I are saying that people like you and need you."

"You need me?"

.   .   .

Our last fair fight, just before Alzheimer's, is about the fact that we fight. It takes place in another blue and white room, this one in upstate New York, a few country houses after the sale of the house in Maine. It is sometime in the 1980s, and we are talking about the Chinese student dissidents, one of whom has been imprisoned. Dad, a barely reconstructed Stalinist, is calling the students "counterrevolutionaries." The Chinese have it a lot better than they had before the Revolution, he says. They have food, they have housing. There is too little to go around in China as it is. Why do they need consumer goods? As for democracy, economic rights must come first. I'm saying that people are willing to sacrifice a lot while a revolution is going on, but once it is won, they expect the goods they were promised. They want democracy. They also want blue jeans.

The argument is fueled by what Freud called the narcissism of small differences. In the big picture, we are on the same side. But we will disagree over the details, and struggle over that last half inch of disputed territory, until one of us is bleeding.

Later, I think, this is a debate about scarcity—about how much a person can expect when resources are few, when everyone feels deprived. In his life, Dad has learned to expect little. Neglected child, adolescent of the Depression, husband whose wife loves him but cannot provide the bottomless affection he longs for, he tries for contentment. Yet his need spills over. I, postwar Baby Boomer, entitled child of peace, plenty, and psychotherapy, want more. Like the young Chinese, my expectations are high, and so are my disappointments.

After about an hour, I yield on one point. Immediately, Dad runs around to the opposite corner, the one I'd just stepped away from, to keep the punches flying. I raise my fists for the next round, then drop them. Suddenly, I am exhausted.

"I can't stand this anymore," I scream, tearful. "You won't even let me agree with you. If all you want to do is argue, I can't talk to you." I add: "I don't want to talk to you. Ever again." And, like a tragic hero in the last act, I fall upon my sword. (Actually, I go upstairs to read.)

When he recounts the event to my brother on the phone a few days later, Dad says, "You know Judy. She wants everybody to agree with her, but she'll never agree with anyone else." Of course, he's right. I am my father's daughter, a girl who won't take yes for an answer.

• • •

Dad cuts the slice of bundt cake Mom has served him in half and half again. He stirs four packets of Nutrasweet into his black coffee, powdering the area around the cup as he tears into the little pink envelopes. "I don't want to talk about it anymore," he says.

"Okay," says Mom. "So we won't talk about it."

"Okay," I say.

"Okay!" says Dad.

He bisects the cake until there is no piece big enough to pick up with a fork and gathers the remnants into his spoon. Then he turns his body fully toward me. "So. What do *you* think?"

I work at gathering the remnants of the subject, if there was one, back into cogency. Dad may no longer be a master of repartee, but now that he's demented he's gotten good at driving other people out of their minds. "Ye-es," he prompts. "Go on . . ."

"You're right," I say, coolly. "You aren't what you used to be."

It takes him a minute. That comment was way too long ago for him to remember. "THAT's what you think!?"

"Dad, I'm agreeing with you."

He chuckles sarcastically. I go back to my cake. He waits, alert. "Ye-es?"

"What I think," I say finally, "is that you *do* want to talk about it." For my nimbleness in debate, I credit a lifetime of paternal tutelage.

Cornered, he strikes. "Do you need me?"

I pause, unwilling to reassure him. "You're my father—"

"Do you need me?"

"Well, I can take care of myself, if that's what you mean."

"You're not me! You don't know me!" He spits cake crumbs.

I parry. "Well, I know you better than I did as a child. I mean, we spend much more time together now than we did then."

"You did that," he grumbles.

"Oh," I retort, constructing an argument far more logical than the one he's flailing around in. "It was my fault you were never there." My sarcastic chuckle is almost identical to his.

Dad is drifting. Rage is his only raft.

"Judy, don't—" says Mom quietly.

"We spend an afternoon almost every week together," I say. Then I taint goodwill with ill: "I can't remember ever spending an afternoon with you in my childhood." Feeling slightly guilty, I cast around for an antidote. "And—" I hesitate, unwilling to say our time together feels good, "and I think we're closer than we were."

He slams his big hands flat on the table, flipping his fork onto the floor and rattling the cake plates. He rises from the table. "I don't need you!"

The kitchen shrinks. Dad fills one end with his fulminating, Mom clutters the other, tossing little scraps of diplomacy: "Jude, he's just trying to—" "Stan, take it easy. Judy doesn't mean—"

I stand in my tight corner, shoulder Dad out of my way, clump through the door into the living room, and wildly start to collect my jacket and bag. "Okay, Dad," I shout back toward the kitchen. "Have it your way. Nobody needs you. You don't need anybody."

But he is hard behind me. I feel his heat and noise like a furnace opening at my back. He muscles around to face me, forces his face into mine, close enough to kiss. Fierce gibberish and spittle hit my cheek. "You *need* me?" That old grimace of sarcasm, now twisted crazy.

"All right," I shout. "Fuck you! People hate you. That what you want to hear?"

We are inches from each other's bodies, our torsos leaning in, then pulling away, hands drawing backward, afraid of striking—a boxing video run in reverse. "DON'T MAKE ME STUPID!" he shouts.

He grabs at my bag and jacket—to harass me or hold me? We are almost equal in size now, he stooped and shrunken, I tall in my heeled sandals. *Now we're close,* I think. *Now we are connecting. This is what we need each other for.* I am shaking, but not crying. My eyes follow the creases beside his mouth down to the wattles of his neck. A perverse energy shivers through me. When Jane Eyre's beloved, the mesmerizingly potent Mr. Rochester, is blinded, "his power dropped and my Soul grew straight," she says. I am stronger and nimbler than my father. My hands could easily collar that neck. *I could hurt him.*

I push past him, slam the front door behind me, and make for the stairwell, my shoes clapping like sparse applause—for what?—on the six flights' descent. In the subway to Brooklyn I scribble what I can remember on a pad of tiny yellow Post-its. The pages flutter into my straw bag, sticking to each other and everything else. They are the beginnings of the book I hope will help me know my father. But knowing him may be no easier than fighting with him

When I reach home, I can barely lift my legs up the three flights of stairs to my apartment. I peel the Post-its from my bag and spread them on my desk, quickly typing some sequence of the events at Mom and Dad's apartment into the journal in my computer. My reconstruction is probably more logical than reality. I often do this with Dad's sentences too: in retrospect I rearrange the syntax, insert missing subjects, verbs, and transitions. It's almost involuntary, the same way retelling a dream constructs a narrative of scattered images and feelings.

I call Mom, worried that Dad's rage might have spilled onto her. She says no; he turned contrite the instant I left. "I'm all alone. You're the only one I have," he told her. "I love you," he said, followed by his twin declaration, "I need you." This she recounts with weary dread in her voice. She tells me, "When you were kids, I used to ask myself, in the midst of the screaming and crying and hitting, 'How can I stay with a man who cares so little about his children?' "

"So how could you?" I ask. As I teenager, when I had absolute opinions about what was acceptable in a relationship (that is, before I'd actually been in one), I used to exhort her to leave him. Now her tone changes. She talks about how supportive he was of her work, how patient with her illness, how funny. She doesn't mention my outburst this evening. But I know that my temper, my messing with Dad's emotions, has only left her more to clean up. She says Dad floated to lucidity, as often happens. "He looked at me that way, with his same old plaintiveness," Mom says, "and he asked me, 'What did I do to my children?' " The funny part, she says, is that he always wanted more children, four or five. "He loved fatherhood."

I hang up the phone, flip through my mail, wash the dishes in the sink. I'm happy to be in my own lemon-lime-colored kitchen with its shelves of bright, mismatched fifties dishes and a clutch of apricot-colored tulips wilting in a vase on the table. It's late, but I call Paul, who lives in Vermont. He answers groggily but is happy to talk. We chat about the tax sale of his neighbor's property, about the emu chicks at the organic farm further down the hill. We arrange Paul's next trip to New York, the exchange of cars and cat. Paul's house is in Vermont, my apartment is in Brooklyn, we both have offices and phones in each other's houses. I live in Vermont in the summer; during the year we go back and forth, sometimes together, sometimes apart. Usually the logistics of our peripatetic relationship irritate, but tonight they seem simple; they center me. As always I ask how our cat, Julius, is. "He's fine," answers Paul cheerfully, as always.

"I had a huge fight with my father tonight," I say after a while.

"How'd you manage that?" Paul asks, laughing gently.

"He's still . . . himself. You know."

"And you're yourself."

"Yeah," I say, feeling sheepish. "I'm myself." We're both silent for a minute. "Well," I say, "I've gotta figure out a better way to deal with it."

Paul laughs again, patient with the obvious. "That would be a good idea, Judith."

2. *Mind*

OUR FIGHT IS NOT in spite of Dad's deterioration. In some ways, it's because of it. For when Dad starts shedding rationality, it not only roils my anger, it triggers my contempt. Yes, my contempt.

Being smart is important in our family. Intellectual ability trumps emotional or practical skill, critical acuity rates above tolerance, which is considered a little soft-headed. When I am small, there's one forbidden epithet in our household: *stupid*.

. . .

I am about nine, walking with my mother on Lexington Avenue on my way to music school. All at once we are surrounded by a group of mentally "retarded" (as they were then called) children with their teachers. They are holding hands in twos and threes, chattering, laughing, shoving, shouting—enjoying themselves like any kids on a field trip. A feeling of faint nausea, fear mixed with pity, wells from my gut to my chest.

Mom takes my hand. I can feel her shudder too. "I've always felt I could deal with a physically handicapped child," she tells me when we're out of the children's earshot, "but I don't think I could stand it if my child were mentally handicapped."

I put this comment away for further consideration. I am far from mentally handicapped. But what if something were to happen to me and I became "retarded"? Would she be able to stand me? Though this prospect worries me, I never question that having a child or sibling "like that" would be too sad to bear. In school, I am polite to the "slow" children in the class. I never tease them, I defend them from teasing. But I do not befriend them. This would be inconceivable.

I am fourteen, arguing with Dad at the dinner table. I'm outmaneuvering him; he's stumbling. It strikes me that while he knows more than I do because he's older, I may be smarter than he. Momentary triumph turns to anxiety. I feel unmoored, unfathered. As I get older, I hold my "superior" intelligence over him. It's an excuse to dismiss his authority, his opinions, and his feelings.

When Mom is miffed by a political attitude or behavior—that working people support tax cuts for the rich or vote for Ronald Reagan—her bottom-line analysis is "People are stupid." It's a joke, sort of.

I am in my thirties and a therapist asks me what I feel. I explain, I analyze. "That's a thought, not a feeling," she says. I scoff. Thoughts are far more trustworthy than feelings.

Does this reverence for the rational make my family extraordinarily cold-blooded?

Hardly. It makes us typical. We are people of our milieu and our time, modern secular intellectual Jews. But we value, and dread, what our whole culture does. Western history makes rational thought inextricable from morality. America prizes the individual above all else. So moral autonomy, arrived at through rational thinking, is the requisite of personhood, and only one kind of person—the rational, autonomous kind—merits full moral and legal consideration. It is no wonder, then, that we call dementia a disease (a disease is a condition that arouses our dis-ease) and no wonder, says the ethicist and gerontologist Stephen G. Post, that we loathe and fear dementia.

"Nothing is as fearful as Alzheimer's disease," he writes, "because it violates the spirit (*geist*) of self-control, independence, economic productivity, and cognitive enhancement that defines our dominant image of human fulfillment." Post, who is a professor of biomedical ethics at Case Western Reserve University and serves on the Alzheimer's Association's national ethics advisory board, calls ours a "hypercognitive society."

In the hypercognitive society, we consider dementia not just a disease, but a living death. "It's like being chained to a corpse," some caregiver once said about living with a person with Alzheimer's, "an endless funeral," said another, and the phrases are repeated like mantras in the support groups and chat rooms. In fact, so much like death do we imagine the loss of memory that we have come to consider death preferable to it. A *New York Times* story about elders' attitudes toward dementia is headlined "More Than Death, Fearing a Muddled Mind."

.   .   .

The first person Dad tells about forgetting is his physician. It is 1987, five years before his meandering speech at the anniversary party, and he is sixty-eight. "Pt can't think of words as well," the doctor records in the notes of a routine office visit. It "took 20 mins" to recall the word *avuncular,* though he "knows all the synonyms." The doctor writes these things down in longhand, with a fountain pen.

I'm not sure when my mother notices. Alzheimer's has an "insidious onset," meaning you're not sure if or when it is starting. Also, they say, Alzheimer's sufferers are good at dissembling, and Dad has always been a master at hiding weakness. He suffered months, maybe years, of pain silently, then one spring evening in 1980 excused himself from a dinner party at home, strolled to the bathroom, and vomited and defecated large portions of his ulcerated stomach onto the toilet, sink, tub, floor, and walls.

When his forgetting began, maybe he thought he could outsmart us, or it. After all, a man who knows all the synonyms can easily get by without *avuncular*.

If Dad is confessing to his doctor that he's worried about his memory, he must be really scared. The doctor registers no alarm. His assessment, on paper at least, is conservative: "One friend noted a slurring of speech," he writes, recording Dad's report to him. "Could be affected by his [dental] bridges. Also ? confusion—could be hearing," the doctor hypothesizes. "No assoc. neural symptoms." The next line reads: "Eating lots of fish."

By January 1993, Dad, always melancholic, is increasingly depressed about his flagging memory. His physician refers him to a psychiatrist at Columbia-Presbyterian hospital, who writes back to the physician that "the picture is probably not of a 'pseudodementia' secondary to primary depression, but looks to me more compatible with primary depression. I gather from him that you and he have discussed the likelihood that this is early Alzheimer's Disease." The psychiatrist prescribes Zoloft for the depression and suggests Dad consult the specialists at the New York State Psychiatric Institute's Memory Disorders Clinic. His letter says Dad is "interested" in doing this.

At the clinic two months later, Dad submits to the "brief mental status testing," a battery of memory and language tests. The evaluating psychiatrist writes in his records, "I feel he probably is demented and that his high scores reflect his pre-morbid function." In his office, he translates this to Dad and Mom: "The smarter you are, the more you have to lose." I wonder which part of this double message Dad hears loudest—the abundance of his personal resources or the depths of his potential loss.

Dad is offered a more complete medical workup to arrive at a diagnosis and begin "treatment." He and Mom discuss this option. Alzheimer's cannot be positively diagnosed, and there is no treatment for the disease (the first drug, tacrine, or Cognex, for retarding the symptoms but not halting the disease, will not be available until two years later, and it will show results that are disappointing at best). Dad sends a copy of the psychiatrist's evaluation to his physician, along with a handwritten note: "So yes, no, at now I just want to be left alone in re above. Lillian and I are involved moving to West Side Manhattan. Incredible what we have collected over the years."

Nevertheless, in the spring of that year, he returns to Columbia for an MRI. Looking back, I imagine he is more eager to know than Mom is. He may believe knowledge will give him, if not power, a measure of control. For Mom, however, knowledge may offer only confirmation of her lack of control. For years, she resists joining a caregivers' support group, telling me she doesn't want advance notice of "the horrors" ahead. In fact, the testing seems only to exacerbate Dad's malaise. Just two weeks after the scan, he writes to the clinic, "Since then I have heard nothing at all about your findings. I have called frequently with no responses, or have been informed that no one was available to speak with me. I would appreciate hearing from you at your earliest convenience." The MRI reveals some minor changes in the brain but is inconclusive. The radiologist prescribes further tests, but Dad, in consultation with Mom, decides to stop there.

Around this time, he begins treatment for hypertension and high cholesterol, which are, incidentally, contributing factors to dementia. He also starts taking a huge vitamin E pill each day because preliminary research suggests that the vitamin may slow memory loss. Anyway, he and Mom reason, it can't hurt.

In 1995, Mom, Dad, and I sit in a conference room overlooking the East River at the New York University School of Medicine's Aging & Dementia Research Center. Dad has undergone all the tests for Alzheimer's. If he has it, which everyone now considers a sure thing, he can become a subject in the center's longitudinal studies, which will make him eligible for some clinical trials of new drugs at other institutions as well. Dad is eager; he wants to do "everything possible." Through NYU, he and Mom will also receive a range of services—social workers, groups, referrals. Mom the administrator welcomes these tools for living competently with chaos.

We wait in large executive swivel chairs, all on one side of the table. The doctor opens the door, stands briefly before us, and introduces himself, like an actor stepping onstage. He is a psychiatrist, or maybe a neurologist, younger than I, pleasant and straightforward. He closes the door, sits at the head of the table, and proceeds through the results of each test he has given Dad. A number of measures indicate progressive dementia, though a true diagnosis cannot be made unless "the brain is autopsied," he says. It occurs to me that such a procedure might be hazardous to Dad's health.

The doctor tells us that Dad has expressed worry about "word retrieval." Mom and I are not surprised. Like most Alzheimer's sufferers, Dad has been having difficulty remembering names and localities—Jimmy Carter, Lillian Gish, Florida, Vietnam. His wide, ostentatious vocabulary is diminishing. Every month or so, he seizes on two or three words that he shoehorns into whatever sentence will approximately accommodate them. *World* becomes a surrogate for all manner of place—*New York, garden, body.* "Your mother is out, working hard, as you know she always does," he says one afternoon on the phone, "up there in the . . . the world." Is she at the Conservatory Garden, her peace group, her piano lesson? After an angioplasty, he points to his groin and tells me the doctors put the tube in through "this part of the world." Just as *world* can mean body, *body* can stand in for its constituent parts. Mom swallows a false tooth. "It fell into her body," Dad tells Paul. His mind continues to arrange word categories, but their contents are interchangeable. He enters the kitchen, where a cake is in the oven. "Mmmm," he exclaims. "Sounds good in here."

Going through his medical records I find a letter he wrote to his physician that year regarding his diet, which they were monitoring to bring his hypertension under control. Dad's prose is as florid as always, but balky with gaps.

Dear Art,
Forgive me for not giving you my recent "Our Foods of the

Days." So then here they are. I do make effort to avoid "Fish," but I dare say it is there in the body of the fish et cet et al. To add this (in writing): Salt Substitute called "No Salt," added: Use it just like salt on all your favorite foods. Ingredients are enormous: potassium chloride; cream of tartar, flavor derived from food yeast; less than 5 mg of sodium per each 1 gram serving—an insignificant amount.

Enough I do hope! In large the substitute is sodium free.

So then let us continue to enjoy. After the Potassium is done I'll return free of a bit (or more) high blood pressure.

As always I do appreciate your concern.

Stanley

Does this letter come fluently or does Dad struggle to write it? The doctor's note, stapled to Dad's letter, tells a mixed story. "Feels well, still giving literacy lessons—playing clarinet.

"Discussed deteriorating memory—no fugue. Does all shopping—gets around well, fearful of future."

·   ·   ·

Reading Stephen Post, I am at first taken aback. *Hyper*cognitive? I've always been offended by people who say "you think too much." It smacks of anti-intellectualism, especially in a country where a lot of people, including those in high places, think too little. While my family's fiercely rational critical stance unsettled me, it also gave me the gumption to argue the world. When I brought home my history books from elementary school, Dad, a former history teacher, incited me to spit out the white-sugar version of America's past I was being fed. He and Mom told me about miners' strikes and lunch-counter sit-ins and the other side of the Cold War; they encouraged me even to challenge my teachers with those then-traitorous revisions. When I discussed the idea of writing this book with Mom, she did not balk. She'd championed my creative and intellectual pursuits since I was a child and was not going to stop now. Books and the liberty to write them are sacrosanct to her, as they were to Dad.

At the same time, maybe it didn't occur to her that the process could be hard for her, emotionally, as it would be for me. Maybe she fantasized it would bring us closer; later she said she'd hoped we would have lunch more often. It is conceivable Mom figured she could support, or endure, my project only by not thinking about it too much; she'd often told me, only half in jest, that denial is an excellent strategy for getting through tough times. I think this means denial not of the facts, but of the feelings about those facts. For years my mother reported on my father's deterioration, but rarely on her own desolation. I colluded in this denial. Intellectually fearless and emotionally timid, I listened to the reports and rarely asked how she was feeling.

You might call us Levines hyper-hypercognitive. As intellectuals we're as typical in America as a cockatiel among the robins in our old Long Island backyard. But, as Post suggests, you don't have to be an egghead to revere reason and tremble at its loss. Our fear of cognitive decline is old and deep, and it reveals more than what we care about in a person. It tells us what we think a person is.

Cogito ergo sum: René Descartes' pronouncement in 1637, in his *Discourse on the Method of Rightly Conducting the Reason and Seeking Truth in the Field of Science,* may be the most influential utterance in all of Western philosophy. Although the idea of reason as God's exclusive gift to humans is at least as old as Judaism, Descartes, a Christian, described systematically *how* divinity lived in the body. The soul, in the *Discourse,* did not require a human body to house it. Although it took up temporary residence, as mind, in the nutlike "pineal gland" at the center of the brain, the soul was transcendent. Considering one of the big philosophical questions of his time—can we assume that what we experience is real?—Descartes contended that the body could not be counted on to apprehend reality:

"Neither our imagination nor our senses could ever assure us of anything if our understanding did not intervene." As it exalted the mind, the *Discourse* demoted the body. And as the body became increasingly a mere "thing," the intellectual historian Ed Cohen suggests, the Western self became a mind, a thinker. Even anti-intellectuals conceive of their subjectivity as William James described it: "We think ourselves as thinkers."

Just like the divinity of reason, the separation of transcendent mind from physical body was an old idea: mind-body dualism can be traced to the Greeks. But as the quintessential Enlightenment document, a "scientific" proof of the existence of God, the *Discourse* would have unprecedented staying power. If Descartes' aim, in a sense, was to make faith superfluous, he bequeathed us godless moderns a faith as firm as an apostle's: *I think, therefore I am* . . . a person.

Today it would seem that Americans are in full-swing backlash against Cartesianism. Flocking to Eastern, Native American, and New Age philosophies, the new seekers value "intuition" above intellection, faith above skepticism; they speak of the "wisdom" of the heart and the body. Embodying a yearning for emotions even in creatures of "pure" intelligence, our fictional human machines from Frankenstein to R2D2 are as sensitive as we are, or more so; at the Massachusetts Institute of Technology, computer scientist Cynthia Breazeal is building robots that are covered in "skin," express "feelings" with their eyes and faces, and shrug their shoulders. In biology, a counter-Cartesian few, most notably the neurologist Antonio Damasio, locate a kind of "thinking" in the body. Also among this group is Columbia University cell biologist Michael D. Gershon, who refers to the enteric nervous system of the stomach as the "second brain."

But Damasio, Gershon, and the American devotees of the Dalai Lama are still in the minority when it comes to the values we assign various parts of the body. "The human body as a hierarchical system is a conceit of Late Antiquity, if not older," writes the art historian Leo Steinberg, and from earliest Christian theology the head of Jesus has symbolized his divinity, the feet his humanity. So, on the ever-raging mind-body question, the strongest tendency, almost a reflexive one, still is to regard the brain and especially its cerebral cortex as site of the "highest" function—mind—and everything going on south of the chin as the "lower" ones. We think of the skeleton and viscera supporting the brain like slaves bearing a monarch on a sedan, lifting the mind toward celestial pure reason, away from the base and bestial instincts and appetites.

As metaphors for humanity, Breazeal's robots are as backward-looking as their names, Kismet and Leonardo. The mind in a box, clean of "lower" functions altogether, is the twenty-first century's image of consciousness, and this age has inaugurated a discipline to serve it. "Cognitive science," a meeting of neurology, computer science, philosophy, and psychology, argues that human intelligence is not qualitatively different from the artificial intelligence of software; we are little more than fleshly computers, albeit highly complex ones.

The thinking-machine theory of humanity is, on one hand, anti-Cartesian: its mind is *nothing but* the brain, nothing if not embodied. On the other, its values—that what counts about us are the impulses traveling across our synapses—are Cartesian through and through. For this reason, cognitive science and the popular excitement its theories stir scare some who care for people whose synapses aren't what they used to be. The recently deceased British psychologist Tom Kitwood, a leader in rethinking dementia and its care, wondered if the views of cognitive science might make "redundant" most of the elements of a widely accepted definition of personhood as a complex of consciousness, rationality, agency, morality, and relationship. He was sure that they render the demented—whose personhood resides in their feelings, their physical bodies, and their relationships—redundant. *I think, therefore I am.* Therefore, if I do not think, I am not, or maybe I do not deserve to be.

. . .

"Mr. Levine, do you know the name of the president?" The soft-spoken Swiss psychiatrist at NYU is testing Dad's memory. They sit on chairs in a small room, practically knee to knee, and I sit beside them.

Dad laughs, as if to dismiss a silly question. At the beginning of Alzheimer's he used to get this one right. Now, ten years later, it's unclear he knows what a president is.

"Thank you, Mr. Levine. And do you know my name?"

Another trivial question. Dad tries to engage the doctor in more interesting conversation. "And we are there," he comments, looking thoughtful.

The courtly doctor waits, listens politely, then writes something in Dad's file. He hands Dad a pen. "And what do you call this?"

Dad manipulates the object into a writing position, then looks around for something to write on. But he doesn't name it. "It's there," he says.

"All right, very good." The doctor takes back the pen and places it with a number of other items—a paper clip, a small pad of Post-its, a rubber mallet—on his file folder cover, which he holds on his knees. "Which is the pen?" Dad picks up the pen. The psychiatrist notes, "So you know what the thing does, but you can't recall its name." He turns to me and tells me what kind of recall this is, but I promptly forget it.

Dad is uncomfortable. He seems to sense he is not doing well. Again, he changes the subject, rambles a bit. The doctor returns gently to the questions at hand. The chat does not seem to have won Dad any extra credit.

Dad is taking a version of the Mental Status Exam widely administered to the demented. Among the results that indicate either temporary or long-term memory loss are:

> *Doesn't know age*
> *Doesn't know President*

Doesn't know how long at address
Doesn't know rater's name.

This test gauges not only memory, but memory expressed in words, and the words and ideas being tested have powerful symbolic resonance. It's rare to read a popular account of a person in cognitive decline that does not mention, as a tragic detail, the fact that he has forgotten the name of the president. But there are critics of the president question and more generally of the tests, not only their efficacy but the assumptions and values written into them.

Why should someone living in a nursing home without access to a newspaper remember the name of the chief of state? And why should he remember the rater's name at all? "Our own experience tells us that we remember what we deem important to us; we recall on a need-to-know basis and we filter out what we consider to be of secondary or lesser personal significance," write Nancy Harding and Colin Palfrey in their provocative book, *The Social Construction of Dementia: Confused Professionals?* A friend tells me that talk show hosts go out in the audience and ask people the name of the vice president, and "a *lot* don't know it!"

Dad's mind is no fine filter. What gets through and what's left behind may have only a little to do with what he needs to know. But, Harding and Palfrey contend, the needed information and the words to express it are more likely to find their way through the mangled mesh in a congenial context. Language is an instrument of relationship, after all, and as everyone who has ever had a stimulating conversation knows, it is enhanced by relationship. So is memory. "Do you remember me?" Dad often asks someone he doesn't remember. The other person usually gets the hint and introduces him- or herself, renewing a word (a name), a memory, and a personal connection.

One afternoon when I pick Dad up from his program, Dahlia, a social worker, shows me a mural she and he are working on, a long swath of butcher paper covered with densely crayoned areas outlined in felt-tipped marker. She describes his concentration and pleasure during the project. "He sings, he laughs. He sweeps the marker wide, like this. And he talks. It seems a little easier when we're involved in art," she says to me. Dad grins as I praise his work. Dahlia turns to him. "Right, Stanley? The words come easier, don't they?"

"It couldn't be better!" he says, his customary phrase of conviviality.

Many psychologists concur that it is harder to elicit such positive results from a test administered in a lab by an unfamiliar tester—a context that is no context, a relationship that is no relationship.

But the context is bigger than just this room or that one, and the tests tell us as much about the tester—us, generally speaking—as they do about the subject answering the questions. The values assigned to particular kinds of intelligence are culturally specific and even subject to fashion. In the United States, the ability to cipher mentally, once considered an essential marker of smartness, has been rendered virtually obsolete by the calculator. Still, the unbalanced checkbook is a flag of distress in every account of mental decline. Perhaps this is because the literal "net worth" of a person can be read in its bottom line. We see among the scattered digits the self, dwindling in value as it wanders in dementia. Meanwhile, in China, the anthropologist Charlotte Ikels found, "the prospect of dementia [does not] cause much alarm to either the elderly or their family members." Why? "The essence of [Chinese] personhood" is not demonstrated by rational thinking; it shows itself in moral rightness, the ability to conduct oneself in a proper way. So as long as a senile person behaves more or less appropriately, she is not thought of as troubled or troubling. Besides, the majority of the Chinese elderly, especially women, have little or no formal education. They aren't expected to know the name of the president, much less balance a checkbook.

Of course, words aren't digits. In the beginning was the Word, and while the value of other faculties may wax and wane, the word shines constant. And not just the word, but the word arriving sensibly after the word before it and before the word after it. "Language's written or spoken articulation . . . becomes an externalization of an ordered and well-balanced mind, and those who express themselves in a 'strange' manner in the context of day-to-day living are candidates for the category of 'diseased/deranged,' " assert Harding and Palfrey. "The whole edifice . . . of social normality is founded upon the cultural imperialism of rational language."

More than social normality comes with language; personhood does. Perhaps the classic narrator of the journey from word to reason and thence to humanity is Helen Keller. Having lost her sight and hearing at the age of eighteen months, she did not acquire language until she was six. For her, the Word was Genesis. Everything before that was prehistory.

"Before my teacher came to me, I did not know that I am," begins Keller's 1904 autobiography, *The World I Live In*.

> I lived in a world that was a no-world. I did not know that I knew aught, or that I lived or acted or desired. I had neither will nor intellect. I was carried along to objects and acts by a certain blind natural impetus. I had a mind which caused me to feel anger, satisfaction, desire. These two facts led those about me to suppose that I willed and thought. I can remember all this, not because I knew that it was so, but because I have tactual memory. It enables me to remember that I never contracted my forehead in the act of thinking.

As a small child, Helen encountered objects and relationships through her three remaining senses, touch, taste, and smell. And yet she claims that without words, she did not think or even will. Others only "supposed" she did.

Language alone could give her consciousness; personal pronouns gave her a self: "When I learned the meaning of 'I' and 'me'

and found that I was something, I began to think. Then consciousness first existed for me." Thought in words "first rendered my
senses their value" and expanded her emotions from the primitive
experiences of anger, desire, and satisfaction to hope, anticipation,
wonder, joy, and faith, presumably more elevated feelings. She calls
the process of learning language "the awakening of my soul."

Keller is the epitomic Enlightenment figure, the filthy, screech-
ing *enfant sauvage*, driven by appetite and aversion, who is brought
into the human fold by reason. Reason is carried in language; the
word delivers her from evil. As a child, she felt the cold and taste of
ice cream on her tongue and knew she longed for it. Later, though,
she discounted the value, even the reality, of that early desire
because she could not name its object, ice cream. In glorifying the
rational mind and language, she implicitly repudiated the body's
senses as sources of knowledge and, more important, of subjectivity.
In intellectual activity—"as I read and study"—she found proof of
Descartes' truth: that in human reason lies God.

Because her story is written in the heartfelt, refined first-person
prose of a remarkable personage, it is tempting to read what Keller
says as an authoritative description of how reason, organized lin-
guistically, creates subjectivity. But she is nothing if not ideological.

"Yeah, it sounds great, doesn't it?" says Antonio Damasio, who
heads the neurology department at the University of Iowa College
of Medicine, when I meet him at his weekend apartment in Chicago.
"But it's totally wrong. That's not the way it works at all."

Damasio is one of the chief critics of Cartesian dualism in the
field of neurology and also an elegant popular writer. In *Descartes'
Error* and *The Feeling of What Happens*, he uses both neurological evidence and his own, more speculative theory to refute the idea that
cognition is superior to emotion and the senses or even independent of them.

The way Damasio describes it, the mind is not a floating spirit,
not a chemical reaction confined like combustion within an engine
in the three-pound mass of gray matter inside our skulls. It is not a

program inscribed on the brain that runs the body like software in a computer. Rather, the mind lives in the body, but not like a vapor inside a jar. The mind is part of the jar. And even the mind's nimblest feats—from deciding which car to buy to dreaming up symphonies—are impossible without the teamwork of the humbler stuff down below: the bone and muscle, blood and chemicals we call the body, and the processes that have been keeping us warm, oxygenated, and out of the way of falling objects since we crawled from the mud.

Chief among these survival mechanisms, says Damasio, are emotions, the body's minute-to-minute alterations that cue us in to changes around us—the queasy stomach of anxiety, the hot face of shame. Signals of those bodily changes travel from the viscera to the brain over the neural circuits and through the bloodstream in hormones and peptides. While the brain is receiving these signals, it is also sending its own out over the same pathways. The body reacts: the facial muscles pull into a smile or grimace. Signals of that musculoskeletal alteration zip back to the brain; it acknowledges pleasure or displeasure. The brain zips a message down the same passageways to tell the body to seek more of the pleasure that made it smile or flee the source of its vexation. The loop occurs instantaneously and constantly. Damasio conceives of "neural maps" in the brain that translate the bodily sensations into conscious awareness, turning emotion into "feeling."

"Emotions and feelings may not be intruders in the bastion of reason at all: they may be enmeshed in its networks, for worse *and* for better," Damasio writes in *Descartes' Error*. "The lowly orders of our organism are in the loop of high reason." The moral of his story is precisely the opposite of Descartes' or Helen Keller's. To Damasio, *We are, we feel, and therefore we think.*

It is clear to anyone who has ever known an animal that thought and communication can exist before, outside of, and beyond words. "I think in pictures," writes the autistic memoirist and stockyard designer Temple Grandin. "Words are like a second language to me.

I translate both spoken and written words into full-color movies, complete with sound, which run like a VCR tape in my head." Surmising that she thinks as animals do, Grandin designs slaughter facilities in which the animals don't see their fellows going to their demise, thus preventing their own panic.

The painter Willem de Kooning died of Alzheimer's disease largely aphasic, but the discernment of color never left his eye nor did the feel of shape abandon his hand. Some critics consider his last paintings as good as the earlier ones, and in some ways superior, more direct and free. Proust tells us that before language, the "I" finds itself through the senses—the aroma of a cup of tea, the sensation of an uneven cobblestone underfoot.

"Sometimes I think," said Paul Valéry. "Sometimes I am."

.   .   .

If he could argue, Dad would side with Descartes. To him, language *is* the mark of humanity. Reason *is* divine. Unlike Grandin or de Kooning, unlike a composer or an athlete, my father is a word man. Long before he felt the wind pulling a hull beneath him through the waves, he learned to sail—by reading. Now he lies in bed each night pretending to peruse the *New Yorker* and falls asleep with his glasses on. As often as he can, he displays his fanciest words—*notwithstanding, daresay*—which poke through his utterances like showy perennials in a garden gone to weed.

I am, obviously, a word person too. I hardly know what I feel until I write it down. In the therapist's office, I felt, as instructed. But I did not just sit and weep or laugh. I used words to describe my feelings, because I need to name them in order to understand them.

So it is with a certain skepticism that I embark on an experiment. While I note the language Dad's mind is forgetting, I start to collect instances of what his body remembers.

Jack Smith, an Irish immigrant musician and artist whom Mom hired as a twice-weekly companion for Dad during the early stages of his disease, tells me about rowing on the Central Park pond with him. Dad took the oars like a pro, Jack says. "He did all that fancy turning stuff." With graceful arms, Jack mimes the alternating strokes of an experienced rower. "It was as if twenty years dropped from him and it was all still there, in his body. I almost began to cry."

Another time, Dad and I are walking in the shady, serene garden of the General Theological Seminary. The gardener is delicately picking the winter debris from around the brave little snowdrops. The air is cold, but the dirt smells warm and wormy, like spring. Dad kneels on the brick path to tie a shoelace.

"You did that very well," I comment.

"What?"

"Tying your shoe."

He looks at me crooked, as if to say, *Yeah, so what else is new?*

I note that he's not only remembering some old things, he is learning new ones. Since he's been going to his day program, he has made friends (and a few enemies), adopted the routines there, and learned to navigate his way to the community room and back, across several streets, through a maze of alleyways and buildings that all look alike. One day, he elopes from the apartment and turns up at the center. The workers call my frantic mother and she goes to collect him. Then Dad gallantly leads her home.

I dutifully report my anecdotes to Mom, who receives each with a cupful of salt. I tell her that Jack feels Dad's confusion is linked to his distress at losing his mastery. I quote Jack: "All that talk about money!" Later, when words lose nearly all their meaning, Jack will amuse Dad by engaging him in "spaceman talk." But, Jack tells me, and I tell Mom, he tries "to listen to what Stan is saying through his code."

"Oh, Jack," says Mom, waving a dismissive hand. Jack, a spiritual seeker, lives literally like a church mouse: nearly penniless, in a room under a stained-glass window inside a church, earning his keep by cleaning and opening the sanctuary for services. Besides caring for Dad and the church, Jack also stacks fruit for a greengrocer in the early mornings. In the rest of his time he meditates, runs, and creates music and art that rarely find an audience. He appears to subsist on wheatgrass and joy. Jack's fasting powers, along with his infinite kindness, confirm to me that he is a reincarnated saint, and Mom also admires and likes him immensely, and is grateful for what he gives to Dad. Still, the Marxist in her is leery of his spiritual leanings and hence his analyses. "You never know with Dad what's going on inside," Mom says.

My mother is in the mainstream when it comes to considering people with Alzheimer's inscrutable and in second-guessing all their words and behavior. But many clinicians would endorse Jack's efforts at interpretation. Oliver Sacks gives us many examples of people who continue to think and feel long after language has fled. Tom Kitwood, psychologist Steven Sabat, philosopher Rom Harré, and many others therefore argue that it is the responsibility of the able-minded to try to understand the demented. It's certainly possible to figure out what the wordless mean—the parents of babies get very good at it. Yet because people with Alzheimer's are considered inarticulate and incomprehensible, their voices are markedly absent from the literature of the disease (Thomas DeBaggio, a writer in the early stages of the disease, is the exception, and the eloquence of his *Losing My Mind* would seem to belie its own title). In general, comments Philip Stafford, director of the Center on Aging and Community at the Indiana Institute on Disability and Community, "it is as if no one had thought to ask these people about the nature and experience of their illness."

Not only oversight silences the voices of the demented. Ideology does. For if we believe there is no thought without the record of thought in language, we also believe that without memory, the mental record of individual or shared experience, there can be no experience of self or of sharing in the present. "Our memories define us," reads a holiday fund appeal from the New York chapter of the Alzheimer's Association. "They create the totality of our human experience. Memories unite us. Shared remembrances bind families, friends, and communities—indeed the entire world. By destroying memory, Alzheimer's disease dissolves identity and erodes our connections to one another."

Yes, memory—history—unites us. But without memory is identity lost and with it, relationship? To Post, such well-meaning rhetoric articulates all that is wrong with a Cartesian view of humanity that locates the self, both its identity and its ties to others, exclusively in the thinking faculties. "Our theories of personhood highlight what is not," he says, "rather than what is."

·   ·   ·

Cartesian theory articulates Mom's most acute experience: what is not. "I can't have a relationship with someone who can't carry on a rational conversation," she tells me. I point out that she does have a relationship with Dad. It's just a bad relationship. Unsurprisingly, this does not comfort her.

What we're fighting about isn't theoretical. It's highly personal. Dad's dulled reason is distancing him from his wife, but it is letting me come closer to him. His intellect was the bayonet with which he kept me at bay; I fought back with my own smartness. Now his weapon is blunt, and since he can't understand my barbs, they're useless too. We never really had a meeting of minds. With one mind retreating, can we meet another way?

That is beginning, gingerly, to happen. Each time I talk to James on the phone he asks, "So, is he making any sense?" I find myself answering,"Not really, but—"

I'm not measuring Dad's or our collective well-being solely in terms of the sense he is or is not making. I have a relationship with a person who can't have a rational conversation. And compared to what it was before, it's a good one.

On a warm September afternoon, Dad and I stop in at the galleries on the edge of Chelsea, not far from his and Mom's apartment. At first, I am uncomfortable. I hardly feel thin enough or chic enough to walk into these whitewashed high-modern temples of gentrification on my own, much less with a doddering boulevardier in a ski parka who talks to the paintings and flirts incomprehensibly with the receptionists.

Soon, though, I begin to relax. The fact is, it's interesting to look at art with Dad. You can be demented and enjoy nonrepresentational work; a little senility might even enhance the experience. When I'm with him, I enjoy a kind of contact dementia. The rational mind snookered, I respond directly to the colors, shapes, and images, the irrational reason of the contemporary visual.

We walk into one of the whitest, highest temples to see the work of the painter Terry Winters. Having begun his career scribbling intriguing organic shapes in watery brown and gray paint on flat surfaces, on these immense canvases Winters is applying thick layers of wild color to create mysterious tunnels of spaces. At first, Dad plays the anxious naif. "What? What am I supposed to—"

"It's anything you want it to be," I say. "There's no 'supposed to.'"

He considers the painting again, then moves away and stares intently at it, a mostly blue canvas whose swirling lines weave whorls over and through each other, pulling the eye into a distant vortex. Dad says, "In here there are worlds inside, and it's there and they are there, in there and there." He moves close to the painting, touches it ("Don't touch!" I scold, and he glowers at me). "The boy is crying, he's dreaming," he says, in the tone of a storyteller to a small child. Then, with the sly earnestness that indicates he still has a sense of irony, "—but don't be sad. Don't worry. It will all come out."

"Come sit with me," I say after we've examined a few more paintings. The seat of the wooden bench in the center of the room is low, and when his buttocks don't meet it at the customary height, he falls fast through the last few inches of air. "Where is she?" he asks.

I assume he means Mom. "Mom's out. You'll see her later."

"She's out?"

"She went to the doctor. We'll see her later."

Although he doesn't seem to be processing the information, he is apparently thinking about his wife. After a while he says, "Sometimes Lillian is very angry. I think lonely. I feel I don't know how to"—he searches for the words—"hold her right."

She is lonely. She has told me so a thousand times. Of course it's easy for me to spend an afternoon a week with Dad, Being Here Now, even finding the experience interesting in its boring way. But it *is* hard to have a relationship with someone who can't have a rational conversation, or understand a joke, or engage in a satisfying dispute, and it is especially hard for my "hypercognitive" mother. The dark, inward-pulling canvases seem to illuminate what is happening to my parents' marriage. After a fifty-year conversation, the convolutions of language, the misbegotten arguments and frustrating silences are sucking away whatever love is left. Dad is lonely too. He cannot hold his wife and he cannot talk to her. Perhaps he senses that to her talking *is* holding.

Dad moves to a canvas of deep blues and purples. He swings one arm in wide stiff circles. "It's back and back and back back," he says.

My gaze refocuses from the picture to my father. He is standing sideways to me, his sneakered feet and straight-kneed legs pulled together as if zipped. His spine draws a wide semicircle from his waist around his ever-more-pronounced hump; his neck and head are cricked like a serif at the end of the spine. People slide between us, conversing in the sophisticated idiom of gallery-goers. They are slender, dressed in black, straight as declarative sentences. And my father's body is the shape of a question mark.

3. *Acquaintance*

WHO IS MY FATHER?

Of his early life I have been told a small suite of fables.

His mother disposes of his beloved Fritzi; she tells him that five is too old for a boy to have a doll. When he is six, he visits his estranged father. A caged canary flies out the window. Little Stanley is punished, tearfully protesting his innocence, and never sees his father again. He is a sweet child; his Aunt May sings to him. A good student; his teacher Margaret holds him. He becomes a serious teenage pianist; his mother refuses to buy him an instrument but the same month purchases a mahogany box of fine silverware, which he inherits.

I have heard these stories all my life. Tales of a blameless boy hurt and misunderstood. A smart boy, a good boy, loved only when lucky. The metaphors are impeccable, the structures balletic. Can they be true?

Clues are sparse. Dad's mother, Bee, is a public school teacher, socialist, and amateur poet and painter. She can sketch an haute couture suit at Bergdorf Goodman's and stitch it up on her own sewing machine. Her apartment is decorated with fragile knick-knacks, the upholstery protected by tatted antimacassars attached with menacing staple pins. Everything in it reminds a child not to touch, not to squirm.

My grandmother divorces soon after her child's birth. She may not have chosen motherhood. "She bore a child and then the burden/To fit him into the shaft of life—/That he might trod alone," she writes in a poem called "Lament." The child, my father, is professionally photographed when he is still in gowns. Her own snapshots capture him conscripted into scenes of childish fun, apparently against his will. Here is Stanley scowling in a sailor suit, holding a toy drum. "A pacifist?" the caption reads. Here, on a tiny wooden tricycle, clutching the handlebars with desperate round fists, his face crumpled. "Get me off a' dis!" writes Mother gaily. I find only two pictures in which my grandmother is holding her son, at a distance from her erect body.

After Dad's infancy, the photographing becomes haphazard. In another poem, entitled "Bondage," she declares, "The navel cord in plaintive voice/Shames strength and makes man/Weak. Enslavement to the Matriarch." No enslaving Matriarch she. At five, she sends Stanley to sleep away at Camp Wamego, where he is voted Best All Around Camper. In the commemorative photo he looks crestfallen. Meanwhile, the record of her own travels increases. She is photographed, in elegant shoes, before the Leaning Tower and the Eiffel Tower, the Spanish Steps and the steps of the Mexican pyramids.

I know these pictures well because there are so few of them. Mom has spent a lifetime editing the family's history, deleting unattractive house gifts, toys, books no longer read. I rescue Bee's recipes as Mom is about to drop them into the trash. "They're our history!" I object, gathering up the index cards of instructions for Sophie's Tzimmes, Belle's Delicious Babka, and a half-dozen versions of pot roast. "Oh," scoffs Mom, "I never make those rich foods anymore."

After sixty-five years and a dozen apartments and houses, Mom's closets hold a half-dozen manila envelopes of photos, cards, and a few drawings by my niece and nephew, one box of slides, and a couple dozen case reports that Dad wrote as a school psychologist.

The one complete archive is a box of Dad's wartime letters, bundled with 1940s string.

At first I explain this compulsion to throw away as Mom's distaste for clutter, which I share. But I come to think of it as the paradoxical legacy of loss. The Depression sent Mom's family from a big suburban house with a Steinway grand piano to a series of rooming houses and house-sits in Manhattan. Then came the War and the Holocaust, and after that, just when security seemed attainable, Joe McCarthy and his anticommunist posse plundered my parents' circles of their reputations and their livelihoods. When that was almost over, the revelations of Stalin's crimes smashed even their Utopian fantasies.

Many of their friends recover from these losses by making money and stuffing their homes with things. But to both my parents, it seems, attachment remains perilous. When Bee dies in 1968, they sell all but a few of her possessions immediately. They keep her paintings, the morally tarnished silver, and the Mexican glass jar, my favorite. A few years later, a stranger calls. It is Dad's father's son from his next marriage, announcing that my grandfather has died. As blithely as he walked out on his first son's life, this man walked out of his own, hit by a bus after a tennis game. The other son asks Dad to waive his claim to his father's estate, and Dad signs without asking the amount.

When she talks about the Depression, Mom always mentions her family's piano, sold when they tumbled from the bourgeoisie. Yet when she recounts the fate of the European Jews who could have fled before the War but did not, she says, "They couldn't part with their grand pianos." They clung to their comforts until the SS kicked in the mahogany doors.

To us children, this nonchalance toward material things is liberating. No tabletop is so fine that a wet glass cannot be placed on it, no glass so precious that its shattering is unforgivable. But what does it mean to grow up in a home where there are so few keepsakes, kept for the sweet sake of keeping? If nothing is too beloved to cherish, is nothing—or no one—unbearable to lose? Or is loss so costly that the very act of cherishing must be avoided?

.   .   .

Bee and Stanley live in the East Bronx near Tremont Avenue, in a small wood-frame mother-daughter house on Elsmere Place and later a block away, on Fairmount Avenue, in a six-story apartment building with a few flourishes of goldlike Art Deco–like ornamentation. Fairmount, neither fair nor a mount, is flanked by Saint Thomas Roman Catholic Church at one end and the Gethsemane Baptist Church at the other. In between stands the squat Alamo–like Messiah Lutheran Church, over whose door a terra-cotta crest reads "Seek and/You Shall/Find God's Love." Suffice it to say the neighborhood Christian kids do not dispense God's love on my small, bookish, Jewish father.

Still, Dad manages to have fun. He plays in the vast, treeless new Crotona Park, where the air is so full of baseballs that the kids field with their mitts on their heads. He becomes a graceful skater on the park's rink. And when he can sneak off, he dives into the Bronx River, its waters oily and rusty from the junkyards and used-car lots on its banks.

In the high-ceilinged gray fortress of Public School 44, little Stanley skips forms 2A and 3A and graduates the eighth grade in 1931 at the age of twelve. The pages of his graduation autograph book are inscribed with the same doggerel that appears in my own sixth-grade book: "There are golden ships and silver ships, but no ship like friendship." "Take the local/Take the express/Don't get off/ 'Til you reach Success." The writers sign, "Your Friend."

Were they his friends? Only his teachers address him personally. "To Stanley, my most Apt Pupil," writes Marjorie C. Clancey. "May you continue to have the charm that has won for you the admiration of teachers and students and may you never lose the earnestness and sincerity that endear you to all." Most wish him happiness, but none notes any evidence that he has attained it yet.

Several adults take it upon themselves to commend Stanley's mother as the architect of his virtues and the pillar of his security. "Never forget the part your mother played in the building of your character," one teacher reminds him. Bee's longtime companion, the dour, dapper "Harold Stein, M.D.," praises Stanley's sturdy character, too, which "holds the keys to your happiness." Harold adds, "Always consider your mother your first, best, and truest friend."

Dad honors his mother by consecrating the opening page of the book to her, on which she squeezes out a maternal valediction:

> To Stanley, my son—
>
> I hope you will retain the character you have now for the rest of your life. Remain unspoiled, reliable, and sincere. You will get as much out of life with these as anyone seeking success and riches.
>
> My greatest wish is that you will have the stamina to face life with all its irregularities. You will thus possess happiness in your own making.
>
> > Mother

With all this talk of happiness, the book is a stiff little monument to scholarly toil and filial duty. The word *love* appears nowhere in its pages.

Between his June 1931 graduation from P.S. 44 and his enrollment in the tenth grade at Evander Childs High School in the Bronx in September 1932, there is no extant school record for Stanley Levine. This, I conclude, is the year he is sent to live with his cousins, the Robertsons, in rural upstate New York. During that year, Bee may live with "Aunt" May, a frequent guest in their home, and possibly her lover. Bee's poems are full of illicit passion denied—"That I might cry aloud—/My love, unto the clouds/ Nor blush for fear of condemnation!"—but also "Of a great love gratified./ Preferred by far/To Clergy's mate/Marital exhibitionism /Veiled in hate." She did not live with Harold, whom she seemed to tolerate more than like. Perhaps he was her veil.

The Robertsons must be the closest thing Dad has to the families he reads about in the Edwardian children's books in the public library. Two married parents, three sisters, and three brothers, surrounded in the family pictures by the accoutrements of upper-middle-class confidence and genteel, perhaps gentile, leisure: large dogs, tennis rackets, Adirondack chairs. In every photo the Robertsons slump companionably against each other; in every photo an uncle or boy cousin has an arm draped around Stan. The Robertsons smile, and sometimes their half-orphaned cousin manages half a smile too.

Stanley returns to the Bronx and starts tenth grade at Evander Childs, where he excels in the all-academic course. He is rarely absent, never late. At Evander, the students are drilled in elocution to bury the first-generation working-class "deeze" and "doze" of "Tremon' Avenyuh" in the deracinated sound of "education." Dad recites the drill to James and me—"Hoe Noe Brone Coe"—both ridiculing and boasting of his classless, "*goyishe*" diction.

At the age of fifteen, still small and soft-cheeked, he enters City College. "He was introspective and analytical . . . sort of a strait-laced guy," says one of his best friends, Jerry Cohen. "He had this fey sense of humor; it was his way of resisting without saying something directly. Jerry also says, "I think of him as sort of emotional, romantic."

Dad finds both analysis and romance in the communist American Student Union. At meetings, says Jerry, "he was always arguing for whatever the left position was. I don't mean ultraleftist. He would stick to his position. He would try to present the winning argument that would not be abrasive. Though it might turn out to be abrasive . . . We [put] a lot of heart into the movement. The period itself was so emotional."

Dad has told me he was a political leader, an outstanding student, and a triumphant tennis player who forfeited a professional career because, outside City College, tennis was for rich gentiles; the

clubs barred Jews even as ball boys, and there was no prize money.
But the college publications, which detail ferocious political debates
between the socialists and the communists, the Leninists and the
Trotskyists, the dean and the provost, do not mention Dad. In the
sports pages there is no word of Stan Levine.

Nor is he an exceptional student. City College has no tuition,
but the exigencies of work in the still-thin late-thirties economy
force him to enroll in the night division, and his grades there are
execrable—one B, the rest Cs, Ds, and Fs. The yearbook marks his
graduation with a postage-stamp photo of a dreamy, handsome face
and a brief entry: "1940, BS. Astronomy Club, executive committee
American Student Union. Freshman Tennis team. Student Council
Committees. Dean '39."

Each day in the City College archives, discovering these unin-
spiring truths about my father, I come home feeling both vindicated
and deflated. He wasn't who he says he was. I knew it! The liar! But
I also notice a hollowness in my chest, as if some pride, or maybe
just security, had been excised. When I call Mom and tell her what
I've found, all she says is "Oh, dear."

Somehow, this undistinguished student and unsung activist
wins the heart of the dazzling president of the Hunter College
Night chapter of the ASU, Lillian Golden. She has many suitors,
among them a well-known history professor and player in left-wing
politics, who later defects to the other side. Her letters to Dad at
first are reluctant, soon longing. They live with their parents. When
they aren't at classes or on picket lines or working or looking for
work—during their courtship he is, among other things, a machin-
ist, a predawn newspaper deliverer, and a coat check in an Eighth
Avenue dance hall—they are looking for apartments and helping
their friends look for work or apartments.

His poor eyesight would give Stan a deferment, but he wants to
fight the Nazis, so he volunteers. Invited to enroll in the Officer
Training Corps, he declines, preferring to fight alongside the army's
working class, the GIs. He asks Lillian to marry him. She is unsure.

She cries when she wakes up on a day she won't see him; "we are so dependent on each other," she frets. But they are both alive, in adjacent boroughs of New York City! How will they bear being apart? He woos her with assurances, from time to time he bursts into panic. Just weeks after their Las Vegas–style Bronx Orthodox Jewish wedding, he is in uniform.

When he gets to Camp Rucker, Alabama, the faithless wedding has earned this atheist Jew divine retribution—or at least the retribution of the second most powerful force, the U.S. Army. According to family legend, sufficient proof of marriage has not been supplied and Lillian's much-needed soldier's-wife's benefits are held up. Dad sends for the document, which arrives after a few weeks, whereupon the sergeant calls Dad into his office.

"Soldier!"

"Yes! Sir!"

"Soldier! What the god-day-um hay-ull is THIS?" He raises his arm and allows a long parchment scroll, illuminated in Hebrew, to unfurl—the *ketubah,* or religious marriage certificate. Dad refrains from laughing. Mom gets her benefits.

"Your father was an idealist," says Morton Lietman, the landlord of a huge apartment complex in Queens, who met Dad sleeping head to smelly foot during a three-day ride to boot camp. When stationed in the South, Dad steps aside to let a black man pass before him on the sidewalk. "Everyone stared," Mort recalls. "You didn't do that in the South in those days."

They are transferred to a top-secret camp in the Arizona desert to train to man a fleet of high-tech tanks. Life is hot and isolated, and the commanding officer is, according to Mort, "a Southern racist, Jew-hating sonofabitch." Dad resists, but not with the quiet humor that Jerry Cohen describes. One night, he cuts the guy lines of the kitchen tent "so that it suffered a collapse," says Mort. "That was an outstanding occurrence." He wheezes and lights another cigarette. "Mainly due to his outspokenness, your father did more than his required share of KP duty." We grin at the image of this wise-ass guerrilla of the sand dunes, sabotaging both all-American Nazism and the tedium of basic training.

"He was madly in love with your mother," says Mort. "He was the most faithful—the only faithful!—soldier I've ever known" (a later letter from a friend to my father referring to "your Paris adventure" casts doubt on this claim). Still, Dad exhibits unusual sobriety in all ways. Says Mort, "He didn't even get drunk."

Throughout his tour, he writes my mother four-, five-, six-page missives, sometimes more than one a day, but is restricted by the censors from saying anything about the operations in which he is engaged or even revealing his whereabouts. So he throws himself into the world she details, the disputes at meetings and at work, the eternal apartment searches. Occasionally, he weaves a fantasy of their future. "I know how important work is to you, dearest. I want you to continue it as long as you want, even after we have a child." He promises to "share the load." He rarely complains; in one letter he mentions an earache. But there is no hint of the cocky prankster in these sentences. This soldier is earnest, romantic to the point of parody. "I love you my Darling, my darling dearest, how I love you and long for you. I love you!" This goes on for page after page. Her letters are informative, loving but not gushy. His are a monotony of desire.

Morton Lietman is wounded on the beach at Normandy and shipped home. Dad's tank battalion, the 748th or "Fighting Rhinos," lumbers across France into the Battle of the Bulge. He spends the winter of 1944 with a family in Belgium, playing bridge. In the fall he is deployed to the Hürtgen Forest, 32,000 acres of thickly tangled firs and perpetual darkness on the Belgian-German border. Corporal Levine spends two months with three other men, gunning from inside a hot metal box. Outside, the tree limbs are so low that the men must stoop to move. The knee-deep mud, hiding land mines every eight paces, is littered with wrecked equipment and bodies. Sleet, snow, and rain are unceasing, artillery fire so intense that the trees burst apart. Dad's crew defecates out the door at the bottom of the tank. After three months, with 24,000 Americans dead and 9,000 wounded or gone mad from battle fatigue, the Hürtgen Forest campaign is deemed an utter debacle. General James Gavin, who commands the 82nd Airborne Division, calls it "one of the most costly, most unproductive, and most ill-advised battles that our army has ever fought." My father takes home a Bronze Star.

As a child, I hear Dad mention this forest only a few times. I imagine a fairytale woods, full of elves and witches. Over the next fifty years, Dad hikes a thousand trails with my mother, but he never goes alone. After Hürtgen, my father fears forests.

After the War, the photos are of groups. Handsome, happy friends pose beside lakes and lie on lawns before Catskills bungalows; they are bundled in scarves and hats on picket lines, drinking wine in shabby apartments. Mom wears red lipstick and a woven Navajo jacket, her luxuriant black curly hair cut short. With his fleshy lips and sinewy soldier's arms, low-slung Stetson and loose-dangling cigarette, Dad possesses all the elements of forties male glamour, plus the gleam of the revolutionary. My parents gaze at each other. Dad is smiling. He is laughing! "They were so happy and in love," their friend Shirley Miller tells me over a grilled-cheese sandwich at her house in Great Neck. Joey Krantz, a towel merchant and amateur musician, reads to me from the notes he has prepared for my visit. "They played duets on the piano. They were deeply in love."

Mom works for the union during the day and is up a stepladder giving street corner speeches in the evenings, with Heshie Miller fending off hecklers at her feet. Dad is teaching history to high school kids. "He was even optimistic about that," Shirley recalls. "He was working in the worst school in Manhattan, but one day he came back and said he thought he was doing well." She laughs. "He told me he knew because the school walls were covered with graffiti saying 'Fuck Mr. So-and-so,' 'Fuck Mrs. So-and-So.' But they never said 'Fuck Mr. Levine.' "

Mom and Dad spend a week at Mrs. Trott's Cabins in Maine with Gloria and Leo Goldstein. Gloria remembers the last night of their stay. "We stood out on this dock and talked about the future, which was stretching endlessly in front of us. Your parents were so happy and so earnest and so in love. We were all so buttressed by our desire to change the world, to do only good in the world. That night was beautiful, and suddenly there was the aurora borealis, just bursting out in the sky. We felt heroic." As friends, says Gloria, "the four of us had that time completely wired into our brains so we can never forget it. Subsequently, whatever happened, whatever frictions developed, we knew we were cemented together." The four become best friends for life.

Dad does housework. And when the children come, he pitches in with the child care too. James bleats with colic day and night. Dad walks him, changes diapers cheerfully. Mom tells me he is more interested in babies than she is. But once James is out of diapers, the doting daddy wants his mommy back, James's mommy. "Your mother was so in love with Jamie," says Gloria. "I think your father was jealous." Another friend remembers, "We went camping with all the kids. James wanted to put up the tent—he must have been six—and Stan pushed him away." Still, by all accounts he is what would later be called a "liberated father." We move to the suburbs, near Dad's job, and Mom commutes to work in the city. So it is he who attends teacher conferences and ferries us around in the car. "We all talked about the Woman Question," says Babs Mishkin, using the simultaneously elevating and diminishing Communist Party term for sex discrimination. "Only Stanley put his money where his mouth was."

Mom and Dad talk endlessly. They talk in the bathroom, while Dad shaves. They talk while they are both reading. They don't just take a hike together, they talk about the hike they are going to take, then talk about the hike while taking it, then review the hike once they get back, and call their friends to tell them about the hike. Their talk, though, is almost always of hikes, of politics, of music and friends. What they do not talk about, Mom says, is themselves and their feelings. Their marriage faces outward, not inward, their intimacy built more on a unanimous interpretation of the world than on an understanding of each other.

They laugh intensely and they argue intensely. Combativeness is the style of their circle. "Some of your father's know-it-all stuff went along with our politics," says Rila Nemerov, a therapist who has known my parents since college. "If there was a need to be arrogant, the politics played into it." But it is also the style of that generation of *men* of the left. Unsurprisingly, Dad's male friends object less to his tendency to bulldoze the opponent than his women friends do. I press Jerry Cohen about his statement that Dad could be "abrasive" in meetings of the American Student Union. Did this disturb anyone? "He was looking for the truth. We were all looking for the truth," Jerry answers. I, the postmodernist, interject with a light laugh that we've since learned there is no One Truth. "We had the truth," says Jerry, unsmiling.

If Jerry feels their side had the truth collectively, throughout his life Dad behaves as if he possesses it personally. "So anyway," he says at the end of a conversation, "the point is . . ." No matter how long or complicated the argument, no matter how many people are involved, there is only one point—his.

The man who puts his money where his mouth is on the Woman Question also puts his libido there. Babs, still beautiful in her nineties, tells me, "He always wanted to dance with me at parties. Once he pushed up close to me and whispered, 'You know, you're a very handsome woman.' " When she rebuffed him, "he made it clear that Gloria was more receptive." She says, "In a sense, his flirting was a put-down of women. He could play with them and not have to take them seriously." Gloria says she was not receptive either. She thinks that if she had been, "he would have been afraid to do anything about it."

When I'm in my teens, he talks so glowingly and often about Greta Norton, a special ed teacher with green eyes and a pixie haircut, that I suspect he is having an affair with her. Lying in the ICU after his ulcer attack, he confesses that he was in love with another woman, and hints that it was Greta, but assures me he did nothing about it because of feelings of guilt and love for Mom. Does he want my sympathy? Am I being conscripted into voyeurism? "Don't talk to me about this," I snap. "If you want to tell someone, tell your wife."

His flirtation can be tinged with misogyny. Michaela, Babs's daughter, remembers Dad "playfully" grabbing her mother's wig off her head at a party and laughing at her balding head. Mom does not remember the incident—"and I wouldn't forget something like that." She swears Dad would not be so cruel. James has no trouble believing it. "The sick fuck," he says.

His women friends at work, who have no loyalty to my mother, are freer to enjoy Dad's collegial come-ons. Greta Norton concurs that my father flirted with every woman he met, including her, but says they did not have an affair. "I never saw it as making passes at me," she says. "I took it as that's the way Stan is." The way he also was, she says, was "sincerely interested. In feelings, in my feelings, in my views about things." Says another female colleague: "Your father liked women and women liked your father."

Dad is sexily affectionate to Mom, too, but he is oddly less self-assured with her. "He idolized her, but he couldn't keep up," Shirley Miller says. "They loved to play and listen to music together," Joey Krantz notes, "but she was a better musician." Over the years Dad grows increasingly dependent on Mom, more infantile. "Even before his Alzheimer's, Stanley looked to her for direction on what should be done," Heshie Miller says. Dad is noisy and late; Mom is efficient. He breaks things; she tidies. As a child I think (incorrectly) that my mother earns more money than my father does.

His anxious competitiveness turns to domination. "He would talk over your mother," observes a coworker who spent time with them socially, "as if to invalidate her point or as if his point were more prescient or profound." Says Mom: "I can still feel his hand on my arm. At all those dinner parties, the minute I would start talking, he would reach out and put his hand on my arm—'Lil, Lil, Lil'—to silence me. I can't tell you how many times in the car driving home, I vowed never to go out in public with him again."

In 1969, Dad inherits $5,000 from Bee and he and Mom buy a house on an island in Maine. They lay stone walls and transplant day lilies from the dirt-road ditches; mow the meadow of alder and sow it with timothy and wildflowers, opening a languid slope to the granite edge of the sea. They paint the floors white and rescue iron beds from the dump. My parents make a personal paradise in what is already paradise.

At fifty, their children gone, they are newlyweds again. In a photograph taken on the deck, she sits on his lap, her arm around his shoulder. His face distorted in a ferocious smile, he holds a clawlike hand inches from her breast. She is laughing wildly. While I'm visiting, we're driving to the dump in the van and Mom makes a comment about his driving. "Up yours, sister," he jokes. "Anytime," she answers with a dirty grin.

Dad buys a sleek, understated, classic sailboat, a Hereschoff Marlin. Mom tries to share Dad's enthusiasm but, uncomfortable on all but the calmest water, stays home and learns to bake and hook rugs. This only inflames her anxiety. While he is conquering the high seas, she is reliving the letterless months of the Battle of the Hürtgen Forest, checking the clock every five minutes past his estimated time of arrival.

Finally (usually within a half hour) Dad drops his tattered L. L. Bean bag in the garage, strides into the kitchen, and tosses his hat onto the round oak table. She has scurried to the door the instant she heard the car in the driveway. Relieved, she scolds him. He is irritated, apologetic, and hungry. With each foray onto the water, he escapes her maddening gravitational pull, then falls gladly back into it. They kiss the kiss of the long married, mutually grateful for this ritual of vexation and forgiveness.

Although he never completes his Ph.D. in psychology, he calls himself Doctor Levine. He is a pretender in both senses of the word: a man who feigns, a man who claims the title. It may be the central metaphor of his life—the pretend political leader, the make-believe tennis champ. "I think he would have been much happier had he gotten the Ph.D.," says a sympathetic Heshie Miller. Shirley disagrees: "He would have felt more important, but I don't think basically it would have made him happier. He wants to be heard. He needs it, he needs it constantly. That's what the doctor thing is about."

"He was always ambivalent about success" and about the people who hand out credentials of success, Mom says. While in clinical psychology graduate school, my grade-school friend David Teicher sees Dad at a party. "When I told him what I was doing, he got that sarcastic gleam in his eye," David says. Searching around for psychologists David might know on Long Island, Dad finally hits on someone. "He said to me, about this guy, 'He's got a *gorgeous* practice in Great Neck.' He kept saying that: 'a *gorgeous* practice.' It was as if he both envied it and had contempt for it." He wanted to be confirmed in the church he blasphemed.

David says he puzzled over Dad's behavior and concluded it was both competitive and conspiratorial. "If you got the joke, you were part of his little club." You were funny, smart, savvy, edgy—worthy. "But the joke was also at your expense. I always felt he was judging me, and his opinion of me was important, even though I hardly knew him. But I never could tell if your father was mocking me or approving of me. He had a way of including you and putting you down at the same time."

Now Dad remembers himself not just as a doctor but as a widely esteemed one. "And Dr. Levine and Dr. Levine!" he says. "It was always, Can you see us, Dr. Levine! Dr. Levine! So high up there," he says raising an arm and lowering it slowly to indicate how the mighty have fallen. "And I came all the way down from so far! Dr. Levine!"

James can't stomach it. "DOC-tor Levine," he spits, lampooning respect.

Some of Dad's former colleagues, especially those who sweated to get their degrees, resent Dad's pretense. One informs me that what he did—"impersonating a Ph.D. psychologist"—is illegal. And yet, by many accounts, he is a talented diagnostician, a sympathetic and authoritative counselor, a committed advocate for his patients.

Pavel Krinski, a pediatrician and psychiatrist with whom my father worked, is one of these admirers. "Your father was a balanced and generous man, human and accepting, whom I remember with great fondness," he says in a rich Eastern European-accented voice on the phone. These are adjectives I would not use about Dad, I think as he speaks. I drive out through rush-hour traffic to visit Dr. Krinski in his office in the back corner of a shrub-covered house in central Long Island, just yards from a mall-lined highway. Hearing my knock on the screen door, Krinski removes his thick glasses and beckons me from behind an enormous computer screen to a chair beside him. From where I sit, I can see his body, from untrimmed gray beard to withered legs and slippered feet.

A listener by profession and an Old World host, Krinski plies me with questions about myself, my work, my childhood. "I am interested in childhood," he says, "because I did not have a childhood." The motherless child of a Jewish bank branch manager in a small anti-Semitic Czech village, Pavel was raised by governesses. "My only friends were in books." At sixteen, he was transported to Auschwitz, where he survived by passing himself off as a locksmith, useful enough not to be wasted in terminal labor. Emigrating to the United States, Krinski and his second wife, a lively Argentine Jewish doctor, had children and became gourmet cooks. My parents always spoke of him as a man who loved culture and seized pleasure greedily. Yet during the hours we spend together, he neither smiles nor laughs.

"It was a delight to chat with him," he tells me of my father. "We talked about things of the world, and opinions. Usually he had a very strong opinion about things. I like that. I don't like people who don't dare to say what they think." Krinski tacitly endorses Dad's abandonment of his efforts toward a Ph.D. "He was not overambitious and he looked down a little bit at people who sacrifice everything to advance in their field." If Shirley Miller attributes Dad's relinquishing his studies to a "lack of self-esteem," Krinski sees Dad as a flouter of bureaucratic bullshit. Discoursing for some minutes about the trivial requirements of the Ph.D. dissertation, Krinski conjectures that my father was too busy with important things to "go back and revise the statistics" to please some nit-picking academic committee. "To put it very bluntly, your father was not an ass-kisser."

I read through a thick folder of onionskin typescripts, reports Dad wrote as a chief school psychologist for the special-ed system of the Long Island schools. At first I notice his prose. The "literary" flourishes: "Such then is the child at this time." The overwrought, nearly incomprehensible sentences, as Dr. Levine strains to impress: "Food for him was gladly forthcoming out of his winsome request." He is in love with jargon and abstraction, the Delphic messages contained in the folded watercolors of the Rorschach deck; the psychoanalytic dissertation that he does not finish is on Rorschach correlates of reading disabilities. But through the thicket of his prose, light, even brilliance, gleams: "His aggressive succorant needs are persistently inverted to aggressive content. He cannot suck; he will then bite."

He takes pains to be precise. "Paul elaborates and embellishes, but he does not distort." He is benevolent, insisting on the intelligence of the child who tests "low-dull," the potential for progress in the most recalcitrant student. In the angry, explosive child he finds fear, pain, and a longing to be loved. A ten-year-old boy is "brash, impulsive, precipitate, for he dare not tarry long" in the presence of his emotionally untrustworthy family and teachers. Of an obese girl referred to the center for her "marked disruptive, aberrant and bizarre behavior at school" including rummaging for food in the garbage, he says, "Her hold is tenuous, she suffers." This man of words searches the barks and squeals and expressionless faces of autistic children for the meanings they are trying to communicate. Unlike many others in his field, he believes they are communicating.

And this parent manqué is sympathetic not only to the plight of the children, but of their parents as well. If a villain is to be found, Mother is the likely suspect. Fathers, if not altogether absent, are marginal, but they are excused for their shortcomings. He calls one "castrated." Neither Dad's own personality nor his mother's can be blamed entirely for this worldview, which is ascendant in the era of Freudian-dominated family and group therapy. At the time, psychologists were attributing schizophrenia and even autism to the "pathogenic" family, particularly to a rejecting or neglectful mother. But while Dad rehearses the theory of the culpable cold mother, his reports bear witness to maternal devotion and grief, to the labors of mothers longing to rescue their children from mysterious, internal torment.

"His psychological reports were a pleasure to read because he elucidated the more human side of his clients and he remarked and noticed the strains and the various pressures of life for the families. He could see things beyond the facades, the practical," says Krinski. This man without a childhood who has devoted his life to children seems to feel a kinship with his childhood-deficient colleague. "Your father's humanity was absolutely superb."

Krinski is not the only coworker who says these things about Dad. Even those who call him arrogant, conceited, and disrespectful to lower-ranking workers also describe him with words like "profound understanding," "immense talent," and "wisdom." One teacher who worked closely with him for years tells me she was "in awe of Stan Levine."

"He could relax children who were otherwise very tense, with his personality," says Krinski, rummaging over his untidy desk and finding a photograph he has put aside for our visit. In it Dad stands on a wide lawn outside the center, beside an adolescent boy who is flying a kite. The boy is turned from the waist, his eyes and chin following the line that extends to the kite, beyond the edge of the photo. Almost comically skinny, awkward even in the static moment of the snapshot, he appears to be made of two-dimensional planes, like an origami figure. Dad, unaware of the camera, is loose-limbed and graceful in comparison. Standing close, neither looming nor hovering nor, apparently, instructing, he is just *being* with this odd boy.

· · ·

There is a genre of family memoir that is at heart a prosecutorial inquest. The author discovers her father was a bigamist, her grandmother a closeted Jew. *Guilty!* she cries, snaring her ancestors in the inconsistencies of their confessions. Usually, the revelation "explains" her own troubles.

My father did not grow up in "a house of poverty," as he wrote in an early-Alzheimer's writing group. His mother had a job even during the Depression, and he had a middle-class childhood, complete with summer camp and piano lessons. At City College he was neither an ace student, nor a political leader, nor a tennis champion. I learn these things from several sources, and when a reporter discovers the same thing several times, she begins to consider it a fact. But in life, and even in journalism, two conflicting facts can both be true.

Dad was not economically poor. But, single child of a single and rejecting mother, emotionally he was poor. He didn't lead the revolution or even the tennis team, but he was a fervent activist and until recently the player of a powerful net game. James's girlfriend Leila offers a memory besides Dad's intrusion on their adolescent lovemaking. She was in her twenties, just released from the hospital after a near-fatal bout of anorexia, when she ran into my parents. "Your father looked into my face, at the creases of anxiety and sadness between my eyes. And he reached out and touched them with his finger." What did she feel from him? Says Leila, "Tenderness."

Dad's friends don't deny his obnoxiousness. They love him in spite of it and because of the rest: his wild humor, warmth, and steadfastness. "Stanley could be a horse's ass," says Shirley Miller, "But he really is a good person."

Have I misjudged him? Measured against a child's desires and fantasies, maybe every parent is destined to come up a fraud. Did Dad trick us? No more than he tricked himself. "He is producing a play every day he wakes up," Greta Norton says. "I never saw him just flowing, just being. Part of the theatrics of his being 'on' all the time was a seeking, a search. You were always asking, 'Where's Stan?' I think he was asking the same thing."

Where's Stan? He is both on the lawn beside the boy with the kite and outside the bathroom waiting to strike his nine-year-old daughter. He is the devoted husband and the wannabe Don Juan, the brave GI and the self-possessed professional so self-doubting that he flaunts a credential he didn't earn. Says Pavel Krinski, "There are people who do clinical work, and they are official and they are not urging to bring out the child. Children sense that—they are very good judges of people. You can't fool children easily." My brother and I were also children, and we were not fools.

But neither we nor the kite boy were right or wrong. We all knew my father. He was all of these men—all were his selves.

4. Quarantine

October 1996

I am teaching journalism to undergraduates at a Jesuit university in Manhattan. The students are mostly parochial school graduates, decently educated and dutiful. Their sentences have the commas in the right places, but their attitudes toward knowledge are less than jesuitical.

I tell them a journalist's job is to doubt (some write this down word for word in their notebooks). They should doubt even themselves. "As beginning writers, you're told to write what you know. In this class, the starting assumption is we don't know anything. What a journalist does is find out what she doesn't know from people who do—and then check up on each person by asking somebody else. Doubt everyone and everything," I say, giving these faith-fed Catholic kids a dose of secular Jewish skepticism. "For instance, just because the cops say it's true doesn't mean it's true."

A boy raises his hand. "My dad's a cop."

"Don't trust him," I say, and he laughs a little nervously.

After the three-hour session, I call my answering machine to find three consecutive messages from Mom left an hour and a half earlier, within forty-five minutes, each escalating in fervor. She is at NYU hospital on the East Side, undergoing intestinal tests, and cannot leave the ward. Meanwhile, out walking by himself on the West Side, Dad has fallen and re-broken the wrist he broke a few years earlier when he fell playing tennis. A passerby found him sprawled on the sidewalk and took him to the ER at St. Luke's Hospital, a few blocks from the college. A fourth message says that Ruth Greenberg, a friend who lives nearby, has volunteered to sit with Dad until someone relieves her. I try to find Mom by phone at NYU but cannot, so I call her machine and tell her I'll go to the hospital. I hope she gets the message instead of continuing to chase me down. It's the era before cell phones.

I arrive at St. Luke's to find Dad in trousers and a hospital gown, lying on his back on a gurney. He looks like everyone else under the ER's fluorescent light, as if they've drained his blood on admission. His wrist is propped at a weird angle on a pillow at his side, wrapped in an ace bandage but not yet set. I ask him if it hurts. He says it does. With barely enough time to be thanked, Ruth scurries out, late for the next appointment.

I can't find a doctor who will talk to me, but manage to get the attention of one of the nurses. "Why don't you just relax, miss," she suggests. "Nothing is going to happen for a while." How long is a while? "A while."

I pull a metal chair beside Dad. My face is even with his chest. "So, how've you been?"

"Not great." A supine shrug.

"Yeah, what's happening?"

He chooses his words, searching not only for available ones but, it seems, for the right ones. "What is happening to me, this memory loss—I don't really know what will be."

"That must be scary."

He looks up at the asphalt tiles on the ceiling. Several are missing; the pattern reminds me of the crossword puzzles Dad used to be expert at. Now he holds a pen and enters letters in the little squares in the *Times,* pretending. His voice climbs up from his throat, making an effort against gravity and fear. "Sometimes I look ahead and I see myself. And I am standing in front of a tall, black wall."

I say nothing. I am trying to find out what I don't know from someone who does. But the person who knows doesn't know either.

That night I sleep at Mom and Dad's apartment on the Upper West Side. Mom has more tests scheduled for the morning, so I have agreed to stay over and get Dad up, showered, dressed, fed, and to the day program. I lie on the foam foldout couch in the "den," making out the titles of Dad's books. It's the library of a progressive child psychologist in the mid-twentieth century, practical clinical texts interspersed with the signal theoretical works of existentialist, humanist, and gestalt psychology: Reich, Erikson, May, Maslow, Reik, Laing, Perls. They are mostly Ashkenazi Jews like my father, whose American dreams of self-invention brightened but never banished an anxious pessimism born of inquisition, exile, pogrom, and holocaust. Dad can no longer read these books, or any others.

I am not thinking about my father's worsening fate, though. I am thinking about my own.

I know he can still bathe, brush his teeth, and dress himself, though he sometimes does so bizarrely—two sweaters in summer, clashing plaids, and always (if you don't catch him) more than one set of underwear. He can still make his breakfast (a huge mélange of cereals, yogurt, milk, fruit, sugar, honey, and whatever else he can rustle up). He goes for walks alone, does simple errands, returns home. But I cannot keep my mind off what may be next. When will I have to shower my father? I have not even seen him naked since I was a child. Will I have to wash his anus, his genitals? Diaper him? My mind skitters from these images as the neon-green digits on the clock roll toward two. Four more hours until morning. *Shit,* I wail silently. *I am not ready for this.*

When I awake, Dad is sleeping and Mom is at the kitchen table. She's canceled her tests, either because she doesn't trust me to take care of Dad or because she wants to spend some time with me, or both. We share a fondness for early morning and coffee. She recounts her attempt to quit and replace caffeine with an herbal mixture called Morning Thunder. "But I found myself dreading drinking it," she confesses. "I'd lost my reason to get out of bed." We laugh like two drunks warming up to a fourth beer. Then I tell her about my midnight foreboding.

"Don't think I haven't thought about these things many times, Judy," she says. "*Many* times." She puts two slices of bread into the toaster. "We're old," she says.

"I've noticed."

After a while, she says, "I just can't do this." She tells me Dad is shedding skills. He can no longer put in a molly bolt, tie the newspapers for recycling, unscrew a bottle cap. "Look what happened yesterday. There was a crisis and I couldn't be there. I can't take care of Dad by myself. I'm all alone."

If she feels alone, she feels alone. I can't argue. But I do. Yes, this was an emergency, I say, but no, it did not become a crisis. She was not alone. Her friend helped, I helped. I dispute even her sense of doom. We need better backup plans, it is true, but I will continue to help.

She's not really listening, and not reassured. I have never given her enough, she feels—not enough attention, intimacy, or sympathy. And apparently not enough help either. Why should she believe I'll start giving now? In my way I feel the same about her. As far as I'm concerned, Mom hasn't figured out that basic maternal maneuver, to be involved but not, as the therapists put it, "enmeshed" in her daughter's life. If I tell her about something gone wrong, rather than say "Gee, dear, that must be hard for you," she lets me know that the injury to me is an injury to her, but I shouldn't be too blue because, after all, such is life; things don't generally work out. Should I soothe her disappointment or dismiss my own? I've long since stopped telling her any but happy news. She feels shut out, and she is. It's nothing extraordinary, this clumsy mother-daughter dance, but thirty years after my adolescence we still haven't coordinated our steps. Compassion would require us to stand in the other's shoes, but we're wary of stomping on each other's toes. Feeling useless to satisfy each other's needs, we browbeat each other to stop needing.

"In the best of circumstances, Ma," I say finally, "shit happens."

"Well." It's a complete sentence. "More shit is going to happen." I sigh a little aggressively, as if to say, *Why do I even talk to you?* She gets the message. "But!" she chirps, managing to combine bravery and defeat in one syllable. "Who knows?"

"Who knows," I repeat, then smile. "Jewish telegram," I say. We laugh, both knowing the punch line of one of our family's favorite jokes. *Jewish telegram: Start worrying. Details to follow.*

. . .

When Dad got a diagnosis of Alzheimer's disease, it was as if the details had already arrived. All were bad. We knew what Alzheimer's is: "a progressive brain disorder that causes a gradual and irreversible decline in memory, language skills, perception of time and space, and, eventually, the ability to care for oneself" (this is a standard definition, from the Encarta encyclopedia). We would read about the brain's changes: sticky "plaques" made of amyloid protein that clump between the nerve cells, or neurons, and Brillo-like "tangles" inside these cells; and the depletion of certain neurotransmitters, notably acetylcholine, that are crucial to learning and memory.

Alzheimer's, we'd been told, is not normal aging. "Some change in memory is normal as we grow older, but the symptoms of Alzheimer's disease are more than simple lapses in memory," reads the Alzheimer's Association's web page. "While it's normal to forget appointments, names, or telephone numbers, those with dementia will forget such things more often and not remember them later." "Everyone has trouble finding the right word sometimes, but a person with Alzheimer's disease often forgets simple words or substitutes unusual words, making his or her speech or writing hard to

understand." The difference between dementia and ordinary forget-
fulness, the Alzheimer's Disease Education and Referral Center tells
us, is that "dementia seriously affects a person's ability to carry out
daily activities."

Although Alzheimer's is not normal, epidemic numbers of old
people have it. Ten percent of Americans over sixty-five suffer from
the disease, says the Alzheimer's Association, and half of those over
eighty-five. The numbers climb with age and an aging population:
four million today, sixteen million by 2025. So great is the threat
that the eminent American physician Lewis Thomas christened
Alzheimer's the Disease of the Century.

We knew, in other words, we were facing a long, grueling slide.

.   .   .

One week after Dad's fall, Mom calls to announce they are moving
to a "continuing care community," not maybe or eventually, but
definitely and as soon as possible. Early in 1995, their application
for long-term-care insurance was rejected on the basis of Dad's 1993
test results and an assessment by their physician that Dad appeared
to have an organic dementing disease. Only a week before the fall,
Paul had arranged to review the finances with Mom to figure out
how to stay in their apartment and also provide care for Dad.

But Mom cannot wait. She has already applied to a Quaker-run
nonprofit facility in Ithaca, New York, that offers accommodations
at escalating levels of care, from independent apartments to
"assisted living" to a nursing home on campus. Now she has
informed the administrators that she and Dad are ready to move in
and has put their apartment on the market.

"But weren't you going to talk to Paul?"

"Judy, I already understand the finances. It's not that complicated."

"Well, there might be some possibility that—"

"I can't discuss this now, Judy."

"When can we discuss it?"

"This isn't a good time." Is this her habitual deflection of a potentially upsetting conversation, or is Dad standing beside her? We agree I'll come to dinner a few days later.

At dinner, Dad is eager to be helpful. His wrist is Frankensteinian, with stainless-steel pins poking through the flesh. But, ever the host, he takes my drink order, then returns several times from the kitchen to remind himself of what I wanted. He brings me Scotch straight up, though I've asked for rocks, in a wineglass. As Mom serves the supper, he holds the plates with one and a half hands while she puts food on them, and carries them cautiously to the table. When we begin eating, he says heartily, "Lilly, you've outdone yourself!" It's her usual baked chicken.

Mom and I discuss a pro-choice group's lawsuit against Operation Rescue, the anti-abortion activists who have been blocking clinic doors. The pro-choicers have won—the judges ruled that the fetus-rescuers were interfering with the constitutionally guaranteed right to abortion. The million-dollar judgment could put the right-to-lifers out of business, and Mom, the former administrator of a birth control clinic, is elated.

Dad, who has been sitting quietly, busily moving his tongue around inside his mouth, is starting to get irked that no one's paying attention to him. "I have floating teeth," he says.

"Why don't you go rescue them?" Mom says. He leaves to fix his denture.

While he's gone, she whispers to me about filling out the application for the assisted-living community. "He can't read anything. He doesn't understand the words." The portion of the application he wrote was unintelligible. When she offered to edit it for him and rewrote it instead, "he became incensed. He kept shouting, 'That's not what I wrote!' "

"I'd be incensed too," I say, speaking as a writer.

But part of the game in assisted living is convincing the admissions office that you don't need assistance beyond the cheap stuff, like free lawn-mowing and garbage removal, and you are not going to need any. Because if the admissions officers believe you will eventually need full-time residential care, they ask for extra money up front and also charge you once you're in the nursing home. In other words, Mom is moving to the continuing-care community to control her costs when Dad's health deteriorates, but in order to control the costs she is compelled to omit any incriminating evidence of the deterioration of Dad's health. She gave Dad another piece of paper to write his portion, then sent in the one she'd written.

Back at the table, Dad speaks to Mom (who is also plagued by bad teeth) like a daddy to a baby: "And what about that thing you have in your little mouth?" She laughs weakly.

I leaf through the large, glossy brochure from Ithaca. From the bright four-color photographs of healthy white elders with coiffed white hair and Fair Isle sweaters to the pastel leaves of pebbled paper tucked into its pockets, the brochure conveys both cheer and sterile gloom, promises stimulation while illustrating narcosis. For Dad it might be just the thing, capacious but circumscribed, with plenty of people to amuse and a heated pool. Both he and Mom like to swim. But Mom can't live on chlorinated water alone. I comfort myself with the thought that since the community is run by Quakers, there might be a few pacifists among the residents with whom to talk and do politics, and that Cornell University will provide lectures, music, and films. Still, Mom is an Upper West Sider from her stack of primary-election leaflets to her Lincoln Center Chamber Society subscription, her Zabar's shopping bag to her Vibram-soled walking shoes (fitted with orthotics, which she refers to as her "pedophiles"). I can't imagine Mom "relaxing" in the plant-filled "day rooms" or trading her destination-directed city hikes for strolls along a manicured walkway that ends where it started. I can't even imagine the joke about her insoles going over among the inmates, condemned to banal politeness by their shared, self-imposed life sentences.

·   ·   ·

It would be hard to imagine life in contemporary America without colonies of "senior citizens" and nursing homes divided into wards, this one for the well and ambulatory, that one for the frail or demented. After all, reason the institutions' administrators, each of these "populations" has its "special needs." But it wasn't always this way, and what we have now is not unmitigated progress.

Old age was once simply the final stage of the journey. The aged lived among us all, ill or hale, helpful or inconvenient, respected and humiliated in differing measures. But aging has changed. Age now is a medical condition, a compendium of disorders and diseases to be prevented, retarded, and cured. "Like other aspects of our biological and social existence," writes the historian Thomas R. Cole, "aging has been brought under the dominion of scientific management, which is primarily interested in *how* we age"—biologically—"in order to explain and control the aging process." Increasingly, Cole says, gerontologists and social and biological scientists "view old age as an engineering problem to be solved or at least ameliorated." Indeed, with stem cells to rebuild each failing organ like a malfunctioning transmission or fuel pump, we're aiming to cure mortality itself.

When science tells its own history, it portrays this new conception of aging as a natural outcome of learning more about the body. In other words, we are curing old age now because we can. Where dementia is concerned, say scientists, we used to think that getting dotty and ornery were among the inevitabilities of aging, that like the heart or the bones, the brain broke down and ceased to work as well as it once did; indeed, *senile* was a synonym for *elderly*. But then, goes the story, in 1906 a discovery was made. The German psychiatrist and histologist Alois Alzheimer, examining the brain tissue of the deceased Auguste D., identified what he took to be the cause of the patient's paranoia, agitation, amnesia, aphasia, and quick expiration: a pattern of peculiar formations in the brain cells—the "plaques" and "tangles" of dementia. In 1910, Alzheimer's colleague

Emil Kraepelin coined the eponym Alzheimer's disease in that year's edition of his *Handbook on Psychiatry*. And since that day, scientists have been refining their understanding of senility, which, contrary to prior beliefs, is a purely biological process, a brain disease, and not normal aging. Put succinctly by the Alzheimer's Disease Society, Britain's equivalent of the U.S. Alzheimer's Association, "Alzheimer's disease is a physical condition. The mental and emotional symptoms are a direct result of a set of catastrophic changes in the brain that lead to the death of brain cells. This degeneration is irreversible."

For anyone familiar with this narrative, it may come as a surprise that even today, as Rob J. M. Dillman, the Royal Dutch Medical Association's Secretary of Medical Affairs, puts it, "No one is sure whether AD is two or even three diseases—or even no disease at all." Critics of the disease designation of Alzheimer's point out that the "syndrome" is far from uniform among the people who are said to have it. The "stages" of decline outlined by New York University neurologist Barry Reisberg in 1980 don't always happen in the same order or for the same duration, if they happen at all. At the same time, some or all of the "definitive" markers of the disease—the amyloid plaques and neurofibrillary tangles, the acetylcholine deficit, the loss of neurons in the forebrain—can be found in most aged brains. But, as David Snowdon's famous Nun Study found, the brain deterioration may or may not be accompanied by dementia. That study examined the life histories and followed the final years of more than six hundred elderly Midwestern sisters in an effort to understand the physical and social factors contributing to dementia.

The most compelling evidence against thinking of AD as qualitatively different from aging is statistical: the older you get, the likelier you are to get it. According to some estimates, half of people over eighty-five suffer from Alzheimer's. This makes it statistically normal. If dementia climbs with the digits of age, the clear-minded eventually become the minority. Who is to say that they are not the "abnormal" ones?

The controversy as to whether AD is simply a more intense version of what happens to everyone if they live long enough is not new. Alois Alzheimer himself was among the dissenters to Kraepelin's new classification. He was agnostic about the relationship between typical senile (or old age-related) dementia and the syndrome he'd identified in the fifty-one-year-old Mrs. D., and also about the distinction between senile dementia and normal aging. Even Kraepelin—whose category was based on a mixed-age group of just four cases, Auguste D. plus patients aged forty-five, sixty, and sixty-five—noted later that "the clinical significance of Alzheimer's Disease is still unclear," and neurologists might be looking at nothing more than "an especially severe form of senile [or old-age] dementia."

Historians aren't certain why this ordinarily scrupulous taxonomist rushed to create such a confounding classification, but some think his concerns may have been more political than strictly scientific. At the turn of the century, doctors were warring over the origins of disturbances of the mind. Kraepelin was one of the premier promoters of the idea that they were caused exclusively by biological and genetic abnormalities (he is now sometimes considered the father of modern psychiatry). But another rising star was fast eclipsing him—Sigmund Freud, whose powerful descriptions of the familial and cultural etiologies of mental illness would dominate much of the twentieth century.

The nature-nurture question is never resolved, but for the moment Kraepelin and his descendants are winning the debate. Personal characteristics long attributed to psychology, morality, or environment have been declared biologically determined, and determined, moreover, by smaller and smaller components of the human body. Gender is written in our hormones, sexuality or shyness "hardwired" in the brain, we are told; since the Human Genome Project, we've been informed that just about everything about us, from eye color to musical genius, is "coded" before birth in the tiny twists of our DNA. Again, the story is that this way of looking at human life is the logical outcome of knowing more about the body.

But now, as in Kraepelin's time, this view is political, the fruit of hours spent not only in the lab but in front of congressional committees, shareholders meetings, and television cameras. As Patrick J. Fox, codirector of the Institute for Health and Aging at University of California / San Francisco, shows in an illuminating recent history of Alzheimer's, the popular conception of dementia is a case study of the politics of science.

In 1974, the same year the National Institutes of Health created the National Institute of Aging, a neurologist at New York's Albert Einstein Medical Center named Robert Katzman presented a paper proposing that early-onset AD and all forms of senile dementia be considered one disease. He also stressed that the elderly were living longer. In 1910, people over sixty-five constituted 4.3 percent of the United States population. By the end of the century, they numbered 13 percent, or twenty million Americans. The newly inclusive category of dementia, compounded by lengthening life expectancies, had a dramatic rhetorical effect: Alzheimer's became an epidemic.

Over the next decade Katzman worked indefatigably to transform the public conception of "senility," a condition of aging, into Alzheimer's, a pernicious and widespread disease. In 1979 he helped consolidate a ragged collection of local caregiver support groups along with scientists and gerontological professionals into ADRDA, the Alzheimer's Disease and Related Dementias Association. ADRDA's rank and file were mostly women taking care of demented family members. They hoped eventually for prevention or cure, but what they needed immediately was help: home health care, elder day care, and other people in similar straits to talk to. Because they remain its backbone, the Alzheimer's Association is now the single largest provider of such services in the United States. But with scientists at the helm, the interests of the science drove ADRDA.

In the twelve congressional hearings spearheaded by the group between 1980 and 1986, all but one focused on the need for biomedical research. Wielding Katzman's catastrophic projections,

ADRDA's witnesses presented Congress with a compelling choice: "If you don't fund substantial research, you will have this problem for a long time," testified one organizer in 1986. "The only analogy would be polio. Had the money gone into treatment, we would have a magnificent portable iron lung, but no cure for the disease." Eager to focus funding even more effectively (and for the benefit of science careers, visibly), in 1988 ADRDA jettisoned "Related Dementias" from its name and became the lean and mean Alzheimer's Association.

Serving this sole master, the organization has been extraordinarily successful. Scientific interest in the disease has mushroomed. From ten published articles on AD in 1966, the number grew to 2,372 by 1996. The National Institute on Aging was founded with the mission "to coordinate and promote research into the biological, medical, psychological, social, educational, and economic aspects of aging." But thanks largely to the Alzheimer's lobby, biological and medical research came to receive the lion's share of the funds—with Alzheimer's disease the lion king. In 1983, Congress allocated $22 million for research into the disease. By 2001, total federal research funding for Alzheimer's reached $520 million, to say nothing of the millions in private biotechnology investment. Beginning with the Reagan administration, hostile toward social welfare programs and busy cutting the taxes and budgets that supported them, the feds have been agreeable to the biomedical project. Its expenses are controllable and its potential profits, especially to the burgeoning pharmaceuticals industry, vast.

The triumph of Alzheimer's as a grant-getter dovetails with the view that each body is an island and each disease a separate colony of bodies in need. Rather than unite to win for Americans what citizens of other developed nations have—health security for young and old, able and disabled—Alzheimer's advocates joined the battle of politicized constituencies of sick people. Cerebral palsy against breast cancer, breast cancer against AIDS, AIDS against Alzheimer's, each "disease community" vies for popular and scientific attention and government funding. Among the elderly, says Fox, the contest divides people between the "deserving elderly," with heartstring-tugging conditions and good lobbyists, and the "undeserving elderly," whose mundane needs for low-salt recipes or transportation to the clinic win nobody a prestigious chair or profitable patent. Robert N. Butler, the first head of the National Institute on Aging, called this life-and-death jousting "the politics of anguish."

·   ·   ·

November 1996

Katzman's emergency and the politics of anguish have Mom by the guts, and the biomedical model of aging has her by the pocket-book. One of the chief problems is that the programs she will have to look to for aid in financing Dad's care, Medicare and Medicaid, are more about medicine than about care or aid. Neither pays for the nonmedical help of the sort a demented or other disabled elderly person is most likely to need: a massage or shampoo or a game of checkers (much of this is called "custodial care," a phrase that calls up the image of a person being swabbed with a mop). Both programs severely limit reimbursement for at-home or community-based elder services, even medical ones. Although my parents have a relatively fat bank account, they will flatten it in no time if Dad needs full-time care. So the government is hurrying them and all elderly people to nursing homes before their time. To add idiocy to injury, nursing homes are far more expensive than at-home care. But, as is often true, idiotic public policy has private profit propping it up. The powerful nursing home industry lobbies vigorously against any proposed funding increases for at-home care.

No surprise, Mom and Dad's apartment, a roomy two-bedroom in a well-maintained prewar building in the heart of Manhattan's fashionable Upper West Side, sells within weeks.

A family conference is convened: Mom, Dad, Paul, me, and James, who is in town for Thanksgiving. We're supposedly discussing what will happen next. But the real reason for the confab is to give Mom a chance to express her already rising doubts and for Paul, James, and me to assure her she is doing the right thing, which none of us thinks she is.

She rehearses the reasons hers is the reasonable course of action: "Neither of us is getting any younger or healthier." (My interpretation: *Dad is deteriorating. Sooner or later he will need institutional care.*) "I don't feel like shopping and cleaning anymore." *(He can't help anymore, and when he does it drives me crazy because he does it wrong.)* "The assisted-living place is offering good deals now; it will fill up fast, so we have to hurry." *(I'm too nervous to postpone acting.)* "Our friends in the city are all getting sick and dying." *(Fewer people want to visit us now that Dad is becoming more bizarre.)* "We'll meet new people there." *(I'm hurt that my friends are abandoning me, so I'll abandon them.)*

We press. "You sure, Ma?" "You don't have to do this, you know. You haven't sent them any money yet." "Couldn't you wait and see?"

These entreaties elicit ambivalence. Yes, she will miss New York, her friends, music, the gardens, the street life. But the ambivalence is muscled out by fear. She does not want to live with uncertainty, and uncertainty seems to be the only certain part of her future.

Every once in a while, Dad asserts himself. "You know, Lil, I have feelings about this, too." He doesn't see the move as Mom does—that is, for his benefit, his comfort and safety. He doesn't see (or maybe doesn't want to see) that their roles have shifted—he now the needy one, she the provider, he the patient and she the caretaker not only of him but of all their shared business. He wants the move to be a project undertaken by partners, a husband and wife who care for each other. He turns to us and says, "Of course I couldn't live without Lil."

She looks stricken (Paul's later comment: "The Levine women's reaction to need"). "Well, you might have to one of these days," she says.

He puts his hand on her arm and addresses her. "What's important is that you are giving me a lot, and I also give you a lot." She turns from him without answering.

I ask if the place is close enough to town to walk in. Mom says she thinks it is. Dad looks worried. "But you have to know the way," he says.

December 1996

"I'm freaking out." It's Mom on the phone. Dad has been packing to go to Ithaca, prematurely, according to her. He put a lamp in a box and labeled it "Light Work." She's concerned that the movers won't be able to interpret the meaning of this phrase. She told him "calmly" that they didn't need to pack yet. Attuned to her criticism, even when unstated, and frustrated by his own mistakes, Dad blew up.

She tells me she sent him to the post office "with detailed instructions" to pick up change-of-address cards and buy stamps, and he returned with stamps but no cards. She says she went back herself to get the cards on Saturday, "in the pouring rain, and waited on an endless line."

"If it was too early to pack anyway, why didn't you wait until Monday, when it wasn't raining and the line was shorter?" She kicks Dad, I kick her. But I ignore the real message of her complaint.

She doesn't need another fight. "I can't talk about this now," she says.

She calls a few days later, in tears. "I hate living with Dad! I HATE it!"

"What did he do?" I ask calmly, hoping to inspire calm.

"Everything he shouldn't do. And he undoes everything I do."

He's been taking things out of boxes and putting them in other boxes, or putting them somewhere else. Keys and kitchen utensils are forever disappearing, unread newspapers whisked to the incinerator. Dad repeatedly loses his senior citizen's bus pass; each replacement requires a time-consuming round with the city bureaucracy. Mom's eyeglasses are suddenly gone; after an hour's myopic search, she finds them—on Dad's face. When she asks him where these things went, he denies everything and bitterly accuses her of falsely accusing him; humiliated by his own forgetting, he is instantly in a rage. For an orderly person like my mother, this is torture. She says she's beginning to doubt her own perception of reality. "I feel gaslighted," she tells me.

Dad's old belligerence and paranoia are still there, but without the intervening reason and social inhibition that used to mitigate them. Combined with Mom's need for order and control, their chemistry has always been volatile. Now explosions are constant. "In so many ways," Mom tells me, "he's exactly the same as he's always been. The same clinginess, the same touchiness, the same need to be at the center of attention. All. The. Time. I look at how he's behaving now and realize how he was behaving all these years. We were so busy, we never sat down and had an analytical discussion. Now almost every discussion we have, he twists it all up. I feel—" she pauses as if to listen to the contents of her head rattling—"*nonplussed*. Sometimes I'm so enraged and frustrated I just run into the bathroom and cry."

•   •   •

Dad is the same person he always was, but when Mom is going out of her mind, one thing seems to console her: the problem isn't him, it's the disease. "Something is happening to your brain, Stan, and there is nothing anyone can do about it," she says to him one evening after a hot conflagration. "None of this is your fault. It's nobody's fault."

Hers is the common understanding of dementia, and it is reinforced by the history of Alzheimer's disease told in popular articles and books, which starts with the famous histologist gazing through his Zeiss microscope and ends with a geneticist gazing through her electron microscope. Across the screen in the final scene reads the legend *Watch this space for more exciting scientific discoveries!* And, I have no doubt, many are on the way.

Absent from almost every account, however, is a chapter in which amyloid plaques and neurofibrillary tangles do not play star-

ring roles. Told by the historian Jesse Ballenger in an academic article published in a sixty-dollar hardcover text with a dull brown
cover, you are unlikely to read this part of the story in *Parade* magazine. But it may contain a crucial missing link in our thinking about
dementia.

The chapter takes place in mid-twentieth century America, when
large numbers of the indigent elderly were committed to public
mental institutions. With thousands of souls—hence, thousands of
research subjects—entrusted to their care, the psychologists and psy-
chiatrists who worked in these clinics came briefly to have a powerful influence on thinking about cognitive decline. They also had
piles of dead brains to study. But unlike Alois Alzheimer and most
everyone else concerned with dementia during the foregoing
decades, these doctors did not seek senility in slides of gray matter.

Some of them denied any organic causality for dementia at all—
or rather, they believed the cause and the effect had been wrongly
reversed. In 1953, for instance, Maurice Linden and Douglas
Courtney argued that senility was "a social illusion . . . largely a cultural artifact," and that "senile organic deterioration may be conse-
quent on attitudinal alterations." In other words, people's bad
experiences hurt their brains, not the other way around.

The most influential member of what might be called the "psy-
chogenic school" of AD, however, was both a psychiatrist and a neurologist. David Rothschild, who practiced at Massachusetts General
Hospital, scrutinized brain tissue slides; he could see senility was
partly a biological phenomenon. But the overlooked—and to him
pivotal—question jumped out at him from the clinic, not the lab:
why did some people with plaques and tangles become demented
and others not? In asking this question, Rothschild presaged
Snowdon's Nun Study by half a century.

By now, medicine has come up with some good preliminary
answers. Genes, cardiovascular disease, high cholesterol, maybe hormones, nutrition, exercise—these and other physiological factors can

increase a person's chances of ending up demented. But Rothschild's answer also resonates: their personal and social lives make a difference. "Many of [the people who become demented] have not had adequate psychological preparation for their inevitable loss of flexibility, restriction of outlets, and loss of friends or relatives," wrote Rothschild "[T]hey are individuals who are facing the prospect of retirement from their life-long activities with few mental assets and perhaps meager material resources." (Indeed, even those physiological factors are related to mental assets and material resources, to education and socioeconomic class.)

Rothschild felt the balance in dementia research had tipped dangerously toward cells and away from the people they make up. "Too exclusive preoccupation with the cerebral pathology . . . led to a tendency to forget that the changes are occurring in living, mentally functioning persons who may react to a given situation, including an organic one, in various ways," he wrote in 1941. If it didn't implicate Dad's own mental assets, I think this view would appeal to him, a man who believed that autism was caused by mothers and the causes of reading disabilities were legible in the Rorschach blots.

But the patients who lost their reasoning minds didn't lose them only because they were, as individuals, unprepared for the rigors of old age, according to Rothschild and his colleagues. Rather, senility was environmentally caused—a social disease. As the Second World War approached, a burgeoning youth culture was dismissing the elderly as useless has-beens. After the war, employers, aided by new labor laws, were pushing older workers (along with women) out of jobs to make room for the returning soldiers. Soon, young families were moving by the millions to the suburbs, leaving grandparents in the cities, stripped of their formerly crucial, challenging, and often joyful roles in the daily lives of their children and grandchildren. The doctors observing this scene from inside the state institutions' walls concluded that "the locus of senile mental deterioration was [not] the aging brain," writes Ballenger. "Instead it was a society that stripped elderly people of the roles that had sustained meaning in their lives through mandatory retirement, social isolation, and the disintegration of traditional family ties. Bereft of any meaningful social role, the demented elderly did not so much lose their minds as lose their places in the world." *I have no boat,* laments Dad. *I have no money.*

Today there is a small but growing number of adherents to what is now called a social constructionist view of dementia. Most are social scientists—sociologists, linguists, anthropologists—rather than biological scientists, and among clinicians they tend to be social workers, music and art therapists, and nurses rather than physicians. But Rothschild the neurologist-psychologist has a brilliant descendant in Tom Kitwood, who also stresses that dementia happens to the brain—but it doesn't happen only to the brain. To Kitwood, a "malignant social psychology" not only plays a role in eating away at the minds of the elderly but also exiles them from personhood once their minds start to go, and that psychological wallop can be so hard that it hurries the dementing process along. At the rotten heart of this malignant social psychology is the notion that the demented person is not truly a person but the vessel of a diseased brain. Thus, wrote Kitwood with his colleague Kathleen Bredin, "the key psychological task in dementia care is that of keeping the sufferer's personhood in being. This requires us to see personhood in social rather than individual terms."

As I watch my mother and father pack up their lives and decamp to a "senior community" because the huge community of New York City cannot contend with their modest needs, it occurs to me that the same thing is happening to all the elderly. My father may truly be losing his mind, and my mother losing hers along with it. But their loss is much heavier: as old people, they are losing their places in the world.

·   ·   ·

January 1997

Paul and I drive Mom and Dad to Ithaca. The movers, two geeky, strong, and preternaturally nice Ithaca boys, have gone ahead in their truck. It is a gray, frigid day. The drive on the interstate is numbing, the villages we pass through little more than strung-together strip malls. I am kept awake only by the constant vigilance of steering my Volkswagen out of the predatory path of tractor-trailers. The community my parents are moving to is six hours from New York and six hours from our home in Vermont. Mom and Dad won't have a car.

When we find our way to the community, we realize that it is not within walking distance of town, but miles outside it. Notices on the bulletin boards inform us that vans ferry residents regularly to the shopping mall, a place my parents have rarely had the desire or the need to go. The apartments and rooms are less than half occupied, the reason Mom and Dad got a reduced initiation fee. There's no one around. The place is quiet, as if waiting.

We check out the apartment, which is large and light, with a good kitchen and expensive fixtures. Then, while the boys unload the furniture, we take a walk. It is hard going for Dad and Mom: the apartments are all downhill from the main building and the sidewalks are icy, without rails, a strange oversight for a senior citizens' community. The wide lawns are bordered tidily with flower beds, which the brochure pictures thick with impatiens and petunias. The trees, all saplings, look decrepit. Rather than a little village, the compound resembles a minimum-security prison in the middle of a golf course.

After a supper of salt-free chicken and potatoes in the dining room, Paul and I retire to our room in the main building. We both feel old just being there.

The next morning, we set out to meet Mom and Dad in the dining room. Eventually, they will take breakfast in their apartment, but their coffeepot isn't unpacked. We're going to help them get started today. Soon we find ourselves outside a dining room. Somehow, though, we have gotten turned around. These are not the nattily dressed, lively residents in whose company we dined last night. These people are patients. Slumped in their chairs or wheelchairs, many wear bibs and are being fed. Food and juice are spilled around the plates on the table. Some are wearing pajamas. Paul and I hurry away, not looking back.

David Snowdon had a similar experience at one of the convents he visited—he found that the able nuns were served in one dining room and the disabled in another—and his reaction was just like Paul's and mine. Walking the ten feet between the dining rooms "felt like going from one world to another: one up and vigorous, the other quiet and disheartening—at least to me," he writes in *Aging with Grace: What the Nun Study Teaches Us About Leading Longer, Healthier, and More Meaningful Lives*. Then the mealtime policy was changed, and "the results were wonderful to see." In a common dining room, the able sisters helped the disabled, and "the sisters who had some cognitive problems seemed pulled toward the normal end of the spectrum." Snowdon, who notes that malnutrition can contribute to dementia, came away certain that nutrition isn't just about calories and vitamins. "It also depends on where we eat, whom we eat with, and whether the meal nourishes our heart, mind, and soul as well as our body."

No doubt the Ithaca retirement community, like the convent in years past, believes it is addressing the "special" needs of its demented and disabled residents. Besides, it's easier to manage everyone who needs feeding in one room, and institutions, no matter how client-friendly, look after institutional needs. For Paul and me and the other healthier residents at Ithaca, though, the separate ward fulfills another, darker function: it allows us not to look at the demented. But our not looking can have a devastating effect on the demented.

When "they" are elsewhere, they become strangers, and from there, more easily, objects, even to those who care for them. In studying their conceptions of nursing home residents, Eva Kahana, director of the Elder Care Research Center at Case Western Reserve University, "found that staff view elderly patients as management problems, while even frail elderly see themselves in terms of prior social roles." The "managers" of the demented elderly may cease to see them as having current social roles either, that is, as being people with opinions, pleasures, or even physical pain. In late 2003, *The New York Times* reported on two new studies, one finding that people with Alzheimer's are in better physical shape and are less depressed if they exercise for thirty minutes a day, and the other showing that people with Alzheimer's who live in pleasant environments and participate in stimulating activities like gardening or baking are less agitated and aggressive than those who are left to sit alone in nursing home wards. It was apparently news that people with Alzheimer's are people.

Other research is more troubling. A study published in *Journal of the American Medical Association* in 2000 found that nondemented elderly hip-fracture patients were given more than twice as much morphine as those with "end-stage" dementia. Only a quarter of these demented patients—"who often are unable to communicate the presence of pain"—had standing orders for other painkillers. "The authors [of the study] theorized that doctors withheld painkillers out of the mistaken assumption that the patients weren't in pain."

Paul and I find Mom and Dad in another hallway ("This must be the young fogies wing," I whisper to Paul). He falls into step beside Dad while I take Mom's arm a few paces ahead. Neither of us mentions the other dining room.

"Tell me the truth," she says, speaking quietly, though the carpet muffles our steps and our words. "If you had seen this place before, would you have advised me to move?"

I hesitate, then immediately regret my hesitation, which reveals my feeling and forces its expression. "No, I wouldn't have," I say.

Then I regret my answer. After all, the die is cast. More than once, Mom has told me that for her and Dad Ithaca is the "last stop."

Her face falls in my first split second of hesitancy, and further after my reply. I want to tell her it's not too late. She can come back home, where the last stop on her favorite bus line, the Broadway M104, is only Forty-second Street. But I do no more than pull her arm in a little closer. She nods her head slowly, as if to acknowledge a grave mistake.

February 1997

Home decoration revives Mom, at least temporarily. She calls me with progress reports. "The guy came to hang the pictures. We put all the family photographs in the hallway. It's very light, so you can actually see them!"

"The shelves are up in the library. Oy, I never thought I'd be unpacking those books again in my lifetime."

"I ordered a new bedspread—the other one looks so shabby . . . Blue and white—you have to ask?" I'm glad to hear she is busy and seems to be enjoying herself. But I also find myself cursing her efficiency. Once the curtains are up, will she feel closer to the last stop?

She swims daily, as does Dad, plays the piano, and gamely tries to involve herself in the social life of the community. But this is proving difficult. The "in crowd" of longtime residents is impenetrable, she says. At certain tables in the dining room all the seats are saved for the same people every night; there are no empty chairs for newcomers. Even outside this coveted clique, relationships are harder to get started than she had expected. One potential friend lives only a few doors away and she and Mom share a love of music, a passion for politics, and a problem—both their husbands are demented. But the other husband is further gone than Dad, leaving his wife little time or energy for friendship. For her part, I suspect Mom isn't eager to spend time with the man Dad may soon become. Her most promising friendship is already fizzling.

This relationship is a small version of the social dynamics of the place. Beyond the independent-living / nursing-home divide, there's this other, more subtle segregation. Among the well, some carry the tainted aura of illness. These are the people caring for sick or cognitively impaired spouses. They are, first of all, busier than the others in this "leisure" community, because the administration provides no free home-health aides. While the caregivers are not shunned, neither are they are sought out by other residents, who find it easier to set up a card game or attend a concert at the university with the relatively mobile and mentally alert. According to Mom, despite the fact that "they have absolutely nothing else to do besides play bridge," the unencumbered residents do not pitch in to help the caregivers. In this way, Mom says, it's worse than the city.

March 5, 1997

Dad is seventy-eight. I call. "Hi Dad, it's Jude."

Pause, while he collects an image of me. "Jude!"

"Happy birthday."

"Ah yes, yes, and so it is." He tells me he went swimming this morning.

"Did you have a happy birthday?"

"Yes, we are all here, we are all here in this world, and we must help each other. And it's all there! And I daresay we are helping, we are helping one another." His wish that he and my mother would stop bickering seems to have transformed into an ongoing homily for world peace. "We are helping. And it couldn't be better. It couldn't be better."

"Glad to hear that, Dad," I say. I make one more try at segueing back to the birthday. "So, you had a good birthday. Did you get any presents?"

"Lil! Lil?" he calls out. "Did I get any presidents?"

I hear her laughter from the next room, but there's no happiness in it.

.   .   .

"People are distressed, they have needs. It's not just because they are sick but—but because they have needs!" Jaber F. Gubrium, a University of Florida sociologist and author of *Oldtimers and Alzheimer's: The Descriptive Organization of Senility,* fairly sputters with frustration. "To have to biomedicalize this to fulfill these needs is a nasty process, a bad way around a difficult problem." No one would deny that dementia has an organic component, concedes Gubrium. And calling dementia a disease has drawn public sympathy, which has yielded services for people like my parents. Then he sighs. "I'm so annoyed with having to construct it as a disease to get anybody to pay attention."

People are paying attention, that's for sure. But with all the celebrity Alzheimer's patients and the Life Channel docudramas, that attention funnels money to biomedical research. The newsletters of the service-oriented Alzheimer's Association are thick with discoveries and drug trials, but there's not much news on the care front. What have billions of dollars in research grants yielded? As of late 2003, the Food and Drug Administration has approved five drugs: tacrine, marketed as Cognex; donepezil or Aricep; rivastigmine (Exelon); galantamine (Reminyl); and memantine (Namenda). The first four, according to the Alzheimer's Association web page, "may temporarily improve or stabilize memory and thinking skills in some individuals"; the effects of the fifth, says the FDA's advisory committee, are similarly "modest." And modest, says Case Western Reserve University's Dr. Peter Whitehouse, "may be an exaggeration." Whitehouse should know. He was on the team at Johns Hopkins School of Medicine that in 1981 discovered the brain cells lost to cholinergic decline, a breakthrough that enabled the development of the first drug. After that, he directed the college's Alzheimer's Disease Research Center for ten years. He served for years as an FDA adviser. And, he admits, he made a lot of money as a consultant to the pharmaceutical industry.

But like the neurologist David Rothschild, Whitehouse got fed up with looking at cells, not people or communities. "I saw a huge lack of balance. I saw molecular approaches taking over neuroscience and the pharmaceutical companies coming in to dominate the discourse. When I voted [at the FDA] to approve tacrine, I thought, 'What am I doing? Are we going to have a lot of look-alike drugs that don't do anyone much good? Or are we going to start thinking about something else?' I was really beginning to understand my limits and the limits of biological science." Whitehouse got a degree in bioethics and now is a professor of neurology, psychiatry, neuroscience, psychology, nursing, organizational behavior, and biomedical ethics. "Do the AD drugs improve people's quality of life? The answer is, there's no evidence that they do. Do they even save money? The answer to that is, who knows?" Along with a specialization in measuring quality of life, Whitehouse is developing a course on wisdom. "All the focus is on modifying ourselves and not being responsible for the [social] environment," the doctor continues. "There are things we could be doing to improve life instead of investing money in an interesting but not achievable goal of securing or preventing AD."

The historian Jesse Ballenger expands: "In trying to reduce a problem like senility to a very narrow technical fix, we may be reducing old age itself into a spiritless, managed and bureaucratized, and medicalized experience that doesn't amount to much besides an avoidance of disease. That's a pretty hard thing to build your life around."

.   .   .

March 12, 1997

Mom and Dad move back from Ithaca. "I'm not going to exile myself to Siberia to take care of Dad," she tells me. Until he was disabled enough to move into the nursing home at Ithaca, "I was going to have to be his nurse anyhow." And if that is to be her lot, she might as well be in New York, where she can put Dad in a cab and take him to a concert. She has sold the Ithaca apartment back to the corporation. The three-month sojourn has cost them $30,000.

I could blame Mom's impulsiveness for my parents' misadventure. But I'm also mad at Medicare and the disease model of aging that is written into it. The fact is, Medicare and Medicaid were never intended to address the ordinary daily needs of the demented or anyone else. The advisory board that proposed Medicare in 1965, responding to fears of the spiraling costs of hands-on long-term care, identified the program's mission as the "rehabilitation and cure" of disease, not the physical or emotional well-being of the old.

Stephen Post decries the *"geist* of self-control, independence, economic productivity, and cognitive enhancement that defines our dominant image of human fulfillment." And here are the only federal programs designed to care for the bodies of the aged (presumably so they can fulfill themselves in their waning days), whose rules discourage spending on any bodies not likely to recover self-control, independence, and productivity. For example, until the Alzheimer's Association lobbyists got the regulation changed recently, the government automatically denied people with dementia reimbursement for rehabilitative services such as physical therapy after a hip replacement. The bureaucrats figured they'd be throwing good money after bad, since the recipient wouldn't remember on Tuesday to do the exercises the therapist taught him on Monday (this just in: demented people can recover from hip surgery). But it's not only the demented who are losing self-control, independence, and productivity. Every potential Medicare recipient is. The bodies of the aged, after all, are aging.

By a *mechaieh*—what joy!—after twenty years on the waiting list at the Penn South co-ops in Manhattan's Chelsea, Mom and Dad are offered an apartment. The same two young men move them back into the city, with equal courtesy and efficiency. They ask no questions. They get an equally good tip.

I exit the subway on West Twenty-fourth Street into a red-brick forest of nearly identical thirty-story buildings. A plastic bag bobs across the front lawn and snags in a scrawny privet hedge. When I reach their lobby, I find Dad on a bench, dispatched by Mom to bring me upstairs. I notice he is losing participles. "What they're demand of us," he says, apropos of nothing.

He guides me through a hallway tiled the color of Gulden's mustard and up a slow elevator to the sixteenth floor. Mom is waiting at the door. "Forgotten but not gone!" she says merrily. We hug and I enter a small, dark foyer giving onto a long living room, which is almost as dark. The room's one, northwest-corner window provides a few feet of river view but casts light only a yard beyond its sill. The floor is a parquet of chipped, wood-veneer tile. The bedroom is also long and rectangular, the kitchen in need of renovation and hardly large enough to swing a rat in. But Mom is flitting through the rooms like a bride just carried over the threshold. In the kitchen, she reels off the improvements she will make. She scurries around the living room showing me where each piece of furniture will go. She recalls Ithaca with a shiver. "I felt like a bird in a net," she says. "Oy! All those old people!" Her laughter turns serious. "Next time I get that idea, remind me to kill myself first."

After their elegant West End Avenue apartment and even the high ceilings and soft winter light of Ithaca, this place is a cave. I foresee more trouble, or another move. Still, we agree that beyond the miracle of the available apartment, they have landed in one of the last redoubts of communitarian idealism in America.

Penn South, founded in the 1950s by the International Ladies Garment Workers Union, is a "NORC," a "naturally occurring retirement community." Despite what my mother refers to as the accelerating "die-off" of the older co-operators and the influx of younger families of all ethnicities, the co-op houses a critical mass of aging Jewish leftists and former union activists. "The politics there run from social democrat to anarchist," a friend whose mother lives here tells me. "They don't know from the Republican and Democratic parties." For my parents, who have several friends in the buildings, it's a kind of homecoming.

Because the founders were socialists and some on the board still are, they put their energies to collective use, organizing everything from nursery schools to communal seders; the complex even generates its own electricity. There's a large active senior center, which runs an affordable adult day care program for people with memory loss. It's housed just a couple of buildings to the north, and Dad can spend three, later four, full days a week there. The cost of their one-bedroom apartment is $10,000, which they pay outright. Maintenance is assessed on a sliding scale depending on income; they will pay less than $600 a month. If Dad needs more care, they can afford it.

Besides returning to her piano lessons, her gardening in Central Park, and her friends, Mom is excited about resuming her political life, which she can now do without leaving home. She soon joins the Concerned Citizens of Penn South (What are they concerned about? I inquire after her first encounter. "Everything," she says in an *oy-vey* tone of voice. Another time she describes a Concerned Citizens meeting: "It was brainstorming without the brains").

I ask Dad if he's glad to be back. "I want to come back," he answers. He has always expressed Mom's feelings when he's unsure of his own. I'm not sure of Mom's feelings, though. On one hand, back in Manhattan she's like an astronaut stepping onto the tarmac at Cape Canaveral. But there's something faintly hysterical about her enthusiasm. It's as if she wants to feel relieved, but knows she has only exchanged one set of problems for another.

They walk me to the elevator. Alerted by our voices, the next-door neighbor emerges from her apartment. She is a little gray-headed Jewish lady, exactly Mom's size, wearing the same sensible shoes, the same worn wool sweater. Mom introduces us. Her name is Mrs. Mehl.

Mrs. Mehl barely glances at me; she has no time for pleasantries. She steps up to Mom, nose to nose like the Caterpillar confronting the shrunk-down Alice, and launches into a Caterpillar-like harangue. She starts with my parents' too-loud radio-playing and proceeds to prohibit Mom from practicing the piano before ten in the morning. Without a breath, she continues into a detailed jeremiad against the building management. "There are lawsuits—you'll see. Lawsuits! They're not returning people's equity." Mom looks over me, mouths *Help!* Finally, Mrs. Mehl turns on her heel and marches into her apartment. I tell Mom that *miel* means "honey" in French. Although he probably doesn't get the joke, Dad laughs with us.

I smile as the elevator closes, but my happiness tastes of worry. When Paul and I left my parents in Ithaca, I admitted to him that I'd played a role in their decision to move, if only by default. Mom felt alone. For a long time, she did not request help, but I also didn't offer. Ithaca scared me. Although the facility was well-run, pretty, friendly, and relatively affordable, Mom was putting herself in voluntarily social quarantine because of the compromised state of her husband's brain. For his part, Dad was going to end up in that other wing, assisted but hardly living.

Still, their move freed me. I would have had to deal with Mom's misery and Dad's deterioration, but over several hundreds of miles of phone line. I will not have to support them financially. Like others of their generation, they are proud not to be a "burden" to their children. But as they brave aging among the brutal young, the person left to assist their living is me.

5. Care

IN MAY OF 1998, Leo Goldstein's skin turns yellow, and he is diagnosed with pancreatic cancer. There is nothing that can be done; he will die within months. I drive Mom and Dad to visit him in Westchester on a Sunday afternoon. It is a cool, sweet-smelling day, and the rhododendrons in the Goldsteins' front yard are in bloom.

Leo is dressed, sitting in the easy chair in his room behind a portable bed table on which is propped a seven-hundred-page literary mystery. Finding out whodunnit, he says, is his incentive to stay alive. The private nurse is just leaving. He tells us that on her first day she got so lost in the labyrinth of their housing development that she arrived two hours late. Still, he let her go early. "Go, go!" he urged, waving her away. "Get lost!" I hope she got the joke, since Leo's gruff manner can belie the innocence of his wit. He is rarely demonstrative; one glass eye makes his gaze elusive. But perhaps because he's never hot, the warmth of his love seems imperturbable. For Mom, he is a soft rock.

Although the Goldsteins' marriage has become more a comfortable mutual alienation than an active love or even an active fight, their affection reawakens in his last months. Gloria reads to Leo and rubs his feet. She has the bed table rigged with the book stand, since holding a book tires him. His appetite is poor, so she keeps the refrigerator stocked with Dove Bars, his favorite ice cream. She fusses tenderly, bringing him tea and a sweater, asking him what CD he'd like to hear. For the first time in years, she says, they have long talks. I feel envious on Mom's behalf.

At lunch, Leo talks about his travels to Wyoming and Oregon, about fishing with his son in the blue-ribbon trout streams of the Rockies. Dad, who has been sitting quietly, comes alive. "And we went up and going up and it wasn't there," he says. "You could hardly place up. Do you remember that, Lil?" She recognizes he is talking about Zion National Park in Utah and a section of a trail that winds beneath a rock overhang so low that hikers have nearly to crawl under it. He remembers Zion, but keeps looking around his best friends' living room and asking, "Jude, have you been here before?"

In the last few months, Dad and I have established a routine. It hasn't been easy. I resist spending time with him, and Mom doesn't press. I could be wrong, but she seems even to resist my doing it.

"Keep telling myself I'm going to put aside a few hours a week to be with Dad. Keep putting it off," I write in my journal in April 1997, just after their return from Ithaca. In May: "Told Mom I'd take Dad once a week. Called today to make arrangements. She can't fit me into the schedule this week or next. What is going on?"

Early June: "Chinese takeout at M&D's with Paul. Mom went out. Dad calls the spicy food 'a little sharp.' Paul gives him some fried noodles: 'Here, that'll counteract the sharpness.' Mom wanted to change date. I couldn't make it—she said don't come. Doesn't want to trouble me? Doesn't trust me? Control? Competition? Leaving for VT in two weeks. Thank god."

Late June: "Thinking about Dad. Three months respite! NO NO, didn't mean that. I'll do it when I get back."

July: "Mom on phone. Depressed, tense, angry. At me because I'm not there? Promised her to start with Dad when home."

Now each Thursday when I'm in New York I collect Dad at the day care center. I pull up a chair next to him and tap him on the shoulder. "Ah! Hello," he says, taking a few moments to establish who I am. Although I have ceased to have a name (he sometimes calls me Lil), I am nevertheless a familiar and appreciated, if not always adored, person. He is usually seated beside Ewa, a former Olympic swimmer who now sits speechless in a wheelchair. Her profile forms a caliper, with a toothless mouth pulled in between a downward-pointing nose and an upward-pointing chin. All of us think of Ewa as his girlfriend, or at least of him as her suitor. He holds her hand and kisses it, and like the high school beauty queen with the besotted freshman nerd, she tolerates his attentions with amiable noblesse oblige. "Do you know this extraordinary person?" he says to Ewa. As if to help Dad, the social worker Dahlia offers, "Yes, that's Judy, Stan's daughter." Ewa looks up with her wan, sucked-in smile.

I help him with his coat and out the door. Like a cat, he enjoys pausing in the passage between indoors and out.

"How's your group?" he asks me when we are on the walkway that winds through the trees and gardens of the housing complex.

"Fine. How's yours?" For some months, I tried explaining to him that I don't have a group, but have given up. Sometimes he asks, "Are you in school?" This indicates to me that he has some idea that I used to be a girl, and that he used to have a relationship to this girl.

"No, Dad, I'm forty-six years old. I'm not in school anymore. I'm a writer."

"A wri-ter." He moves the word around in his mouth, identifying an unfamiliar flavor. After a few minutes, he asks anew, "So, how's your group?"

"Fine. How's your group? Is it going well?"

Dad still has a monologue about "his group" that recalls his professional life as a school psychologist. He remembers that it is his job to figure out what is wrong with children and families and what to do for them. "They have no parents, you see, and they are coming in and just on the side. And they're having. But I say and I'm say"—he shrugs the Yiddish shrug—" 'What the hell!?' " He is vaguely describing the home health aides who sit with their charges at the center from time to time. "But don't kick them up. Because it's an extraordinary, I mean I could, 'Get the hell outa here!' " He pauses, as if to consider the clinical sequella of kicking them up. He pulls his brow into a thoughtful wrinkle, then speaks one of his stock sentences: "I'm not completely sure what to do about it."

"Hmm. That's interesting," I interject, trying to spool him in. We nod to the old women on the benches, watch the children chasing each other across the bolted-down, liability-resistant playground apparatus. I imagine Dad and me in white coats, our hands clasped behind our backs, strolling the hospital on grand rounds, discussing our observations of the patients. Now the doctor is the patient. He wears a silver bracelet like a diabetic or a hemophiliac, except his identifies him as a client of Safe Return, which enables police and hospitals to contact his caregivers and take him home if he wanders.

When we arrive at their apartment, sometimes Mom is home, sometimes not. It's better when she's not. Dad doesn't like competition. When we're alone, I make tea and put out a plate of cookies. We walk, Dad greeting each dog and squirrel warmly, to the Chelsea Market at Fifteenth Street and Ninth Avenue, where I buy us coffee and an expensive pastry at Amy's Breads. Then we make our way west to the Hudson River and into the monstrous sports complex-cum-marina-cum-mall called Chelsea Piers, where we stand at the rail and squint southwest into the sun over the harbor.

"There she is!" he always exclaims.

"Yup, there's the Statue of Liberty."

He counts the tugs and ferries, which were many and varied before September 11, tries to read the words on the hulls. "He's bringing it in now," he always says, whether one is approaching or not.

We inspect the docked sailboats and yachts: "I'd have it," he says, when I point at one $100,000 fiberglass tub. "It's a beautiful piece."

"You like that one?"

"It's a quite nice."

"You think so? I think it's kind of ugly."

"Yup."

We stroll around the overgrown planters, stand hypnotized by the techno music and the pendulum-like swoops of the kids in the skate park. Once in a while we walk a block north to Pier 63, home of the retired metal fishing boat *Frying Pan,* a kayak club, and various temporarily moored sailboats and houseboats. There we visit Bob, age fifty, sixty, or maybe seventy, a former sea captain and current proprietor of an outdoor bar that resembles a beachfront hut on an underdeveloped Caribbean island: a tin roof over a bamboo-sided counter, a few Naugahyde bar stools, and a cooler, all arranged on a square of green Astroturf.

"Ah, Stan! Skipper of the Bullseye!" says Captain Bob, identifying Dad by the boat he owned. Morning or evening, rain clouds or sun, he offers us a drink.

We discuss the weather, boats, and life. Bob uses seaman's terms, like *knots* and *ketch* and *schooner.* Perhaps I'm mistaken, but at one point, I think I hear Dad say *yar.* It's a word whose meaning I've never quite known, but an old favorite of Dad's. Maybe he doesn't know its meaning anymore, either, but it and the rest of these words are shibboleths, gaining him entrance to his own past world, the world he shares with the captain.

Sometimes, in the middle of the conversation, he'll turn to me with anxious nonchalance and ask, "Have you been here before?"

"Yes, Dad, and so have you. This is the Hudson River. This is Bob, your friend." It's as if he comes unmoored and needs his lines tightened to the dock.

Or, walking home, "Do you remember me?"

I tell him that yes, I remember him well. We have known each other for a long time—my whole life! I tell him my name is Judy, and I am his daughter.

"Happy Father's Day, Dad," I announce, arriving for Sunday brunch with a bouquet of irises.

"Day?" he asks, as I carry the flowers to the kitchen to put them in a vase.

"It's your day, Dad. Father's Day."

"Father?" Indignantly: "Father!? I don't have a father!"

"I know you don't have a father, Dad. You're *my* father."

"*You're* my father?"

"No." I laugh. "You're *my* father."

"My father? I don't have a father."

"I know, Dad, I'm your daughter." It's no use, but it helps to remind myself of this fact.

In October, Mom calls to tell me Leo has died. Gloria, his children Jill and Alfie, and even the dog were at his side. He was conscious; they all said good-bye. "I told Dad and he was blank," Mom says. But at the funeral, Dad sees Gloria and says to me, "He must be sad." I'm not sure if he means Gloria or Leo—but I think he knows what has happened. At the small, simple chapel at the crossroads of their village where the funeral is held, Dad painstakingly signs his and Mom's name in the guest book, "Stanley and Lillien Levine."

Leo's teenaged grandson, Tony, remembers playing Guys on the Edge with his grandfather, a bath-time game that involved knocking plastic Army men from the tub rim, in combat, into the water. A local mechanic describes a friendship that grew around fly-fishing. Recounting her frequent lunches with Leo in the city, Mom says he was perhaps the only person with whom she could discuss "everything." That *only* excludes Dad, I infer, and Dad is included in the everything they discussed. "I will miss him terribly," she ends, and her steps drag the terribleness of a diminishing world back to the pew where Dad is waiting, neither comfort nor even company.

I, who have not prepared any remarks, am moved to stand up and declare that I always felt Leo's love for me was "unconditional," unlike "the complicated relationships with my own parents." I regret my words almost before they are out of my mouth, embarrassed by some Tourette's-like compulsion to say unkind things about my parents in public. I comfort myself with the knowledge that Mom can't hear much and Dad won't understand, or at least remember.

A month later, just before Thanksgiving, Paul calls to tell me that Julius, our healthy seven-year-old cat of the breed Paul has christened Domestic Orange Jumbo (or DOJ), is famished and thirsty and eating and drinking constantly, but quickly losing weight. He has dropped nearly half of his fourteen pounds. When he tries to jump onto the counter, he misses. This is funny, until it isn't. Paul takes him to the vet, who says he has diabetes and his body has gone into keto-acidosis: unable to metabolize the sugars in his food, it is staving off starvation by eating itself up.

I take the train to Vermont and go directly to the veterinary clinic, where Julius lies in a cage, scruffy, bony, and watery-eyed, with tubes attached to his shaved front legs. Each day, I return to sit beside him, dabbing little pieces of canned food on his paw to encourage him to lick it off in his desultory self-grooming, and weep.

We take Julius home on Thanksgiving, still in iffy health, and share a stripped-down dinner with two friends at their home. It is the first Levine-Goldstein Thanksgiving I have missed in twenty years.

In early December, the wind is blowing off the Hudson during Dad's and my late-afternoon walks, and the sailboats are in dry dock. Battalions of geese V southward, honking taxi drivers on their way to a pit stop at the Jamaica Bay Wildlife Preserve. As we stand at the railing, I watch a duck dive under the pewter ripples and think about the fish below. My mind drifts to Leo the fisherman, "cemented" in friendship to my parents for life and therefore cemented to me. If Julius's near-death approximates that of a child, Leo's is the closest I can imagine to the death of my own father.

I watch my father now, honking with the geese. I wonder how I will grieve for him, or if I will miss him enough to grieve at all.

.   .   .   .   .

Like most things about aging and illness in America, the idiom of Alzheimer's has love written into it. To the social workers and talk-show hosts, Dad is the "loved one" and we—family, professional, and minimum-wage custodian alike—are the "caregivers." The terms *loved one* and *caregiver* are gloved in velvet, but they wield the iron-fisted power of manipulation. Loved one labels the sufferer with the very passivity that is the condition's curse, then consoles him with a promise of succor.

Who will provide it? The *caregiver* becomes nothing but. She is there to give care. An early self-help book called her lot *The 36-Hour Day,* so apt an appraisal of the emotional and physical overburden of the caregiver's role that it instantly became a catchphrase in the Alzheimer's community and the book a perennial best seller.

Caregiver is nunlike. It reminds us not only of what we are supposed to do, but implies how. "I don't have to do the things I am doing. I want to do them!" writes Lyn Roche in *Coping with Caring.* "I don't give out of obligation. I want to give. It's my turn to give. It is what I choose to do and it feels good. I am motivated by love." Something about the repetitiveness (or maybe it's that exclamation point) makes this "daily reflection" hard to read as anything but a command. Another book title combines caregiving's physical end-lessness with this emotional injunction: *Love Never Sleeps.*

"Loved one," spits my resolutely antisentimental mother. "I hate that expression." Yet Mom does love Dad, has loved him body, mind, and spirit for more than fifty years. Her second and third thoughts about their marriage have sifted down only recently onto that bedrock of love. Since the age of nine I have been asking myself if I love my father. At Leo's funeral I more or less told a hundred people that I felt more loved by Leo than by my own father. I am at the best of times a reluctant daughter. What motivates me?

I feel the plainest poignancy toward Dad, and terror for him as he faces that "tall, black wall." Yet these are anonymously humane feelings, not specific to him, not specific to him as a father, *my* father. I realize I am trying hard to think of him as father, and all of us as family. That's why I keep reminding Dad of a relationship that might be abstract to him even if he had the ability to think abstractly. We never used the word *family* to describe the four individuals whose names appeared on the Levine tax return. I hardly uttered it until the 1980s, when the Christian Right coined "family values," and then I always flourished the phrase with a sneer.

Nevertheless, Mom found out in the Ithaca "community" that *caregiver* is code for family member because nobody else, least of all any policymaker, seems to care much about giving to the elderly. What will enable me to enact that verb straddling emotion and practice, *to care?* Family is so precarious a start.

. . .

Family is precarious, and as we embark on this nearly doomed familial project, it grows ricketier still. The more time I spend with Dad, the more conflict I fall into with Mom. She is irritated when I disagree with her about his capacities or his care, as if her authority is being undermined. She is responsible; the buck stops with her, so this is reasonable. But we're squabbling about more than how to care for him. The discord, it seems, is about how to *feel* about him and about each other.

When I'm with the two of them, my loyalties feel split. Mom wants respite from him; she wants to relax with an "adult." That leaves response to his demands—whose adamance increases with Mom's diminishing attention—up to me. But when I do pay attention to him, she is piqued, as if I am neglecting her. At the same time, she's vigilant in his defense. While she neither solicits nor seems to want Dad's love, she protects him against lovelessness. After a visit from James she calls. "Jamie could barely manage to speak a word to Stan," she says, sounding as disheartened as she is incensed. I comment that my brother hates his father. "Well," she answers, "he could pretend to like him for a day."

Between her and me a sort of Oedipal drama is unfolding—call it Electra by default. The daughter inherits the father, if only because the mother doesn't want him anymore. Of course, no tragedy worth the name is so efficient. Mom doesn't want Dad, but she doesn't want me to have him, either. Or maybe she doesn't want him to have me. Some of our moments of truest intimacy, Mom's and mine, have been our shared disappointment with Dad. In the scarce emotional economy of our family, if I start to love him, will she lose us both?

Before Christmas, Paul and I meet Mom and Dad for lunch and music. This year it's Richard Westenberg's Musica Sacra singing Bach's Christmas Oratorio at the Fifth Avenue Presbyterian Church. It's a yearly ritual and we all love the music. Beyond that, our experiences are not shared. Mom suffers no sympathy for the opiate of the masses and is impatient with the faithful, especially the well-heeled Upper East Side faithful like the members of this congregation, upon whom their god has obviously, and to her mind inordinately, smiled. My own reaction, especially during holidays, is to envy believers the comfort and joy they find in believing; I wish I could have faith in something without questioning it. Paul is a lapsed Catholic, but the values of his small-town Catholic education sank in, and he remains one of the truest Christians I know, his actions ruled by a love of justice and a universal respect for other people (when he represented our town in the state legislature, I used to say his specialty was suffering fools). And Dad, since Alzheimer's, seems drawn into the cool, fragrant spaces of any sanctuary he passes. Inside he can parrot piety. He even appears to believe in . . . something (though half the time he also feels compelled by some leftover political instinct to poke fun at God, preferably within earshot of some serious worshiper).

Dad loves the music, but today he's not happy about the lunch. Too many people talking too fast make him feel overwhelmed and excluded. He sulks or pesters Mom, resisting her ordering him a sandwich from the menu, which he can't read, and spitting bitter sentences into the middle of the conversation. "She's such a good talker." "Don't I get some coffee?"

As we walk to the church, I converse with Mom and Paul talks with Dad, cheering him with his interest. At the church, there's a fracas about who will sit where. At first Dad doesn't seem to have a preference, but he's riled when we begin to file into the pew, perhaps because he has not been consulted. The little rebellion in turn annoys Mom, who wants Paul and me between Dad and herself, a momentary buffer, but isn't up for a fight with Dad. I settle Dad on the aisle and turn my back to Mom to talk with him, pointing out the stained-glass windows.

Soon he is chatting up the woman in the pew in front of us. Either she doesn't notice Dad is senile or that he's wearing two clashing plaids and a pair of slightly dirty jeans, or she's simply a true Christian like Paul, tolerant and loving. She nods attentively as Dad prattles on. A slender black man, dressed in an elegant brown suit, slides in next to Dad. Dad leans on him companionably. The man jerks back but says nothing. Dad engages him. His icebreaker: "You see, what's going on with me is I have this memory loss." The man examines the soft brown leather gloves in his lap. "I used to be famous," Dad continues.

During the concert, Dad riffles through the hymnal and the libretto. From time to time, he bursts into song; he's listened to this piece his whole life. I don't know if Mom can't hear him (her ears are failing), is deliberately choosing not to deal with him, or is following the caregiver's creed of absolute permissiveness. I shush him when his voice grows too loud, but not too harshly or too often. The man beside him grows increasingly aghast. By the final chorus, Dad is leaning again on the man, who demands with his eyebrows that I do something about it. I shrug: *Sorry*. The performance ends, and the congregation coughs and fidgets, waiting for the sermon. As the chorus files out, Dad shouts, "Brava!"

A large, copper collection plate is passed from the other aisle, from Mom to Paul, Paul to me, me to Dad. He looks at the over-flowing plate, perplexed, searches the air for clues, then reaches up and plucks a dollar from the heap of bills, like a cookie from a plat-ter. I glance toward the finicky man to see if he's looking. All clear. Mom and Paul are engaged in conversation. Quick as a pickpocket, I stuff the dollar into Dad's shirt and grin at the caper the young Stan Levine would surely have appreciated. The ragged, godless Jew appropriates the wealth of the gilded cathedral. The demented hoodwinks the deluded. I won't tell and Dad won't remember. But we're partners, partners in crime.

July 2000

Spring passes. I sublet my apartment and decamp as usual for the summer in Vermont. Mom and Dad take the train up to visit us, and we meet them at the station.

"How was the trip?" I ask.

Mom rolls her eyes. "Long."

Driving to our house, she sits in the front seat of the car with Paul and I sit in the back with Dad. He drops off to sleep and wakes up every once in a while to ask, "Where are we?"

"We're in Barre," Paul says. "We're coming into Woodbury. We're on our road now, Stanley. Almost there." He might as well say, "We're on the moon." Away from home, from known objects and routines and habitual conversations, Dad's internal dislocation moves into the external world. He is altogether outside time and place.

For Mom, though, the time and place are a joy. It is high summer. The *ver* of Vermont—which lasts, in our northern reaches, about ten weeks—is in ravishing display. When we pull up to our place, the pond lilies are half-shut in the waning light, the bee balm buzzing with visitors. Mom is ecstatic to have three whole days of what she calls "adult companionship." But she also loves the coun-try. I sometimes hope she will move to Vermont after Dad dies; I imagine her in a ratty straw hat at ninety, contentedly weeding. I don't consider her dying before him.

Already disconnected from everything that orients him, Dad also seems to feel her tether loosen. He clings tighter. She attends to his needs: helps him out of his jacket, shows him the bathroom, counts his pills, (eventually) answers his questions and comments, which become more frequent and insistent. She has become more efficient now that he needs more help with everyday tasks, but the main emotion she shows is faint irritation. "I'm no longer his wife," she has said. "Now I am his caregiver." For her, too, away from home and its implication of intimacy, the transformation is pronounced. Detachment may make the tedium of caretaking more tolerable for Mom. But I wonder if it also makes them both lonelier.

That evening after supper, Paul goes upstairs, Dad takes a book to "read" in the living room, where they are sleeping, and Mom and I sit at the table, catching up over tea. After a while, Dad emerges and stands beside her chair. She finishes what she is saying to me.

Then she asks him, "What would you like, Stan?"

"Can't I talk too?"

"Dad, Mom and I are having a private conversation," I say.

"And I can't?"

"Why don't you put on your pajamas?" Mom suggests.

"Why don't you put on *your* pajamas?"

He's obnoxious, yes. But it's also an appropriate protest, succinctly put. Dad is eighty years old, and he does not want to be treated like a child. He will not be sent to bed while the grown-ups sit in the kitchen, drinking grown-up drinks, talking grown-up talk.

Things go downhill from there. The next day starts out well with a drive to a nearby lake, where Dad paddles around happily and watches the children dig moats in the sand. But a trip to another lake in the afternoon is too much. "Weren't we here?" he shouts. He stops on the path to the beach and refuses to move.

The next day, Paul takes him to the shed and figures out a way for Dad to help him do a little repair job. Dad comes back into the house exuberant, his old self, the putterer. Then Mom sends him to the living room to change into his swimsuit. When he does not come out, she goes in and discovers he hasn't undressed. She offers to help him, but he doesn't want her help, which itself seems to accuse him of helplessness. "I can't do anything," he yells at her. *I have no boat. I have no money.* His outburst turns to a plea: "Why am I living?"

Later, she tells me that her answer was "the usual": he is liked and needed—his group depends on him, they are waiting for his return. She does not say she needs him, because of course she does not. Or that she loves him. Is that what he wants to hear? Why is he living if not to participate, welcome and useful, in the daily commotion of relationship?

When I repeat my father's query to Paul that night, he says, "It's a good question."

.   .   .

Why am I living? How can I live? These questions, which Paul suggests are pertinent not just to Alzheimer's sufferers but to everyone, stand in high relief in the stripped-down existence of the caregiver.

In finding answers, the caregivers' culture cherishes the personal search, the personal story. Yet it also offers answers. And just as the disease model of dementia creates a tidy category by cobbling together diverse data and excluding confounding eccentricities, the world of the support group and the advice book advances a homogeneous Alzheimer's Experience and subtly compels certain feelings about it. As in twelve-step programs like Alcoholics Anonymous, the participants come to belong—both to feel like members and be accepted by the group—by singing their own unique verses, then joining the chorus in an anthem of heroism, love, and tragedy.

When sociologist Jaber Gubrium spent time in Alzheimer Association support groups, he observed in some that the shared understanding "varied with the flow of storytelling and the comparison of relevant experiences." But many groups enforced a "ruling narrative" that brooked little divergence. "Newcomers quickly learned that the personal stories that made the most sense and that were believed to be realistic were those that conformed to local understandings." The resulting "unity in disunity"—which is how he also describes the disease classification of Alzheimer's—not only gives people a strong sense of fellowship, it also creates the comforting impression, which may be an illusion, that they can learn from others what to expect.

What if a member's feelings and expectations do not conform to the common story? In one group a woman Gubrium calls Dee maintains that she is not lonely taking care of her husband and doesn't think she will have to put him in a nursing home. Ruth replies, "You're denying. We all try to deny it."

In the caregiver narrative, love is both assumed and prescribed. Confessions of anger, even homicidal rage, toward the person with Alzheimer's are applauded as steps toward honesty in the service of good care and, equally important, good self-care. Still, such animus is considered evanescent and situational, never the quality of the ongoing relationship. Negative feelings are not a response to the person himself, moreover, but to the disease, and the disease is *not* the person—it is an intruder that robs the Alzheimer's sufferer of his personhood. Scoured of his idiosyncratic self, the sufferer becomes a standard-issue Alzheimer's Patient, an agglomeration of symptoms recognizable to all caregivers, and one of a group commonly referred to as "they" by the caregivers. Neither the notion that the patient inevitably comes to resemble the rest of "them" nor the caregiver who adheres to this notion is implicated in the theft of the sufferer's personhood. The loss of personhood is understood as a fact—and the patient's loss is the caregiver's, too.

To be a family caregiver is to provide unstinting service under unbearable stress, period. A paid worker can be deemed insufficiently kind, intelligent, or competent—and fired. But the family caregiver is assumed to be doing the best job she can. Indeed, the job she is doing is rendered good by the love that motivates it (negligence, ignorance, and thoughtlessness are the sins of the *other,* non-caregiving, family members).

To reconcile the assumed love with the active hostility a caregiver may feel for the person with Alzheimer's, she is instructed to adopt a stance of emotional neutrality—not to take it personally, for instance, if the cared-for person hits her, swears at her, or orders her out of his house. Together, the feeling of love and the practice of emotional neutrality enhance patience and thus promote consistent care. "Loving is different than like," counsels Roche. "I can dislike something someone does and still love the person. I can do things I don't really like to do when I am acting out of love." This love-laden neutrality is meant to ease the gradual estrangement that dementia can effect. But emotional restraint hastens that separation, too. The cared-for may be loved but—because he is no longer truly a person—he is not related to.

In the support group that Mom has recently joined, I get the impression she is celebrated as a maverick because she doesn't buy the "loved one" rhetoric. Her unsentimental humor probably gives others permission to express some less-than-loving feelings. Whereas the tone in the more public Internet chat rooms is almost reverent (prayer is often recommended), the support groups may cultivate a darker, snarkier culture. Members can rage at the "loved one," joke about him, and, since caring for a person with Alzheimer's is "an endless funeral," even wish him dead. Still, there's "the disease" to hold responsible. Lars Tornstam, a leading Swedish gerontologist, notes that the disease model of Alzheimer's reconciles the contemptible figure of the "weak elderly," a useless burden in a productive, independent society, with the piously venerated "wise elderly"; the result, comments anthropologist Elizabeth Herskovits, is "condescending pity." Put another way, disease facilitates a satisfying and yet guilt-free exercise: the caregiver gets to vilify the "loved one" without blaming him.

Mom tells me the group admires her insight and frankness, and when I briefly meet her co-supporters in the New York Alzheimer's

Association's hallway one afternoon, several tell me the same. But iconoclast though she may be, Mom is also a joiner. Like everyone else who finally makes it to the group rooms, she has come in out of the lonely cold: she wants comradeship. Like theirs, the line of her life has become a wild scribble: she wants a diagram. I hear her begin to revise the story of the last ten years of her life to fit the official Alzheimer's story. First, she sheds her role as wife (a word that implies a proprietary relationship) and takes on the official title of Caregiver. Then, as she starts to retell the events, it is as if she has done nothing but care for Dad and all that has transpired between them was "about" his dementia.

It is impossible to unravel the strands of their deteriorating marriage from the tangles of Dad's deteriorating brain. Yet as an explanation of what is so hard to explain, I can see why she might prefer the Alzheimer's narrative to the real last chapters of her relationship with my father. The Alzheimer's story is told from one point of view, that of the caregiver, who is also the hero. The cause of all distress is the patient, barreling toward the edge of dementia's cliff. Yet there is no villain besides a conspiracy of chemicals: "Something is happening to your brain, Stan. It's nobody's fault." In the story of Mom's marriage, by contrast, both narrators are unreliable, the plot is tedious and confusing, and the resolution will never come. Both tales tell of love and disaster—and what more compelling tale can there be? But in the Alzheimer's story all are innocent. And in the story of my mother and father, no one is.

. . .

Paul and I drive Mom to the ferry in Burlington that crosses Lake Champlain to Plattsburgh, New York, where she will catch the train to Westchester to spend three days with Gloria Goldstein. We watch her small frame grow smaller as she walks onto the gangplank, carrying a Sportsac overnight bag across her chest. Dad says good-bye, unaware that she won't be back.

She has never traveled alone, and his visit with us is the first time they have been apart for as long as he can remember, though he can't remember most things more than a few minutes. This makes it both easier and harder. He forgets she is gone, then experiences her absence anew. "Where is she?" he keeps asking.

Back at the house, while I make a salad and set the table, Paul and Dad grill chicken and vegetables on the deck. Dad helps Paul by holding the plate, handing him the spatula, delivering salt from the kitchen.

I warn Dad not to let the cat out while he enters and exits the house. I tell him Julius will need his insulin injection soon, and if he gets out we won't be able to find him, perhaps all night. But of course, Dad does not understand. He pulls the screen door open, and from the center of the kitchen I see an orange tail zip across the doorsill. I push past Dad, yanking at the door so that his fingers are wrenched back in the handle. "Hey!" he yelps. As the cat slips over the edge of the deck into the rose bushes, I grab at his body, catching hold of one hind leg. He yowls and struggles as I reel him in, all legs and claws, and stride into the house.

"I told you not to let the cat out!" I scream at Dad. "Don't let the cat out! Don't let the cat out! Don't let the cat out!"

"Judith, okay!" Paul stops me. I mutter an apology to Dad and press my face into Julius's soft, creamsicle-colored belly.

That night, I relive the event over and over. I am ashamed at my impatience and violence toward Dad. After all, I have been with him only half a week. But I can feel the pain of my beloved cat, as all his weight pulls on one twisting leg. When I replay that image, I could cry.

The next day, Paul takes Dad to the Fairbanks Museum in St. Johnsbury, a bulky, brown, old-fashioned all-purpose institution displaying a variety of what used to be called Items of Interest—rare minerals, colonial dolls, photographs of tribal Africans. Its major attraction is a huge collection of taxidermy-preserved creatures from tiny finches to a massive polar bear. Dad visits with each animal in turn, conversing. But he seems most compelled by the

Bengal tiger. He crouches close to the animal and touches its hard stuffed muscles. He gazes into its glass eyes. "I'm very, very sorry," he says, "but I can't help you right now."

On the third day, Paul and I are catapulted from our bed by a blast of Beethoven. "Are you awake?" I ask him, a sleeper as imperturbable as Rushmore. He laughs and opens his eyes. I announce the obvious: "My father." It is the morning I am to drive Dad to Gloria's to reunite him with Mom. I pull on my robe and stumble downstairs, stomp over to the stereo, and brusquely push his fingers from the knob, shutting the music off.

"Take it easy," he huffs. "It's . . ." He pauses to decipher the face of his digital watch. "It's . . . four o'clock!" He is fully dressed, shoes tied, hair combed. His suitcase is packed, positioned squarely in one quadrant of the tautly made bed.

"I'll see you in a few hours," I say more calmly and make my way back up to bed.

Upstairs, Paul and I lie on our backs, listening to the loops of footsteps as Dad searches for the bathroom. At five, Paul goes down to make coffee. At the bottom of the stairs, he encounters Dad, waiting like a child on Christmas.

"Crazy day," says Dad amicably.

"Sure is," says Paul, with his easy laugh. "It sure is a crazy day." Neither he, Dad, nor I have a clue how crazy it will be.

I pack sandwiches while Paul gets our things into the car. The ten-year-old Volkswagen has 160,000 miles on it, no air-conditioning, a moon roof whose windshield has flown off, and ceiling fabric that hangs unstuck, secured by pushpins. It is August, just past sunrise and already eighty degrees. Paul waves good-bye and good luck.

"Where is she?" Dad asks, as he has been asking for the past two days.

"Mom's at Gloria's house."

"Where?"

"Gloria Goldstein's."

"Do you know where she is, dear?"

"Yes, we're going there now."

"Where is she?"

"We'll see Mom in about six hours."

He looks at his watch. "Eight one seven," he says. "Where are we going?"

"We're going to Gloria's to see Mom."

"Eight one eight."

By ten, it must be ninety out. The hot wind beats in our ears, drowns out the radio but barely dries our sweat. Dad reaches through the moon roof, cups his hands and pulls them toward his face, as if splashing it with water. But by some stroke of aerodynamic mischief, this action sets up a small cyclone inside the car, which pulls down the ceiling fabric and scatters the pins. The fabric becomes a billowing, flapping spinnaker, blocking all sight. Driving seventy-five miles an hour, I bat at it with my right hand, which does no good.

It also does no good to ask Dad to keep his hands in the car, but I do. He checks his watch four or five times, then raises them again. I roll up the windows for a few torturous minutes. Dad snorts at his crazy, punitive daughter. I roll them down again. The wind comes back up, his hands reach up, the fabric pulls down, I stop to find the scattered tacks on the floor and throughout our baggage and tack it back up.

Finally, after a half-dozen stops to secure the spinnaker to the ceiling, I whip the car into a service area, pull out my pocket knife, and slash the fabric down. The pioneer who has skinned the bear, I strut into the store for a couple of celebratory iced teas. I screw off the top and hand one to Dad.

"DON'T!" I shout, too late, as he shakes the bottle, sending sticky liquid onto my clothes and the car's floor, but, miraculously, not himself.

"It's okay," he says, climbing out of the car and pointing to the half-full bottle. "It's . . . available." There's enough left to drink, and he's perfectly dry! I wonder, as always, whether his solipsism is the dementia speaking, or just the same old Dad. Or both.

I take Dad's arm as we cross the parking lot. Always on the qui vive for infantalizing slights, he pulls it away and mockingly takes mine. "Okay," I say, snatching my arm back from his derisive protection, in the process depriving him of mine. "Get run over. See if I care."

We reach the shady grass in safety, eat our sandwiches in peace and even a sort of battlefield comradeship. He forgets our tiff. "Have you been here before?" Dad asks, conversationally.

"No," I answer, "but I know where we are." He examines his sandwich. Being with him is like the first experiences of meditation: I'm vigilantly observant and fatally bored. *What if I abandoned him here?* While I idly entertain the idea, the image of my weeping father wandering toward the interstate swoops like a hawk onto my little black joke. Walking back toward the car, I watch for vehicles but do not take his arm—respect for his dignity or a small abandonment?

I buckle him into his seat belt. He allows this docilely, which inspires my tenderness. "Ready to roll?" I ask.

"It couldn't be better."

Now it is I who looks at my watch. It is one o'clock. Within two hours, I will finish my three-day shift with Dad and Mom will take over her endless one.

· · ·

Caregiving is women's work. When paid, it is underpaid; its workers are almost exclusively female immigrants and American women of color. Of family caregivers for people with Alzheimer's, more than 70 percent are women—wives and, among adult children, almost exclusively daughters and nieces. The ranks of the cared-for, meanwhile, are either too young or too old or their bodies or minds too feeble to possess the sine qua non of earned respect, autonomy. In a value system that lionizes might and patronizes or exploits weakness, both the givers and the recipients of care are simultaneously sentimentalized and undervalued.

Caregiving is a unique species of interpersonal work, says Diemut Elisabet Bubeck, of the London School of Economics, who has analyzed caring as labor. Caring is not service, a relationship in which the provider does something that the recipient could conceivably do but chooses not to—for instance, a worker cooks or serves a meal in a restaurant. By contrast, says Bubeck, the caregiver "tend[s] to the needs of a person who cannot provide them for herself." Whereas services, negotiated in money or other forms of exchange, can be exploitative or fair, the caregiving relationship is by definition unequal. Built into it are the greater need of the cared-for and the greater ability of the carer. For this reason, Eva Feder Kittay, a feminist philosopher at the State University of New York at Stony Brook, calls caregiving "dependency work."

Kittay also calls caring a "labor of love." This is not only because it is so often motivated by love, but because it is a job composed of loving acts. You can bathe or feed a person without emotion, for sure. But caregiving is the provision of thousands of small kindnesses, and it requires the greatest kindness of all: attention. Nel Noddings, a philosopher and educator who teaches at Stanford University, calls the undeviating attunement to another person's moods, rhythms, and desires that is necessary to caregiving "engrossment." And because you can't be engrossed in another at the same time you are engrossed in yourself, it is a practice of self-denial, self-sacrifice. More than anything else, it may be a talent for selflessness—and a joy taken in it—that distinguishes the greatest of care workers. Many are religious.

Dependency—essential inequality—makes caregiving a site of power. But even bolstered by a full complement of love, "engrossment" can feel more like indenture than mastery. Mothers often say their lives are "dictated" by the cries of their children. But at least they can (within limits) cry back. Caregivers of the demented are advised to maintain a level of patience that would put any mortal on a waiting list for beatification. The required patience is, moreover, of a certain kind—patience with chaos. "I've always been in charge and in control. I am learning an important thing: I must let go of control," reads the July 20 entry of *Coping with Caring*. Alzheimer's caregivers are advised never to correct or argue with the person's mistakes, never to scold the person if he clogs the toilet or breaks a dish, always to distract and comfort him when he becomes obstreperous and move cheerfully onto something else. For Mom, to let go of control is to be controlled. She feels deprived of her very personhood. "He can do everything he wants," she complains, "and I have no civil rights."

The chaos that Alzheimer's personifies and the injunction to go with its raggedy flow may be one of the hardest parts of this experience for Mom. Not only is organization her professional forte, organizing for others is often her way of showing that she cares. A visit to Mom and Dad's house in Maine always involved a full schedule of hikes, berry-picking, swimming, sailing, gardening, and eating meticulously planned meals, each activity pushing hard upon the next. To care by *not* controlling is anathema to her.

Mom expresses her care for other people not only by organizing them but by being interested in them. But interest isn't the same as engrossment. She wants a person's opinions, his arguments, his news. Dad's opinions are garbled, his arguments are infantile, and his news is chiefly bad. To be engrossed, Mom wants a person to be engrossing. As a child, I worked hard at this.

Bubeck calls the toll that caregiving exacts on the body, the psyche, and the pocketbook its "net material burden." For some, love and spiritual satisfaction balance the burden of care. But perhaps for fewer than we think. On a program about dying and death, Bill Moyers reported that about 80 percent of caregivers polled said the work made them stronger, but only 39 percent said it has brought them closer to the person for whom they were caring. Relying on the caregiver's "unremitting love or tolerance," says the philosopher Harry R. Moody, imposes "a standard of saintliness, not ordinary human virtue." Mom, like most ordinary humans, cannot pour herself into loving service and feel replenished by the trickling spiritual rewards of having poured. She wants reward of a more mundane sort: pleasure, companionship, and help with the dishes.

She often notes with irritation and envy, and also a hint of disdain, that selflessness does not afflict the men in her Alzheimer's support group, even though men who join such groups "are more sensitive and caring" than average. "They can shuffle off the responsibility. They can make the decision to put their person in a nursing home, not feel guilty about it, and go on with their own lives." The women, on the other hand, "can't let go." Studies on gender and the effects of dementia on relationships affirm Mom's impressions. One found that wives experience more distress in taking care of demented spouses than husbands do. The researchers conjectured that the women feel trapped by expectations that they will care for their husbands indefinitely.

I ask Mom if she harbors any feminist resentment about having to care for Dad. She doesn't answer yes or no. "This person is a wounded bird. I have to help him," she says. Then she adds, "He was always enormously supportive. Of my going back to work, with my Crohn's." In other words, he did it for me, he was an egalitarian husband. Now I should do it for him.

But part of her unhappiness may be that she does not feel particularly good at helping him. She often says she was not "naturally maternal" and preferred older children to babies. But her guilt was the feminine guilt of the fifties: she needed the adult contact and satisfaction of paid work, but she felt like a bad mother for leaving James and me at home. An image that haunts her is me, four years old, sitting "dejectedly" on the curb watching her leave for work.

Selflessness is both a feminine virtue and a female vexation. My mother, dangling between duty and desire, femininity and feminism, feels the obligation to give. But she also wants something back.

·   ·   ·

By the time we get to Gloria's, we have all melted down—Dad, me, and the car. Hugging my mother clumsily, he seems relieved.

"How was it?" she asks, embracing him warmly but briefly. She looks my way.

"Fine," I say and shrug. "Anyway, we made it." She nods knowingly.

Dad is noticing none of this as she guides him into the house and I follow. The rooms feel empty without Leo's lumbering charisma. "How was the visit, Stan?" she inquires.

"Fine," he says cheerfully. He doesn't seem to recall the hellish trip. It is only memory, I realize, that necessitates forgiveness.

After a snack of iced tea and cookies, Gloria calls me into the kitchen. "Maybe it's time to—" Her sentence detours around the words *nursing home* or *institution*.

"My mother will know when it's time," I reply. "My father still loves his apartment. He has his stuff, his friends at his day program. All he has left are his wife and his home." *And his children,* I think tentatively, but do not say. "We can't"—I am abashed to say *we must not,* it would sound so preachy—"take that away from him."

· · ·

If my parents chafed under their parents' unloving demand for love, my own objection to the idea of Family is more ideological. I detest the hierarchal bonds of the institution, which imply the subservience of woman to man and child (especially female child) to parent. Yet as I struggle to care for my parents, and Dad's decline irritates the never easy relationships among us, I long for compulsory love. It would make the other obligations of family so much easier to fulfill.

What motivates me? I contemplate this in the night after the incident of the escaped cat; I wonder about it again when I consider releasing Dad to the six-lane highway. I have asked myself, on our weekly walks to the Hudson River, *why am I here?* I'm not sure Dad even knows I'm anyone special to him.

I'm surprised when an answer comes to me: *filial duty.* Duty is little acknowledged in our century. Our modern, psychological worldview describes the family as an engine fueled by passions, sexual and otherwise. But duty is almost the opposite of passion; it is sober, steady, a value more than a feeling. It is fealty not to a person (though people are often its beneficiaries) but to an idea—to Ancestry, Country, God. Not only do I come from a family that is allergic to such sentiments, I am of a generation that rejected such abstractions as religious dogma and patriotism; in high school my friends and I were even cynical about school spirit. My feminism makes me doubly suspicious of sacrifice, the cousin of duty, for while men's duty is intermittent—fighting wars, taking the kids to the ball game on Saturday—women's duty is never done.

While taking on an obligation is a mark of maturity, it also competes with the quintessentially American desire to be free of the family. Freedom is entwined with self-reliance, which requires that no one rely on you, either. "The word [duty] grates upon our moral ear," wrote Lionel Trilling, because we wish to believe that "right action [can] be performed without any pain to the self." Familial duty is not a passion; but this mixture of convention and compassion, obligation and mercy, is hardly dispassionate. It can hurt.

As my incipient filial duty rises, its sources become clearer. My parents did not command personal love, but they communicated unwavering duty—to humanity. They taught the Jewish commandment *tikkun ha'olam* (which they never named, much less in Hebrew)— repair the world—and they taught it by example. They repaired the world on those long trips to Washington, during those evenings of stuffing envelopes and canvassing for candidates. Dad did it night after night during the Vietnam War, putting his professional expertise as a psychologist to work as a draft counselor, coaching inductees in the bizarre behaviors that might win them deferments from military service in the war he believed to be immoral. But my parents' duty was not just to all the anonymous Oppressed People, it rang close to home as well. When her own mother was old and sick, Mom and her sister looked after her doctors' visits, bills, and apartment. At the end, Mom visited her mother daily.

Duty asks a continual reassertion that its recipient—the party, the country, the person—is worth the pain of sacrifice. My mother's feelings toward her mother were as ambivalent as mine are toward Dad. Why, when she felt so wronged by the obligation to love, did my mother do it? Finally, to the person answering its call, duty is a tautology: you care for your parents because they are your parents and they need care. Duty is like faith, belief without evidence. In fact, duty is paid when evidence of worthiness is scant, even in spite of evidence of unworthiness: *my country right or wrong.* When my friend Rachel was a child, her mother berated her endlessly and whipped her for minor childish infractions. As the mother aged, she fell even more profoundly into paranoia and rage, and finally senility. Yet Rachel gave gentle care to the old woman until she died. How did it feel to deliver the necessary daily kindnesses to this woman? Rachel's answer is an astringent comment on filial duty: "I felt the limits of my love."

Still, like Mom, I want something back. And in spite of the limits of my family's love, sometimes I get it. A week after I return to Vermont after delivering Dad to Westchester, Paul and I receive a letter from Mom. She tells us that while at Gloria's she realized "this kind of 'vacation' is no longer viable" for her and Dad. Coming home, she sees it is time to get more help—to ask Jack Smith to work another day and "find someone else as well, as back-up and fill-in." The three-day respite was a revelation, and she is going to try to go away one weekend every month or so and leave Dad with Jack or a home health aide. She continues:

> How can I tell you what your being there, your support, under-standing and sweetness means to me? My answer is the same as when you asked what the Penn South Concerned Citizens are concerned about. The answer is: EVERYTHING! I particularly appreciate it because I think I know how jealously you hold your time, with your own work, a million projects to get done

around the house, and the desire to bike, and swim and see friends. I remember vividly how I really didn't want anybody in Maine for most of our time there, when every moment to do our Maine things was precious.

I love your place. It, like the two of you, has a special quality. It is a joy to be there.

In the final paragraph she promises—"I'm putting it in writing"—to replace our tattered couch with a new one when (if) we complete our long-planned renovation. She's attempting, against the odds, to tidy up our home and keep us on schedule. This, as much as anything else, lets me know she cares.

Love would make the fulfillment of duty easier. It might balance Trilling's pain to the self. But for me, at least for now, duty will stand in where love goes missing. "Love is an act," a disgruntled boyfriend once hurled at me in a fight. In other words, *Don't just talk to me about love. Put your money where your mouth is.* Years ago, when my father was working with severely troubled families, he told me, "No matter how miserably they fail, most parents try their best. Most parents, even the worst ones, love their children."

I do not know which is more true—that one can love and not act lovingly, or that compassionate acts of duty *are* a kind of love, or might as well be.

6. *Body*

IT IS MARCH 4, 2001, the day before Dad's eighty-second birthday, and I am spending the weekend with him while Mom visits her sister in Washington. I've looked forward to this, eager for it to go well both for Dad's sake and for Mom's.

I have resolved to be Buddhist about it, taking each moment as it comes, and with so many hours to fill and no place else to go, there's no reason to do anything but. Not to lose track, however, I've also been keeping a running account of my anxieties. *Start worrying. Details to follow.*

"What do I fear, anyway?" reads a journal entry from a month earlier. "Tedium? My anger, his? An emergency? His disappointment?" Later, I began a new section: "More Fears." On this list: "His body? Something yucky (sexual?)"

I drive into the city and arrive at seven-thirty in the morning. Mom buzzes me up. She is as nervous as I, but already putting her coat on when I reach the door. Everything is prepared: meds, itinerary, phone numbers (Aunt Valerie, doctors, police), food in fridge, petty cash in drawer. Dad has already eaten his cereal, the dishes are in the dishwasher. I shoo her out the door, and she is happy to be shooed. While Dad spends three days a week from nine to three at the center and an entire day with Jack Smith, my parents are still together three other days, plus every night. This weekend is the first respite Mom has had in almost seven months, since Dad stayed with Paul and me in Vermont. For me, it's the first weekend alone with my father, ever.

I tiptoe down the hallway. Dad is in the bathroom, supposedly showering. He's left the door open, but the shower is running, so he doesn't hear me. I observe him from the rear. His head is feminine in a plastic shower cap, his progress halting. He moves slowly into each act, trying to recall what comes next, advancing toward the tub, staring at it, pulling aside the curtain, staring into the tub. His torso bent forward above his narrow, naked buttocks, he's a spotted brown skin, empty of muscle, on an armature of bone—an overcooked duck, drained of savor.

I leave him to his ablutions to search for coffee filters in Mom's tidy but oddly organized and, since Dad's illness, uncharacteristically dirty kitchen. After twenty minutes, I hear the water stop in the bathroom. It's funny what Dad remembers how to do. I have found the coffee filters. Two small triumphs.

He is as eager as I am to please. After his shower, he sits on the toilet in his robe, humming companionably as I scrape at his face with the razor, negotiating his upper lip, the folds of his neck. He bends his head as I pull a comb through his thick silver hair. I help him dress. Arms slack, he watches my fingers slipping the shirt buttons into their holes.

I respond with solicitude equal to his compliancy. With the blade at his throat, I am so gentle as to be almost ineffectual. I don't insist that he change the grimy, days-old undershirt he's chosen (though I manage to dissuade him from putting on the second and third undershirt). I zip his fly, pulling the fabric away from his body so as not to touch his genitals.

"Come have coffee with me."

"Caw-fee," he pronounces, chuckling at the sound. He pads behind me to the kitchen, sees the pot, and matches object to meaning. Between sips, he smacks his lips and wipes the table with a scrunched-up napkin. "Okay, dear, dear," he says. I hand him a sponge to wipe the spills, and he dabs at the sponge with the napkin. "That's good, that's nice, okay, dear," he murmurs as he works, taking care of business, taking care of me. With a clean napkin, I dab a drip of coffee from his jaw just under the ear.

It's cold and blustery, so I bundle him into his down jacket and navy blue watch cap. He insists on wearing it with one ear exposed. When I pull the hat over his ear, he swats my hand away. "What are?" he spits.

I pull the hat a little more roughly, and this pushes his anger further. "Are you making them better?" he asks sarcastically.

I give up, hoping I'll be able to persuade him to pull it down if he gets cold outside. "Okay, Dad. It's fine."

More nastily: "Fine?"

By the time we're out of the building, he's in good humor again. In the light I notice I've missed half the hairs I meant to raze; they bristle at his frayed neckline. I haven't done that well combing his hair, either. It's flattened at the back near the crown and sticking up on one side. From the chin down, he is a bum who's spent the night at a mission, a bit cleaner but still grizzled and a little grungy. From the forehead up, he is a disheveled little boy, roused from a nap.

Since I arrived, few words have passed between us.

•   •   •

Caring for Dad increasingly means caring for his body. Knowing him means knowing his body. His personality perseveres in his body: the literally in-your-face aggression, the Catskills comedian shrug, the pipe-smoking intellectual's eyebrow raise. His needs for affirmation, humor, tenderness, or respect are communicated—and fulfilled by others—through his body and its accoutrements: a hand held, a shirt laundered.

Increasingly, Dad lives in what neurologist Antonio Damasio calls the "core self," in "core consciousness." The Cartesian model defines consciousness as that which is alive through language, reason, and creativity—Damasio calls this "extended consciousness," whose faculty is the maintenance of the "autobiographical self." But core consciousness is still consciousness. It "provides the organism with a sense of self about one moment—now—and about one place—here." The core self "is stable across the lifetime of the organism; is not exclusively human; and it is not dependent on conventional memory, working memory, reasoning, or language." As anyone who has shared life with a cat or a dog knows, core consciousness includes emotions. It allows even global aphasics—people without any spoken language—to communicate and know themselves. "As you familiarize yourself with the tools at such a patient's disposal," writes Damasio, "it will never even cross your mind to ask if that human being is or is not conscious."

·   ·   ·

We walk to my car. "I had one of these," Dad says.

"Yeah, you had a car. A Honda."

"Hon-da."

I buckle him into the passenger seat. "We're going to the Aquarium in Coney Island with Emily," I tell him, thinking Coney Island may jog a memory. It does not appear to.

On the Brooklyn Bridge, he looks out the window and asks, "Have you been here before?"

We pick up Emily, an old friend who worked hard to make peace with her alcoholic father before he died and is enthusiastic about my efforts with Dad. I help him out of the car so that Emily can get in. On the sidewalk, I introduce her, though they have met several times. He feigns recognition. "Oh, yes! It's—you!" A hearty laugh. "Do you remember me?"

"Sure, I remember you, Stan," she says. "How are you today?"

"How are we day?" A long pause before he warms up. Then he launches into an account of some kind of "work" he did, maybe yesterday. "I sime this pushing and pushing and pushing. And all day this thing. I'm saying to myself, 'Jesus Christ!' " A look of playful exasperation. "And then we are, there we are. 'How are we going?' I'm asking myself. You have to ask yourself." A sigh and a chuckle. "Such is life."

"Such is life," Emily agrees.

"But it couldn't be better." She laughs. He clearly likes her.

"So, Dad, should we go to the Aquarium?"

Suspiciously: "Do you want to?"

"Yeah, I'd like to. You?"

"*You're* going?"

"Yes, we're all going," I say.

He doesn't like being led around to strange places. "You go," he says. "Go!" He starts walking away from the car. I feel a familiar fear for his safety. Shit, I say to myself. I shouldn't have let him out of the car. I follow him and take his arm. He yanks it away and walks on.

"Dad, we're all going."

"You wanna go? Go, go. I'll stay here."

Emily and I look at each other. "I'm going, too," she says. He regards her quizzically. "We're all going," she repeats.

She wins the day. "Okay," he says grudgingly, to her, and glances over at me as if to say *Happy now?*

He squeezes into the back seat (another mistake? Will it be hard to get him out?). I lean in to buckle his seat belt. This he lets me do.

We drive to Coney Island. When left on his own, Dad's face slackens, as if thinking were an effort that wanes when no one else is demanding it. But when we get out of the car, after his usual discomfiture on arriving in a new place, he brightens. "Hello, little fellow," he says to a Rottweiler who is neither little nor a fellow as we cross a vest-pocket park. He stands inches from a homeless man propped on a bench. "My friend!" exclaims Dad into the alcohol-redolent face. I hold my breath, hoping the guy won't wake up and bite Dad, but he's too drunk to be roused. As I cajole Dad along, he greets the pigeons with jaunty politeness.

I notice a cluster of old men at a concrete table in the corner of the park, jackets open in the thin sunshine, newspapers folded, drinking coffee and eating crullers from a Dunkin' Donuts bag. The pleasures of friendship: this is what sustains life, I think. I imagine Dad at eighty-two with his mind intact, playing chess in the park. He used to be a good chess player. A wave of sadness passes over me.

I steer Dad toward the pedestrian bridge. He turns to Emily. "We'll have to up in it," he says in a businesslike but reassuring tone.

"Okay," says Emily, nodding like his lieutenant.

"We'll discuss the money in later years," he adds in his joshing voice, and moves closer to her. She laughs as he leans into her and takes her arm. "But don't worry. I'll take care of it." He's flirting. My annoyance turns on like an instinct. Forget it, he's harmless, I say to myself. *Harmless*. Neutered.

We walk down to Nathan's for the hot dogs and French fries, which, because of Mom's restricted diet, Dad doesn't get to eat at home. He consumes them a little hesitantly, either in guilt or fear, drizzling mustard and ketchup over his hands, chin, and the front of his jacket. I dab at him with napkins as he eats, and when he is done wash his hands and face with a wad of napkins dipped in a large cup of water.

As soon as we enter the Aquarium, I ask him if he needs to go to the bathroom. He has recently had his first urinary "accident," at the daycare center, and I don't want it to happen here. He agrees to go. We find the men's room near the white-whale tank, and Emily and I stand outside while Dad disappears behind the concrete wall. Five, ten minutes pass. Emily and I keep looking at our watches. We deliberate about what to do. "Do you think he's okay in there?" "Give him five minutes. He'll be out soon." "One more minute and then I'll go in?" Men enter and leave, in a reversal of the usual sexual wariness eyeing us as we loiter by the entrance and peek around the barrier.

Finally, I go in, excuse myself to the other occupant, and find Dad standing in an open cubicle trying to tuck his shirt into his pants. Instead of tucking it in, he is smoothing it down outside the belt. At first he insists he can do it, but quickly drops his hands to his sides and lets me push the shirt inside, then zip and snap his jeans and buckle his belt. He washes his hands and allows me to help him dry them. We emerge into the windy salt air.

We move slowly through the exhibits. As he wanders, I keep an eye on him, never letting him get too far away. In the cool, dark hallways of lighted tanks, he stands for a long time before a display of corals and other plantlike underwater animals opening and closing their primitive mouths while tiny, flat, bright fish flit among them. He is enchanted, as I am. "It's a very hat that they gate for you, dear, dear," he says to me. A child looks at him curiously. "It's a beautiful piece," he says to the child, pointing to a midnight-blue fish.

At the seal tank, we watch the animals dipping and rising in the oily-looking water. Dad narrates: "They're very good friends each other." He points to the smaller of two, making a U-turn toward the cave. "He's clowing through." Both seals splash and slip under the waves. "You see. They sort of dysectrate."

"I see that," I say.

"But you don't have to worry, because the money is coming out." He chuckles.

At feeding time, we make our way to the corridors under the large-animal tanks. A crowd of spectators presses around the shark tank to watch the attendants push ragged fish flesh on metal hooks under the fishes' long noses. The children know sharks are scary, so they scream each time one shoots by, indifferent as a torpedo. Dad looks on blandly.

At the sea-turtle tank, he becomes more animated. He mimics the creatures for no audience but himself, pulling his elbows into his torso, flicking his hands back like paddling fins, stretching his neck forward, and opening and closing his mouth silently. When we exit the aquarium, we all get ice cream cones and I watch Dad open and close his mouth around the soft, white mound. They resemble each other, the turtles and my father, with their downward curved mouths and wattled necks, their benign agendas.

I have channeled my worries into the exigencies of Julius, whose schedule of insulin and feeding (in Brooklyn) must be spliced into my time with Dad and his medications and meals (in Brooklyn and Manhattan). I drop Emily off at home and take Dad to my apartment. When I unlock the door, I hear the familiar "Brrrrrddttt," Julius's hello meow. I pick him up and my tenderness wells as I feel his head butting against my chin. Ah, unconditional love!

While I attend to the cat, Dad walks around my living room, rearranging things. Obeying some internal sense of order, he turns a chair ninety degrees, moves it back to its original position, then turns it again. He picks up the books on the coffee table and places them on the secretary across the room. I watch him fingering the shells and stones in a little bowl. Then he comes to the kitchen table and starts opening my mail. I take the envelopes from him and into my office, where I stand, breathing. Having come into my office—an excuse—I yell to him that I am going to check my e-mail, which means nothing to him. I feel suddenly exhausted, a tiny inkling of Mom's daily life.

When I return, he is snoring at the kitchen table. I put on water for ravioli. He wakes up. "Are we?"

"We're going to eat."

"Have you been here before?"

I laugh. "Yeah, Dad, I live here."

"Ah." He pours salt out of the shaker onto the table. "Are we having?"

"Yes, we'll eat in a few minutes."

He withdraws to the bathroom, where he remains for a worrisomely long time. The smell emanating from the room tells me he is moving his bowels. I don't want to help him wipe himself, though I know he uses wads and wads of paper and still doesn't achieve the goal very well. So I'm worried that he will stop up my sensitive toilet, but I also know it's unlikely he will let me help him.

Finally, he appears, his trousers unzipped and his arms laden with bottles and boxes, soaps and tubes from inside my medicine cabinet and under the sink. Eleven hours and thirteen minutes into our time together (I've been counting), I lose my cool. "WILL YOU PLEASE LEAVE MY STUFF ALONE?!" I yell. *Most parents, even the worst ones, love their children.* When Dad said that, I thought, *he's making excuses for himself.* I gave him no credit for trying. Now I'm trying, and doing about as well as he did.

A shampoo bottle, then a tube of toothpaste, drops to the floor. I lunge for the tumbling toiletries. "Give me the stuff. Just give it to me." My voice is stern.

Dad inspects his shoes as he grasps the last items to his chest. He loses a plastic bottle of Tums and looks up with anxious eyes. "Are we getting along?"

I move closer. He cowers, almost unnoticeably. Does he think I am going to hit him?

In *Maternal Thinking,* Sarah Ruddick calls mothering, the primal act of caregiving, a conscious nonviolent practice. The mother (or child-caring father) is tethered day and night to a smaller, weaker, relentlessly demanding, and often resistant person over whom she has total power. She often feels like hurting the little miscreant but deliberately refrains from doing so. This intimate rejection of might-makes-right, says Ruddick, is a model for international relations.

Like a mother, the caregiver of the frail elderly must relinquish her power. She must deliberately refrain from doing harm, the temptation of which is evident in the wide incidence of elder abuse. *I could hurt him,* I thought, my hands inches from Dad's vulnerable neck the night he and I battled in my parents' apartment. But I did not.

"Nothing is more material, physical, corporeal than the exercise of power," writes Foucault. When you care for the aged, or you age yourself, you experience both sides of that equation. Caregiving, which is care of the body, is power. And nothing is more vulnerable to the exercise of power than the body. *I could hurt him,* I think now as he stands in my hallway, a shoplifter caught with the booty. And I have hurt him, a little.

"Yes, Dad, we're getting along fine," I say softly, kneeling. "Here, let's put this stuff back." He kneels too and hands me a bottle, like an apology. Now, though I could hurt him again, I am exercising restraint. Of course, restraint is an assertion of power, too, and so is pardon.

After dinner, we return to Twenty-fourth Street. I try to read on the couch while Dad sits in a morris chair and watches a cable-channel show about disasters. Tonight they are focusing on tornados: the wind is screaming, power lines falling, doors and cows flying through the air, families wet and freezing. Interrupting the regular programming, a news brief announces a major fire in the Bronx, killing three children. Dad seems sanguine. "Mmm-hmmm," he hums to the TV screen. Suddenly feeling like a mother who has looked up and noticed her four-year-old watching a Mafia massacre on television, I turn off the set and coax Dad into his room.

I take his pajamas from beneath his pillow and leave him to put them on. When I return a half hour later, I am surprised to see he has succeeded, though he still has his socks on. No need to fuss about the socks, I think, as I get him under the covers. An hour later, I find him sleeping with the *New Yorker* on his chest and his glasses askew. I gently remove the glasses, dab some drool from the corner of his mouth with a handkerchief on his night table, and settle him down on his pillows. One arm is under the blankets, the other lies flat outside them. I think of his huge hand holding my little hand when I was a child. Now his hand looks small.

I leave the hall light on so he doesn't stumble if he gets up to pee.

·   ·   ·

Nothing is more vulnerable than the body. You think you know this all along. You think you face it each time a friend your age gets cancer. When Julius is ill, I imagine my life diminished of his rusty purr and the small weight of his body landing on the bed at night.

Within several months after Leo dies, my journal records the passing of three acquaintances in their fifties, a friend in her seventies, and two of my parents' friends. A Buddhist friend reminds me at the time that the instant you are born, cells start to die. You start to die.

You think you face mortality as you age. But you don't face it until it faces you. This confrontation occurs twice in March of 1999.

In the first two weeks of the month, two successive mammograms find calcifications in my left breast, sometimes a symptom of cancer. The radiologist says it is not an emergency, but recommends than an oncologist read the film "as soon as possible." Paul is in New York to fly to Portugal for a long-planned sailing trip with friends. He's leaving Tuesday, my oncologist's visit is the following Thursday, and he is scheduled to return that Friday. I've told him to go; another friend can come with me to the doctor.

On the morning of his flight, the phone rings at five-thirty. It is Mom, in the emergency room at New York University Medical Center, suffering chest pains. A neighbor has come in to get Dad to his program. She will tell him simply that Mom had an early appointment.

Paul and I reconnoiter. He decides the planets are not aligned for his sailing trip. We are both relieved that he'll be around for the mammogram verdict. We're independent but, we realize, are starting to appreciate opportunities to depend on each other.

When I arrive at the hospital, Mom is already feeling better. The ER doctor, a skinny, friendly pulmonologist who has treated Mom before, diagnoses the chest pains as a lingering symptom of a two-week flu, but her own doctor, a cardiologist entranced with high-tech diagnoses, has already admitted her and ordered a test that involves shoving a tube down her throat to her stomach. No, she doesn't really need the test, but since she's here she might as well; he'll be able to get a better picture of . . . she can't remember what. And, oh yes, in case they are unable to take her today, she'll have to stay overnight.

I spend the next nine hours trying to spring Mom. When the

cardiologist finally makes an appearance, I have to ask him to stop walking and face me while I talk. He is unmoved when I remind him that Dad, who is also his patient, has Alzheimer's and will return to an empty house. He will not sign Mom out. In her curtained cubicle, she and I calculate the number of hours until Dad gets back from his program. I call Paul to put him on notice.

Mom and I devise an escape plot involving smoke bombs to distract the nurses while I spirit her out. But Plan B works instead. I have begged the pulmonologist to call the cardiologist to let him sign Mom's release. After two hours, he accomplishes the mission. "You're free," the pulmonologist informs Mom, and, already dressed, she hurries out with me before anyone changes his mind.

"I'm glad you're alive," I tell her as I put her in a cab.

"So far," she said, grabbing my face and kissing it. Then she admits she is glad to be alive, too.

It's lucky that Paul is in New York. He has given Julius his morning shot, called Dad's program, and was ready to pick him up in the afternoon. It is lucky that Mom has gotten home on time, and Dad is none the wiser. But Dad is sick, Mom is sick, Julius is sick, and I may be sick. I picture us all crowded into a stalled elevator, going nowhere. At the very least, we need somebody who can climb the stairs.

The next day, Paul and I return to NYU, this time to see my oncologist. He tells me the calcifications are "probably nothing at all" but prescribes surgery anyway. He describes what he will do—an "excisional" biopsy, in which a thin, hooked wire is inserted several inches into the breast, an incision about a centimeter in diameter is cut around the wire, and the calcium-spattered plug of flesh is pulled out. "Like a lollipop," the doctor says cheerfully. I am almost certain I am going to die.

A week before the surgery, I turn on my computer and the screen is blank but for a blinking cursor. Blink blink blink. Nothing else. The near-final draft of a book is on the computer's hard drive, only partially backed up.

I press the keys, I shift-control-delete. I toggle the on-off button and tap the keys more desperately. Nothing happens. Having exhausted the software solutions, I turn to the hardware. I pick up the computer and drop it on the desk (this sometimes works). Then I scream at it (also occasionally effective). When I call the company's tech support, the guy tells me sleepily, "I'm sorry, ma'am, but I don't think you can get anything off that disc." The black box is impenetrable, with three years' work locked inside.

I am suddenly almost blind with headache. A question floats into my mind: *Which would I rather lose, my book or my breast?* The answer comes in a millisecond: *my breast.* Interesting. I value the "book" in me more than the "breast," my rational brainpower more than the fleshly attributes of my sexuality. I am evidently more Cartesian than I thought.

Three weeks later, I am waiting in a small birch-paneled "pre-op" stall off a corridor outside the operating room, wearing a paper johnny and flat paper slippers. The wire, inserted earlier that morning, protrudes from my breast, covered with a loosely attached, thick patch of gauze. The anesthesiologist enters with a clipboard, introduces himself as Dr. Patel, asks me what I'm allergic to, and recites the list of chemicals he is going to inject into me. "It's a cocktail. Feels just like two wheeskey sours," he says.

"Could you use coffee instead?" I ask, already in the throes of a caffeine-withdrawal migraine.

"Cream and shoo-ghar with that, madam?" he retorts, laughing lightly. I'm distracted from visions of death by visions of breakfast.

Paul is allowed to come in. He kisses me and balances the pile of my clothes, shoes, the rings I haven't taken off since I was sixteen, and the glasses I can't see without, to lock them in a drawer in the hallway. "It's been a laff riot," I say, waving.

In the operating room, waiting for the local anesthetic to take effect, I lie flat, naked, shivering, and myopic, anticipating the scalpel. As I slide from the black-tiled room into drugged oblivion, the last thing I envision is the cold, like a fog, seeping into my breast. The boundary between the embodied self and the rest of the world is nothing if not porous.

That afternoon, back at home, Paul sits on my bed and tells me, "You went through that door and were transformed into a slab of meat they were going to cut up. When I saw you, without your rings or your glasses, with none of your 'identifying characteristics,' none of the expressions of your personality, it was like you were just a body. You were naked, and then you put on that paper johnny, which was like a sheet of brown paper laid over a side of beef to keep the flies off. It was like it wasn't you." He touches my hair. "And at the same time, of course, you *were* you. And I thought, I might see your body wheeled away and never see it—see *you*—alive again."

I tell him I felt the same way. I was a body without a history, a lump of flesh whose resident self was irrelevant to everyone but me, and even I could not quite remember who and where it was. I tell Paul I was, as the computer geeks call us noncybernetic beings, a *meat puppet*. "That's how they'll think about Dad soon," I say. "A body."

"A meat puppet," Paul repeats.

.   .   .

Bedded down on Mom and Dad's couch during my weekend with him, I barely sleep. At about five the next morning, Dad wanders into the living room, turns on the light over the table, and starts moving a pile of papers around. I ask him to go back to bed for a while, and like a sleepy child he trundles to the bedroom. I close my eyes and dip in and out of a dream.

In the dream I am packing to move house and my father is helping me. Only it's not Dad exactly, but a friendly Puerto Rican guy with close-cropped black hair and the body of a welter-weight boxer. He is driving an old station wagon. To get to my apartment, I have to cross a construction site in front of my building, climbing over stacks of rebar and lumber and leaping over muddy ditches. As I navigate the course, a worker grabs at my ass. I spin around, ready to slap him, but just at that moment "Dad" pulls his car beside the curb, leans out the window, and shouts to me, "Hey, baby!" He throws a threatening glance at my assailant, whom I glare at triumphantly as I sashay to the car.

When I wake up I feel relieved, then disturbed. Is Dad the virile sexual protector or the sexual harasser? Or both?

I walk back to his room, where he is singing and sorting his papers—a postcard from Nova Scotia dated August 17, 1998; a pamphlet entitled "What You Need to Know About Dating Violence"; a poem xeroxed on mint-green paper, "My heart stood still"; a Winter 2000 circular from the West Side YWCA, church-concert handouts, magazine subscription cards, and urgent fund appeals from do-good organizations. An archivist who can neither count nor recite the alphabet, Dad is up at the crack of dawn, organizing the ephemera of his radically ephemeral existence. He is wearing slippers, but the fly of his light blue cotton pajamas is open. I can see his testicles.

It has been a long time since I have felt comfortable with my father's body. In my infancy, he bathed and diapered me, fed me, and walked me at night. I don't remember this. I remember the torturous tickling, the scary-fun rides on his back in the ocean and on Flexible Fliers screaming down various Suicide Hills.

And showers. Showering with Mom, I sat on the tub floor and busied myself with my plastic tea set, positioning the little cups under the stream of soapy water pouring from her pubic hair. But under the spray with Dad, courtesy was observed. I'd stand at one end and he at the other, his large, loose genitals practically at my eye level. He washed himself, I washed myself, we got out and toweled separately. A Freudian child psychologist but also a "progressive" parent, he probably considered this a good compromise: the child observes the sexual apparatus of the adult male, but the father, by avoiding excessive touch, prevents Oedipal excitement.

When James was about eight and I was five, things changed.

Suddenly my brother became modest, and a large bookshelf was moved to divide the master bedroom we shared. When my brother's penis was withdrawn from my gaze, so was my father's. My parents' bedroom door was closed. At the beach with him and James, I braved the women's locker room alone. Glimpses of Dad's nakedness under bathrobe or up boxer-short leg became illicit, both repellent and magnetic. Unlike the hurly-burly bear hugs and lips-to-skin belly farts of early childhood, his touch was now more reserved, his goodnight kisses more formal. The less of it there was, the more it became the touch of a stranger. Withheld in order to remain nonsexual, it began to feel sexual.

Verbally, he was more profane—or maybe I just started to understand his humor. I didn't like his "dirty jokes." Or his masculine appreciation. Shopping one afternoon when I was thirteen, he stopped in the hardware store while Mom took me to buy my first "training" bra, a garment that is by definition unnecessary but for which I'd begged. When we emerged from the store, Dad was waiting on the sidewalk. His gaze fixed on the breasts-in-training inside my semitranslucent yellow shirt. "You look very nice," he said. I never wanted him to look at me again.

For decades after that we barely touched.

While Dad busies himself in his room and the coffee drips into the pot, I take out my journal and make a list:

> *Things I did for my father this weekend:*

> Fed him.
> Shaved his face and neck.
> Combed his hair.
> Scissored hair from his ears.
> Wiped mustard off his knuckles and chin with a wet napkin.
> Reminded him to go to the bathroom.
> Dressed and undressed him (zipped fly).
> Tucked him into bed.
> Dabbed drool from the corner of his mouth.

Ready or not, I have touched my father's body.

When Mom returns from the weekend in Washington, I put my arms around Dad and hug him. For the first time in years, I hold him close. He is stiff, but this may just be the increasing physical awkwardness of Alzheimer's. He feels like neither a child, nor a flirt, nor a threat. He feels only like a father. And I feel not like a nurse, a mother, a wife, or a sex object. I just feel like his daughter.

.   .   .

A few months after our weekend together, I take Dad for his yearly evaluation at the NYU aging and dementia center. I have now read through several years of his medical records. I've translated the abstract and distancing language—*A fiberoptic colonoscopy to the cecum. Chest X-rays show mild degenerative changes in the mid-thoracic spine*—into the traits of a living, aging body: his skinny butt, his messy bowel movements, his slow, bent gait.

We go upstairs first for an EKG, blood, and urine. Two sweet nurses, one named Candy, get Dad to lie down while they prepare for the blood-taking. They repeat "Lie on your back" four or five times before he does it. He falls asleep as Candy attaches the monitors to his hairy chest and snores through the procedure.

Then they need urine. I ask not too hopefully if one of them can do it. Candy shakes her head no: "The patient's caregiver usually does it."

A couple of weeks earlier my friend Debbie returned from Houston, where she'd taken care of her father in the city hospital. "They had no staff there. No nurses, no orderlies, nothing. I did everything. I fed him, I rolled him over. I put his penis into the bedpan," she told me.

"You touched his penis? Wasn't it creepy?" I'd asked. (Her husband asked the same thing.)

"When you have to do it, you just do it," she said.

Now I hold my breath, knock on the men's room door, and when no one answers, go in with Dad. He takes out his penis and I hold the plastic cup under it. He waits for the urine to come out. It's hard enough to pee on demand; it must be even harder with your daughter holding a cup under your penis. But he is neither modest nor immodest, just concentrating on the task at hand. While he works, I watch closely enough to make sure everything is positioned right, but look away in politeness, boredom, and an embarrassment I consciously work to suppress.

"Finished?" I ask several times.

Finally, he seems finished. I help him zip up, and he washes his hands. When you have to do it, you just do it.

.   .   .

As it turns out, I lose neither my book nor my breast. A friend corrals the errant bytes from the hard disk. The biopsy comes up negative. I am left with a thin scar and a brand-new laptop. When the dressing is off and the stitches removed, Paul inspects the rescued breast and its still-pink raised track. "I would have missed this breast," he allows. But we agree that the fading scar is sexy, in a sadomasochistic way. The body of sexuality has assimilated the body of illness. Its wounds are poignant, marking a history of vulnerability, an impending oblivion—marking its mortality.

Dad's body is not scarred. But the scarring of his mind is written on his body—and in sexuality, how can you separate the mind from the body? In one way, his sexual self is not much altered. He still likes to think of himself as a sexy guy. He still is handsome, still relatively hale. Alzheimer's has opened further his already unbuttoned humor; its hairy chest is showing. But with his wit silenced, he relishes physical humor now, or its approximation. As before, his jokes often involve something vaguely sexual or forbidden. "Nooo, but not down here" he says knitting his brow in mock censure, pointing to his genitals. "No smells, no smells," he says with a sly grin and points toward his anus. Sometimes he mixes the scatological theme with the Jewish theme: "No schmells."

In another way, of course, Dad's sexuality is utterly changed. No longer pushy, he is now beseeching. For Mom, this seems unbearable. He has taken to crying out, somewhat in jest, "Mmaa-mmaa! Ma-ma!" and each time he does, she almost winces. It's not the constant fighting that makes him unsexy now; it's the passivity. Once their struggle seemed a form of eroticism; mixed with humor and love, it drew them together. Now the battle is drained of eros, reduced to maddening childish squabbling.

Again, Dad's dementia has opposite consequences for Mom and me. The loss of his aggressive—or I should say effective—sexuality, like the loss of his belligerent intelligence, is a relief to me. When I was younger, his touch was never abusive, but in the context of his constant lewd joking, it felt sexual, repellent. Now, he sometimes tries to touch my buttocks or breasts, but it's ridiculous. At worst it makes me sad. Yet, without his big brain and his big penis taking up all the space, there's room for me to know him, even to touch him.

For Mom, the big brain and the big penis were a lot of Dad. What is left? She's been separating from him physically a little at a time. She bought twin beds when his violent nighttime twitching, a symptom of the brain lesions, was keeping her awake. She needed the new bed in order to sleep. But I think it was also a gentle way to extricate herself from their fifty-year embrace. During the day, too, she keeps herself apart. She touches him to administer that "custodial" care, but she does not hold his hand or hug him.

Interestingly, sexual estrangement is not the rule with dementia. In a study of Finnish married couples in which one partner was demented, three years after onset almost half continued to have intercourse, and after seven years more than a quarter were still having sex. A third said that the demented spouse expressed more tenderness toward the caregiving spouse than before. The researchers concluded that "dementing illness has a major negative impact on many dimensions of marriage," but compared to the rest of the aging population, sexuality—or at least frequency of intercourse—is not one of those dimensions.

Dementia clearly makes the difference for Mom. She cannot

have relations with someone who can't have a rational conversation. The man in the body she knows almost as well as her own has become alien, infantile, an untouchable baby.

.   .   .

From the main pavilion at NYU, Dad and I have to walk a few blocks to the MRI clinic. He stops every half block because his shoelaces untie. We wait a long time before they take him in for the scan. When he's called, they don't let me in, and he looks back imploringly as two nurses walk him to the lab. I worry about him, having to lie still in the tube as the magnets read his brain. But he seems fine when he comes out. He's joking with the nurses.

He hasn't had lunch and it's almost two o'clock, so as we walk back to the main building I peel the two clementines I've brought and hand him one section at a time. He finds this funny, and as I'm passing him one, he chortles and takes my right hand, with the fruit in it, and clasps it to him. We continue along this way for a few blocks, he clutching my hand to his chest. I feel the fruit crushed in my palm, its sticky juice dripping into my sleeve.

At the end of the day a harsh, hurried, big-voiced physician examines Dad. She scolds me for not attending to the cysts behind his ears. (Later, Mom says the cysts have always been there and are actually getting better.) She scolds him when he doesn't understand her instructions. "Open your mouth." No reaction. "Open your mouth!"

On the way out of her cramped office, holding the heavy door chivalrously for me, Dad catches his finger in the jamb. "Take me out! Take me out!" he cries. I extricate him as fast as I can, but he is bruised and bleeding. A flurry of icing and bandaging ensues. The doctor glares at me accusingly each time she looks up from his hand (is she going to call the authorities to remove him from my custody?). I feel a little vindicated when I notice Dad is getting no more sympathy than I am. She yells at him again—"I told you to hold it still!"—and tells us both we are "lucky" there are no broken bones.

"I'm sorry," I murmur to everyone in the surrounding offices as we wedge past her file cabinets and out of the small room and slink down the hallway. "I'm sorry," I say to Dad over and over.

In the cab home, he holds his injured hand away from his body and touches the bandage with his other hand. "I'm concerned about this," he says in his professional voice, as if he were talking about someone else's finger.

"I'm sorry you were hurt," I say again.

At their apartment, I tell Mom what happened. She grimaces in empathetic pain and takes Dad's hand. "That must have hurt," she says, looking first at the fat, gauze-wrapped digit and then into his face. "Did it hurt a lot, dear?"

Dad regards his large hand in the small cradle of hers. "Mm-hmm," he answers, not looking up, shy as a young lover. It has been a long time since I've seen them touch.

7. Dis/loyalty

June 20, 2001

The phone rings in Vermont. It's Mom. I take it out onto the deck and sit on the steps. A mallard is sliding through the lily pads on the pond. The last of the lilacs are dropping from the shrub to my left. Beside my bare right foot, Julius is chewing at a clump of grass that is left unmowed for this purpose. From his throat comes a purrlike growl that always accompanies grass-chewing.

"I've been seeing someone," Mom says.

At first I'm unsure whether she means a therapist or a beau. But her voice, coy and excited as a girl's, clears up the confusion. I've heard about Sid before, a member of Mom's caregivers' support group. Once, expressing her loneliness and debility to the group she said, "Sometimes I just wish someone would bring me a cup of tea." The next week, Sid brought her a Styrofoam cup of tea. He continued to do so every week, along with books and movie and theater recommendations. I've had a fantasy that after Dad dies, Mom would end up with Sid. Now his wife has died and, as Mom tells it, he is courting her energetically.

"That's nice, Ma," I say. I can almost hear her retreating from my

tepid reaction, a small reprimand. But she rebounds quickly, bub-
bling on about how sophisticated Sid is, how sensitive, how attractive.

"I'm sure he is," I say.

She tells me she knows I'm going to like him.

"I'm sure I will," I say, not sounding sure at all. "How's Dad?"

Mom is only momentarily deterred by the question, or her
answer. She is full of plans. In August, she and Sid are driving to
Vermont and they want to visit us.

"What about Dad?"

Jack Smith will stay with Dad, she assures me, now audibly irritated. I know she wants me to feel as overjoyed as she is. But don't. I
hang up the phone and watch Julius, stalking through the long
grass in the orchard like a tiny lion. I feel confused, sad, a little
afraid.

A few days later, I call James. He's heard too. Like me he is taken
aback, but mainly by Mom's uncharacteristic glee. "This is the first
time I have ever called and asked how she is and she's said, 'I'm
great!' " he tells me.

"Amazing," I say.

"She's completely naive about these things," James says.

I switch from worried child to worried parent, the role he's
assumed. "She's only had one serious relationship in her life," I add.
Mom has told us both that there is "no bullshit" between her and
Sid. Veterans of scores of "honest" love affairs, my brother and I
laugh. "There's always no bullshit between people who are lying to
each other," I say.

The next week Mom calls us both to recommend, in an
emotion-laded voice, the movie *Innocence,* about two "senior citizens" who fall in love and have a passionate affair. "Ma, please!" is
James's response.

I tell Paul about the movie review. We discuss the accommodations in Vermont. Sid has booked a bed and breakfast about an
hour and a half south of our town for the first night. To avoid a

long drive after seeing us, I've told Mom I will find them an inn nearby.

"So are they going to sleep together?" Paul asks, with half a grin.

"Don't even TALK to me about that!"

Soon Mom tells me she is in love. What she feels for Sid is "real love." She says she has never felt this way in her life.

I am forty-eight years old, and after fifty-nine years of marriage my mother is telling me she did not feel "real love" for my father. Again, I do not respond with happy congratulations.

"I'm still carrying my Actor's Equity card. I kiss Dad, I pat him," Mom says another time. But her love for a fully functioning peer must make Dad's deficits loom larger. Whenever we talk, she reports on how much worse he is getting. An old friend and colleague, Peter Jaffe, visited. They went to lunch at the diner across the street. Dad used his stock phrases with the waitress: "What would we do without you, dear?" "It couldn't be better!" The waitress thought he was adorable. "You can leave him here with me!" she exclaimed. Mom says she thought, *Be my guest.* When Dad was in the bathroom, Peter commented, "He doesn't understand a single thing you say to him anymore." Mom tells me about the waitress and Peter's comment twice.

She is sure he doesn't understand anything. I call their apartment when Dad is with Jack and Dad picks up the phone. "I haven't seen you in a long time," he says. "I miss you."

"I miss you too," I say, surprised that I mean it.

"When I see you, I'll run after you," he says. We laugh.

I report this exchange to Mom. "He probably doesn't even know who you are," she says. I feel slapped.

Mom tells Paul that having Sid in her life makes her more patient with Dad. But I'm not sure Dad sees it this way. I think he understands this single thing: Mom is not with him. She tells me he asked her "Where do you go?" She doesn't say whether he sounded angry, sorrowful, or scared.

He has a new refrain: "I was a little boy, all alone. Just a little, little boy."

A year ago, Mom bought twin beds but stayed in the room with him. Now she sleeps on the living room couch. She says he gets up more often in the night, disturbing her. But I can't help thinking that the reawakening of her erotic self renders Dad's body, and his demeanor, repugnant to her.

Dad wanders out of his room one night. "There's nothing in there," he says.

.   .   .

I am confused by the word *we.*

"How's Dad?"

Mom's hearing is getting worse. "We're fine. The new apartment is just beneath—" she names some celebrity. That is, Sid's new apartment.

"How did the doctor's appointment go?" Dad has been to the psychopharmacologist for a new prescription.

Mom: "Elinor is dying." Elinor, Sid's daughter, has just been to her oncologist.

"We went to see *Contact* the other day. It was marvelous."

"Who's we?"

"Sid and I! Who do you think?"

"We're going out to Brooklyn tomorrow to see Rila Nemerov."

"You and Sid?"

"Why would Sid go see Rila Nemerov?"

When I call around looking for an inn for Mom and Sid in Vermont, I refer to them as "my mother and her friend." But sometimes I slip and say to Paul, "When my parents come."

There are other *we*'s, and by implication, *they*'s. One *we* is the group that is "thrilled" about Mom's relationship. This includes Elinor, Mom's counselor (whom she calls her "therapist") assigned by the NYU center, and the majority of the old friends she tells. When she confides in Joey Krantz, in her kitchen on Twenty-fourth Street, he lifts her off her feet and dances her around the room. Some people are initially ambivalent but come around to being happy, if not thrilled (e.g., her piano teacher, who nursed her own slow-dying husband at home until the gruesome end). Then there are those whom Mom hasn't told yet, including her former daughter-in-law, the mother of James's children.

"You don't have to tell Wendy," I say. "You don't have to tell everyone."

"Why do you say that?"

"Because Dad is still alive. You can leave him a little of his dignity."

"That's why I'm not telling everyone," she says. Her tight tone registers my rebuke.

Most of the friends I tell about Sid are also delighted. "Good for her!" they say. "Wow, how old is she? That's inspiring."

James and I discuss developments over the phone. He reveals little more than amused astonishment. I get the impression he's not querying Mom closely about Sid ("I don't want the details, if you know what I mean"), but I doubt he's actively disapproving either. She infers that James is in the very-happy-if-not-thrilled camp.

I, meanwhile, inquire about neither the details nor the big picture. Each conversation between Mom and me becomes a dialogue of pointed non sequitur, as she relates something about Sid and I ask about Dad, she briskly responds to my question about Dad and segues back to Sid, and I maneuver the conversation back to Dad—or anything besides Sid. She is embarking with Sid in a jaunty high-bobbing boat, and I keep heaving Dad in between them. Water pours over the gunwales, they bail and row on. I refrain from blessing their voyage, she refrains from acknowledging that such a blessing might be hard for her daughter, and her husband's daughter, to give. When I interview Gloria Goldstein, Mom's confidante, about Dad's life a month later, she asks me, "Why are you taking your father's side against your mother?"

I call my friend Gina. "Do you think I'm taking my father's side against my mother? Maybe I am."

Gina tells me that after her mother died, her father almost immediately remarried. "He was on to the next thing. He didn't look back." After twenty years Gina has virtually no relationship with her father's wife, "and that is only partly related to the fact that she's a hideous person." We laugh and she continues more seriously. "The funny part is, I hated my mother. But I felt someone had to hold her memory."

Even James says on the phone, "For the first time in my life, I actually feel pity for the old man." He says he has an image of Dad sitting alone in a nursing home room.

．　　　．　　　．

August 10, 2001

Saturday morning a burgundy Mercedes sedan motors up our driveway. Paul and I are standing side by side. He is training the garden hose spray on the white phlox, fresh as winter in the heat-exhausted perennial garden. "Here they are," he says. My mother and her beau step out from behind the rose hedge at the top of the hill. I don't know why I'm surprised, but Sid is an old man. Handsome, slim, almost slight, with a little brittle gray hair and smiling eyes that are puffy underneath, he is dressed urbanely for the country in tattersall and khaki.

"Okay," I say to Paul. "They can go home now."

Sid and I shake hands and tell each other we're glad to be meeting. He hands me a gift box of four bottles of wine, two red and two white, all Italian, and Mom pulls a lumpily wrapped package from her beige nylon handbag. I bring the gifts into the kitchen and unwrap the smaller one. It's two cassettes of Bach cantatas, including Mom's favorite, the "Coffee" Cantata. The card is signed in Mom's hand, "Love, Lillian and Sid." The new *we*.

Paul is giving a tour of recent improvements to what we jokingly refer to as "the estate": the new flower bed, Paul's vegetable garden, which is doing well this year. Mom, a lifelong gardener, crouches and pulls a weed. I lead them to the far side of the pond, where we've cut a trail through the balsams to a smooth black rock on the shore, perfectly sited for viewing our resident beaver. Sid is balky on the uneven, pine-needley path and declines an offered seat on Beaver Rock. Mom, meanwhile, exclaims over the lush moss underfoot and the view into the marsh behind the pond. It occurs to me that he wouldn't have made a good husband for Mom, who, along with Dad, adores nature and has always mistrusted the wealthy (she used to repeat her mother's adage that it's as easy to love a rich man as a poor man, with the postscript that she'd never been able to love a rich man). Sid appears indifferent to nature and is wealthy.

But what's an ideal husband? Dad? Hardly. Now she loves a rich man who probably tolerates nature just fine, as long as it is surrounding a Tuscan village with a quattrocento church and a decent trattoria. Mom and Dad would never even consider the kind of hotels Sid always stays in. The inn I've booked for them costs twice what anyone in my family has ever paid for a night's lodging. But it is one of the best B&Bs in New England, located in one of Vermont's prettiest towns, with excellent food and exquisite English gardens. Why shouldn't she get to stay at such a wonderful place? Sid is also less of a snob than Mom about movies, theater, and music. He does not appear to require that people share his politics in order to like them. This seems to relax her usual vigilance to judge. They laugh a lot.

I put on coffee and cut the blueberry banana cake Paul made earlier this morning. As Mom takes her plate, I notice she is wearing a ring on her right hand, a large irregular white pearl and a round black one, set in copper, a gift from Sid. Her hand looks small and old in this big, tasteful, but also somewhat ostentatious ring, which almost reaches her knuckle. She has never worn any ring but her

Lutheran-plain gold wedding band, which she still has on. Sid, widowed just two months, wears his too.

When she goes to the bathroom, Sid turns to me and says, "Your mother is a remarkable woman."

I answer, "I know. " I'm sure he is reminding me because Mom has complained about my insufficient appreciation. Later, he tells me she's a good driver, as if this warranted mention. My feminist hackles are up.

After they've been with us an hour and a half, Mom pulls me aside and asks, "So? What do you think?"

"He seems very nice." He's intelligent, affectionate, and attentive to her. He also likes to take charge, and Mom seems glad to let him. "Don't worry about it," he says to her frequently. She turns to me and says, "Sid is a worry wart." Never mind the Jewish telegram. Between them, worrying is *only* a joke, not a source of tension.

Sid seems eager to impress, if not necessarily to please, Paul and me. He says, about the people he mentions, "His daughter was a Fulbright scholar." "He's the chief of brain surgery at Columbia Presbyterian." They go off to visit a friend of Sid's and when they come back they both tell us that the son of this man's second wife is only seventeen and already is exhibiting his sculpture in galleries. From the other end of the table, Paul says brightly, "When I was seventeen, I got my driver's license!" Mom and I laugh.

She says frequently of her new relationship, "It's like a fairy tale." I'm waiting for the prince to turn into a frog. Am I afraid he will, or do I want him to?

We meet them at the bed and breakfast for dinner. There we stroll in the garden, which looks west to Mount Mansfield, behind which a blinding red sun is setting. I ask Mom the names of the flowers and she knows them all. She asks if I'd like to see their room. I decline.

Sid chooses the wine. We talk awkwardly about Vermont politics. Though Paul was in the state legislative leadership for years, Sid asks few questions of him or me. But neither of us ask him many questions either. When it gets dark and cooler, Sid offers to go upstairs and fetch Mom a sweater, but she goes herself. The rest of us sit silently, sipping our wine. We're all relieved when she returns.

The next day I go for my daily swim across Nichols Pond, where I meet Melissa, my frequent swimming partner, to whom I've been recounting the saga of Sid. "How's the boyfriend?" she asks eagerly as we wade into the water.

"He's nice," I moan. "I hate him."

Sunday morning, Dad's caregiver Jack calls and asks for Mom. I say she's not here, then quickly amend it to "She just went out." He reports that Sally, a home health aide who was slated to take over from Jack when he went to open the church, has finally arrived, two hours late. Mom has been talking with Jack on Sid's cell phone since early this morning, trying to find a pinch hitter from three hundred fifty miles away. Since there's no tower nearby, half the calls haven't gone through.

In the months since the arrival of Sid, Paul and I have wondered how his presence will change the already fragile system of time, money, and attention that make up Dad's care. Paul suggests that the four of us discuss the new arrangement during the visit to Vermont, and on my request he calls Mom to propose the idea. She calls back and says that Sid would rather not. So it is agreed that Mom and Sid will visit friends on Sunday morning, he'll drop her off at our house around one-thirty and go amuse himself elsewhere, and then return for dinner.

They arrive instead at four, together. Sid is installed on the deck with his book while the three of us repair to my writing cabin, behind some trees beyond the vegetable garden, about thirty yards away.

The warm air in the cabin is decadently perfumed by a clutch of pink Thérèse Bugnet roses in a mason jar. Mom tenderly touches the small cast-iron wood stove that used to be in her and Dad's bedroom in Maine. She admires the stones and bones, nests and feathers displayed on the bookshelf and settles into a low canvas chair in the corner. Paul takes the red rocker with shredding caned seat opposite, and I swivel between them on my desk chair.

Paul introduces the topic. It's as important as it has always been to coordinate Dad's care, he says. But "the dynamics have changed, now that Sid's in the picture. You may be away more," he says to Mom. "We need to know what's going on, what the schedule is, who to call." He's in managerial mode, to which Mom responds in kind.

Before he can finish, Mom begins what sounds like a rehearsed speech. "I have three choices," she says. One, she moves in with Sid ("He'd like me to live with him." She doesn't say if she'd like to live with him) and manages full-time help for Dad. Two, she gets more part-time help and continues to inhabit her own apartment, where she feels "like a prisoner." Or three, she puts Dad in a nursing home. She says she wants to start looking for homes right away because the lists may be long, but agrees to wait until I return in the fall.

She has worked all this out financially. Right now, Social Security, Dad's pension and annuity, her smaller pension, Medicare, Medigap, and prescription drug coverage provided in their retirement packages allow my parents to keep the principal of their nest egg intact and even reinvest a portion of the interest. In four and a half decades of middle-income nonprofit and public-sector jobs and about ten years of investing during the foolproof 1980s and early '90s, they have socked away a half million dollars. Mom has calculated how much she can pay a care worker, researched the costs of nursing homes, and talked to elder lawyers about what can be subsidized by the government.

I learn the next time she and I talk that Sid has written her into his will. But his bequest does not come into the conversation because, in spite of Sid's generosity, Mom does not want to depend on him. She says she needs her own savings to live on, "and I will not spend all my money to keep Stan at home forever." She intends to use up Dad's annuity and pension on his care, and when the annuity is depleted (in about three years, she calculates) turn his pension income to nursing-home fees. But even for a financially healthy couple like my parents, institutional care is unaffordable. Dad's annual $45,000 will cover about half the cost of a New York nursing home. He will have to qualify for Medicaid, which means becoming indigent—the possessor of less than $8,000 in assets.

How can one spouse become eligible for Medicaid without leaving the other penniless too? This problem faces not just poor people but also middle-class ones like my parents. In the past, when clients faced this common conflict between indivisible property and divided needs, lawyers counseled the only licit solution: get divorced. Today, rather than resolve this absurdly cruel dilemma by ensuring all senior citizens a decent retirement, the state lets couples of five or six decades get divorced financially but stay married formally. They may shift assets little by little out of the ill spouse's name and into the well spouse's. The healthy spouse (or "spouse in the community") may keep a certain amount of that money to live on; in New York in 2002, it was $87,500. Then she may renounce a portion of financial responsibility for her partner. This process, which prevents her own impoverishment (provided she dies soon enough), is called "spousal refusal." So much for family values.

Paul and I still have questions. Sid's role is hazy: we want to know if he is contributing to Dad's care, Mom's upkeep, or neither? Mom used to consult Paul occasionally on matters of financial planning, but she hasn't asked lately. We presume he's been replaced by Sid. Mom mentions that one of the benefits of her current plan is that it will guard James's and my inheritance. But do James and I have a say in whether to use that money now to keep Dad at home?

As we try to insert these questions into Mom's monologue, she repeats what she has already said, each time more impatiently. "I already told you, Judy . . ." "The annuity will last for about three years and . . ." The normally solitary and silent space of my cabin fills with the clamor of unspoken emotions. Mom sits forward in the chair. Outside, bees hurl themselves with muted thuds against the window screens. At this point the only certain thing is that

James and I will not be consulted. Paul and I are not being consulted now. We are being informed.

"So what about Sid?" I ask for the third time.

"All he wants to do is help me," she says.

"And so . . .?"

The meaning of her unstated anger erupts. "You know, Judy, everyone is so concerned about Dad. But Sid is the only person who is really *for me*. He's the only person who helps me."

If he is for her and I am not sufficiently for him, then I must be against her. I am taking my father's side. Declared a traitor, I seize the role. "One thing, Mom," I say. "I didn't like lying to Jack about where you were when he called yesterday. I don't want to lie to him and I don't want to lie to Dad."

"Okay, I can understand that," she says. The response is clipped. Is this another act of betrayal? By not protecting her time with Sid, am I denying her a last chance at love?

But I'm not sure who I am defending, Dad or myself. "Mom, I—" My voice quavers with the still unsorted feelings of the months since the announcement of Sid. "You're, you're assuming Dad doesn't understand anything. I think he does understand that something is going on. Maybe he doesn't know exactly what, but he's got to know you aren't with him."

"He has no sense of time. He doesn't know how long I'm there or not there."

"How do you know? You told me he's asked where you go."

"He doesn't understand anyway," she says.

"Maybe he does."

She sighs loudly at my pigheaded denial of her reality. "He doesn't ask anymore."

Or he's given up, I say to myself, probably projecting my own welling discouragement. "Look, I would rather err on the side of his having consciousness," I say. I remind her of the conversation in which Dad said he missed me and she dismissed it with the comment that he doesn't know who I am. She does not remember saying that.

Paul tries to bring the conversation back to the coordination of Dad's care, but I have swiveled the chair in Mom's direction. "Before"—before Sid—"I felt as if we were cooperating about Dad. Now you have other interests, which are not necessarily my interests. Or Dad's interests. Like about lying to Dad. All of a sudden, I'm engaged in this thing and—" my tone shifts from defense to offense "—and I mean, you didn't even ask if I wanted to meet Sid, much less spend the weekend with him."

"You could have said you didn't want us to come."

"But then I'd have to reject him," I say, in tears of anger, because now I feel trapped: I am rejecting him. "You set me up."

Mom looks bewildered but also furious. I'm accusing her of manipulation, of which I'm sure she does not feel guilty. In fact, she probably did not "set me up" on purpose. But it doesn't occur to her that she could have done so unconsciously—that she might want to get back at me for not celebrating her new love. My mother, wife of a psychologist, has never had much interest in the unconscious. But maybe she hears another, equal, insult in my accusation: not that she misunderstood me, not even that she hurt me, but that she does not know me. "Do you think I don't fully understand how you feel about this?" she says. "Don't you think I know what you must feel?"

"Obviously you don't, or you wouldn't have put me in this position."

"Judy, I didn't *put* you in any position."

"You did. You did too!" I shout, like a five-year-old lost in a tantrum. *Mommy, just listen to me!* Paul reaches out and puts his hand on my leg.

"I understand fully—*fully*—what you feel," she says again. This time, it sounds more like indictment than empathy.

I swivel the chair toward Paul, so she cannot see my face. I shake my head no, as if to say, *I can't.* He has mostly been quiet except during the more practical portions of the conversation. My face begs for help.

"Lillian," he says, "all Judith is saying is that you might feel one way—sympathetic, understanding, whatever—and behave another way. Can you see you made it difficult for us when you didn't give us the option to graciously decide to meet Sid the first time, say, in the city for a drink? Do you see it was even somewhat aggressive to bring him here without really asking us?" Hearing the word *us,* I feel protected.

She starts to cry and turns to me. "Judy, why are you blaming me? For ten years I have done nothing but take care of Dad—"

"Well, not nothing, Mom. You've had a life and—"

"I've had no life."

"Okay, you've had no life."

She rises to leave the cabin but does not. She sits back down and stops crying. "Sid and I have decided that whatever our friends or families feel, we don't care. We want this relationship and we are going to have it."

I say, "I'm not talking about your relationship with him. You also have a relationship with me."

She does not respond to this, except to plead her case. "You know," she says. "I only have about two years to live."

"What do you mean?" Does she have cancer?

"I'm not going to live forever." Phew. No cancer, just mortality.

"Oh, so I should excuse everything you do because you are going to *die sometime?*"

She continues on the subject of how little time she has left. "I probably should have divorced Dad years ago. Then he got sick and—" Her voice trails off.

"So now you're leaving him."

"Judy, I am not leaving him."

"You are leaving him."

"I am not leaving him," she says, not with pride or conviction or even stubbornness, but only with fatigue. She is stating the simple, regrettable truth.

The lowering sun has now slipped under the cabin's eaves and into the room. The conversation vibrates like molecules in a heating beaker, caroming between the burden of Dad's care and the miraculous arrival of Mom's happiness—and my desire to deny her that happiness. For a moment I remember that we called this meeting to figure out how to reorganize things so Paul and I might take some of the burden *off* Mom.

After a while she says, "I don't love Stan anymore. I have no feelings toward him."

"You have feelings."

"All I feel toward him is irritation, rage, resentment, boredom, and anger."

The catalog of her alienation lands on my heart, heavy and final. "I know," I say. "I know."

We're all quiet for a long minute. She says, "He's not even a human being anymore."

Paul and I glance at each other with the neutral faces that say we're thinking the same thing. I say softly, "I disagree with you."

"What?"

I speak a little louder. "I disagree. I think he is a human being."

She backpedals. "Well, I don't literally mean he's not human. You know what I mean."

Whether out of shock or sadness, fear or self-righteousness, I am momentarily speechless. Part of me wants to think she doesn't mean it, she doesn't think he isn't human. I want to believe her need to separate from him and her guilt about doing so compel her to see him as a creature without ordinary human perception and emotion, who doesn't know she's leaving and doesn't feel the pain of her departure. Another part of me thinks I have finally heard the truth. Much later, I will reconsider Mom's statement in light of analyses like Stephen Post's; I won't hold her exclusively responsible for dehumanizing the demented. In the cabin this afternoon, though, I take it personally, on my father's behalf. "Yeah, I know what you mean," I say.

"Listen," she says, blowing her nose, her voice almost beseeching. "I feel compassion for him. I feel pity. I am loyal to him." Paul is nodding his head supportively. "I will not abandon him. For the rest of his life, or mine—and I'll probably die before he does, with all this stress—I will do everything I can to make sure he is safe, comfortable, healthy, occupied, and happy." She pauses. "Anyway, as happy as he's able to be." *I am no longer his wife. Now I am his caregiver.* The skilled administrator will apply her talents to provide for every detail of his care. But to transform him from husband to Alzheimer's patient, Mom is divesting Dad of his former self, even of his capacity for happiness.

The anguish described by many caregivers arises from the persistence of the old self and the old relationship. The new self-free identity of the patient can ease some of that anguish. A creature hollowed out of traits both beloved and reviled, the person with Alzheimer's enters the caregiver's life afresh. Historic ties to the old self dictate obligation, which is of course a kind of relationship. But now that relationship can be cleansed of the sadness of perpetual loss. The "endless funeral" is over. The loss becomes final, the sadness becomes grief, and grief is an emotion that evaporates with time. In losing his memory, the person with Alzheimer's allows his caregiver to lose her memories too.

As the screen door slaps shut behind Mom, Paul and I stand. He puts his arms around me and says, "I'm sorry this is so hard, sweetie."

"Yeah," I say, depleted. He takes my hand as we walk across the lawn to the house. I watch Mom climb onto the deck and put her hand on Sid's shoulders from the back. She leans down to say something to him and he touches her arm and smiles. Then she goes into the house. Sure that Sid has heard every shouted word from the cabin, I am again irritated that Mom brought him here, but I'm also embarrassed. Besides being a madwoman, I am a lousy hostess. "You shouldn't have had to listen to that," I tell him when I reach the deck. "I'm sorry."

If I'm a bad hostess, he is a good guest. "No, no. I didn't hear anything," he protests. "I've been reading."

He accepts a gin and tonic from Paul, who grills swordfish on the deck while I make a mango salsa and put rice on the stove. Mom offers to pick the salad greens from the garden, then brings them into the kitchen and returns outside to sit with Sid. At the dinner table we make small talk, and both Sid and Mom praise the food effusively. They stay as long as is courteous, excusing themselves immediately after coffee. We are all exhausted.

I am grateful for Sid's good manners. And as they walk from our lighted house through the dark to his car, I am grateful for his guiding hand at the small of my mother's back.

.　　　.　　　.

September 11, 2001

I have tarried in Vermont at the end of the summer to write a piece about an organic dairy. It is nine in the morning and I am in my cabin, trying to call New York before driving north to Butterworks Farm. Frustrated by busy signals in Manhattan, I manage to get through to the phone company. The guy says, "Maybe this has something to do with it, but I just heard on the radio that a plane hit the World Trade Center."

"You're kidding," I say. We marvel at the stupendous incompetence of the pilot. We exchange good-natured clichés: "Boy, life in New York." "It's always something, isn't it?" "Okay," I sign off. "If it doesn't improve, I'll call you back tomorrow."

I go into the house and turn on one of the three channels our television receives to see if I can get some news about the plane. Five tearful hours later, I turn to Paul and say, "Let's go do wood." We put on our work clothes, load the chainsaw into the pickup, and drive down the hill to Paul's forest to begin the chore of getting the winter's fuel in.

Paul cuts the thick trunks, felled in the spring, to eighteen-inch lengths. I heft them into the truck bed. We drive them to the house and toss them off the truck into a rough pile, from which they will be split and then stacked in the cellar. We drive down the hill and do it again, and again. The labor feels redemptive; the forest, fragrant with fairy-ring ferns and bright with blue-bead lily berries and white dolls' eyes, is blessedly far from history.

Unaccountably, I reach Mom on the phone the next day. "Dad has no idea anything is happening," she tells me. "No idea whatsoever."

"Lucky him," say I. But of course, Dad's not lucky. His ignorance of one of the biggest events in his city's history, his inability to feel its mourning embrace or even its jittery energy, only write his isolation larger.

I tell Mom that like everyone else, I have been e-mailing anyone I've ever had a fight with to make amends. She doesn't have e-mail, so I'm making amends with her now.

"Uh-huh," she says, not exactly accepting my offer. Then she adds, "It makes me realize that what really matters is relationships."

"Yes, I agree."

"That's why Sid and I just want to spend all the time we can together."

Dad is divorced from history, Mom is divorced from Dad. Now that her future is with another man, she is severing one of the last ties Dad has to his own history—his marriage. In the preservation of the self, what really matters is relationships. With whom shall his be?

The next afternoon Paul comes with me to Nichols Pond. The water remains warm even as the cool nights have begun to turn the maples red. We swim to the other side and pull ourselves onto the float in front of a never-used camp. The loons have crossed with us, diving and bobbing up yards away, then paddling back to accompany us. I think they see my white face, black-suited chest, and black cap of hair and think I'm one of them. A late-summer swim is always an unanticipated gift from an indulgent Nature, who knows better than we do how long the winter will be.

I sit on the edge of the raft with my feet in the water, bent at the waist, and bring my nose to the surface. My shadow blocking the glare, I peer into the water at a half-dozen bass gliding among the rocks. The simplicity of their lives—just eating and avoiding the occasional hook—seems attractive. I relate this thought to Paul and roll my eyes when I hear what I'm saying. "God," I comment. "I'm so self-pitying that I envy *fish!*" I pull my legs out of the water and stretch them across the warm planks.

Paul and I talk, as we have been doing since Mom and Sid's visit, about what will happen next. I don't even have much idea as to what is happening now, as communications with Mom have thinned considerably. Still, Paul and I are contemplating our own future with Dad, discussing, among other things, moving him to the tiny nursing home in the next town, on whose board Paul has served.

Paul repeats what he has been saying these last few weeks. "Your mother is not abandoning your father. She said she wasn't and I believe her." She has been trying out caregivers. One woman arrived for an interview two hours late. *Next!* Another spent a few hours with Dad but scolded him for putting the paper towels in the refrigerator. Mom didn't ask her back. "She's stupid, a stupid woman!" Mom exclaimed, telling me the story.

"She's an excellent manager, your mother," Paul says, listening to me recount these events. "She's going to make sure all his needs are met." Dad will be well fed, groomed, healthy, safe, and, as the social workers put it, "stimulated."

"All his needs but one," I say.

His face questions.

"Somebody's still going to have to love the bastard." We both mime alarm and point at each other like Laurel and Hardy. Across the silvery surface of the pond the loons are ululating. "I guess I just wish my mother loved my father," I say after a while. "It's an infantile wish."

He touches my foot with the hand he's been trailing in the water. "Not a bad wish."

We drive back to the house in the early gathering dusk. The

fields are brittle and burnished yellow, and hidden among the stalks the crickets are scraping their legs like amateur fiddlers. I think of Emily Dickinson: "As imperceptibly as Grief/The Summer lapsed away—" A part of Mom's grief is lapsing as new love brings her back to happiness. And for me, two unexpected new griefs loom: the grief of losing the father I am warily beginning to love, and now the grief of alienation from my mother.

8. *Decompensation*

I RETURN TWO WEEKS LATER to a New York stunned and gentled. But the citywide truce has not substantially changed relations chez Levine. I take the subway to Twenty-fourth Street for dinner, Mom opens the door, I take off my jacket and sit on the sofa. The first thing she says is, "You never ask me about my life." Meaning, I don't ask about Sid.

"How's Sid?" I ask, unconvincingly, and she fills me in with equal enthusiasm. I don't have to ask about Dad. She has told me he is worse, and I can see what she means. "Bring your chair in here, Dad," I say when we are ready to eat. Blank stare. "Do you want some water?" "What?"

A week later, on a walk with him, I try to get a battery for his strange new wristwatch (which turns out to be a portion of a personal alarm system Mom has gotten from some agency). I drag him from hardware store to drugstore to supermarket, encountering the bewilderment of every clerk. Dad keeps feeling his wrist where I've removed the band. I tell him he'll have it back in a minute; I'm fixing it. He seems skeptical, then resigned to the incomprehensible trials everyone regularly puts him through. Then he stops on the sidewalk and refuses to move. "So where are you going now? Where is it?" It's as if he's decided that I can't fix the thing, or anything. Or simply that things are not fixable.

Things feel unfixable between Mom and me.

Jill Rosenberg, the Goldsteins' daughter, mentions that her mother is going to Mom's birthday party.

"I heard you're having a birthday party," I say to Mom the next time we talk.

"Yes," she says brightly. "Sid is inviting everyone to a little Italian place in Chelsea." She ticks off the guest list: Gloria, the Millers, the Jacobsons, Sid's daughter Elinor . . .

"And Paul and I aren't invited?"

"I assumed you wouldn't want to come."

"Why did you assume that?"

"Well, you don't seem to be interested in my life."

"You mean Sid."

"You've told me, Judy, that you don't want to have a relationship with him."

"Number one, I have never told you that. Number two, whether or not I have a relationship with Sid, I have a relationship with you. *You're my mother*, remember? Why would you think I don't want to come to your birthday party? Didn't you think it might hurt my feelings if you invited everyone else except me?"

"Okay, okay, I didn't mean anything by it. Come to the party."

Progress is being made, though, in stitching together a life for Dad so Mom can get on with hers. She has hired a caregiver, a warm, smart, experienced Argentine woman named Nilda Palombo. At sixty-eight, Nilda is plump but compact and energetic. She wears a pressed housecoat in the apartment and, though she was a hippie in her younger days, running a tea house in a northern Argentine beach town, she now dons a cashmere sweater, skirt, makeup, and jewelry whenever she goes out, even to the supermarket. She and I share an adoration of cats. She leaves food once a day beside the building's Dumpster for a scruffy white stray. In her photo albums, half the pictures are of the past feline members of her family and her friends' families. She is a fervent socialist who reads the Spanish leftist newspaper *El Pais* from cover to cover, pointing out to me the anti-Bush cartoons and commending articles by Edward Said and Noam Chomsky. "She's got all the right politics," Mom says. In other words, she's one of us. If Dad could understand her tastes and views, he would feel that connection, too. But he feels it anyway.

The plan is that Nilda will come every weekday from nine to five, Jack will spend Friday night and Saturday with Dad, and Mom will be there six nights and Sundays.

But the plan starts to shred almost immediately. When Sid invites Mom to a fund-raising dinner or concert, she wants Nilda to come at night and take compensatory time off during the day or work Sunday and take a day off during the week. Nilda is accommodating. It's a new job and, she tells me, and "I like to work."

Mom asks the same of me. Can I come Monday evening at a quarter to six instead of Thursday? Sid is having cataract surgery during the day, and Mom wants to stay with him overnight. And Nilda's English lesson starts at six. I tell Mom I have French Monday and can't get there until six-thirty.

"Well, that's all right," says Mom. "Nilda can go to her class later."

I object: "If she's taking a class, she has to be at the class."

Paul says I should pick my battles. And if I want so badly to help Nilda, I can reschedule my own lesson.

So again, I'm taking sides. Being fair to Nilda means being inconsiderate of Mom and now of Sid, too. Nilda and I have discovered we can communicate in French (her English is only a bit better than my Spanish), so she appoints me her union steward. She complains to me about the schedule changes, it's impossible to make any other plans. She is sympathetic to Mom: *ta pauvre Maman* is so tired and anxious, she says. But she's always lived at the homes where she's worked. If she's going to come and go at all hours, she needs an apartment nearby.

When I broach the subject of Nilda with Mom, she is irate. She tells me Nilda expresses nothing but delight with the job. Next time Nilda expresses something besides delight, I counsel her to take her gripes directly to my mother. I assure her that Mom, an old union organizer, will be reasonable. Nilda says she will. But when I ask her whether she has, she says, "Oh, no, no, Judith. I don't want to burden her, it's still so hard for her. And I like to work!" Then she complains some more. Finally, Nilda asks Mom for a dependable schedule and a rent subsidy in the neighborhood, and Mom tells me she is demanding too much. I reply that if she doesn't want to meet Nilda's demands, she can find someone else; a number of my friends have had wonderful caregivers for their parents. Though my intention is to satisfy Nilda's needs so she will stay a long time, I succeed only in piquing Mom's nervousness that she will leave. But she finds Nilda a room in the co-op and helps her pay for it and regularizes her hours. Later, she tells me my comment that Nilda was not the only caregiver in New York was "dismissive" of how hard she worked to find a good person. I guess I shouldn't go into labor negotiation.

Compared with these high-level dealings, relations with Dad are uncomplicated. So through him, I attempt to do nice things for Mom. Spending an evening with him the week before her birthday, I suggest we make a birthday poster. I letter HAPPY B-DAY on one page and LILLIAN on the other in Magic Marker, and while I cook a supper of leftovers, Dad sits at the kitchen table, humming, and scrubs at the pages with crayons until the white is all covered and the crayons are stubs. Like a proud kindergartner, he writes his name in the corner. I tape the two posters on the outside of the door.

"Shall we listen to some music?" I ask Dad when we've finished.

"Hmm? Hmmm," he answers, agreeable.

I put on a CD of Richard Goode playing Beethoven's piano sonatas. As the F minor begins, he rises to dance. I take his hands, we spin and sway together to the first movement, then I sit on the couch as he continues on his own, facing me as on a stage. He follows the piece's map of emotion from measure to measure. It starts out coquettish. Dad trills with his fingers, steps mincingly on his toes, his mouth in a tight moue. Fists planted on hips, he mimes pique, then dances a calculated seduction, a sly smile on his lips. Beethoven interjects a series of masculine chords, which Goode renders like a Latin lover, aggressive yet voluptuous.

The second movement has Dad extending his arms, palms up, pleading but evincing small hope of satisfaction, then pulling his closed hands back toward his heart, as if he is resigned to emptiness, his eyes and mouth near tears. The third movement is a lilting waltz, but it steers away from frivolity, skirts sadness. Dad dances with impeccable rhythmic and dynamic attention, now silly, now grave. I stand up to waltz with him, which he does about as well as a dog on his hind legs. Along with Goode, he sings, his usual *Dah-dah-dah-dee.*

The final chord is struck. Dad trumpets the soprano note in his nasal bass. Unembarrassed by his exuberance, elated by his unembarrassed elation, I clap and shout "Bravo!" He kisses me decorously on the lips.

When Mom returns from a date with Sid a bit after nine, I hear her laughing in the hall. "This is beautiful, Stan!" she exclaims when we meet her at the door. The three of us stand back in the hallway and admire the posters, all grinning. Maybe Sid is good for my mother, I think, and by extension, good for my father—and me.

Concerned that I not get on the subway too late, Mom hurries me out. As she hugs me and thanks me warmly, Dad pushes in to gather me in his arms, too.

"When will I see you?" he asks.

I answer as I always do, "Next week." When I arrive the next week, the posters are still on the door.

Other visits aren't so sweet. Dad doesn't like being with babysitters all the time. The evening of Sid's cataract operation, Nilda lets me in as Jack is exiting. She and I go into the kitchen.

"What are *you* doing here?" Dad shouts when he finds me.

"I'm staying with you because Nilda has to go to her class."

"No, you're not."

"Yeah, I am."

"You are *not!*"

"Sorry. I am."

"No, you're not," he says with less conviction. With a defeated but condescending laugh, he turns to go back to his room. "I'm not running it," he says before retreating. He's right. We're the ones screwing up.

He tries weakly to woo his wife back or at least figure out what's going on. He, Mom, and I are in the kitchen. Dad stands close to Mom and asks, half-challenging, "So, how do you feel about it?" He looks at me. "It was acceptable, between her?" Relationship talk.

On a hot morning, he takes all his undershirts from the drawer, spreads them on the bed, and puts on three. Mom has learned not to pursue this particular battle—Dad's wardrobe is a last redoubt of self-determination—but it's so steamy out that she tries to persuade him to take off two of the shirts. Predictably, a struggle ensues. He flings the shirts on the floor and at her. Finally she manages to calm him. She finds a light summer shirt in the closet. "Here, let me iron this for you," she says.

Dad watches her warily as she hurries through the task, now anxious to get him to his program on time. "You'd really like to get out of here," he spits.

Dad's temper is becoming more volatile. He is hitting more people—participants at the day center, Jack, even, once, Mom. After he hits an aide at the center, the aide tells me, "Something in his brain must have done something, and he kept apologizing after that."

"Yeah," I reply. "Like anyone, he feels remorse."

Dahlia and I discuss this last fracas, and though she has not witnessed it, she suggests that it's not just the brain that's out of whack. "What I wanted to know was what happened before he slugged her," she says. "Did she provoke him?" He may be unable to control his impulses, in other words, but that doesn't mean his impulses are meaningless. Indeed, Dad's cycle of easy provocation, lashing out, and sincere contrition are nothing new. The new elements are the speed with which he progresses from feeling to action and the wildness of the action. "Stan is Stan," says an experienced social worker who knows Dad. "With Alzheimer's, there are always disturbances in the personality, but you can still see the personality, and the emotions are there into the very late stages."

In his testiness and aggression, Stan is Stan. But other, sweeter parts of his personality, buried during the intensely frustrating early period when he was most aware of his deficits, are also reemerging. No longer engaged in full-time revolt against Alzheimer's, Dad now has more room to express his graciousness, his yearning to be liked, and his pleasure in the pleasure of others.

Nilda brings out this best self. While he is at his program, she sets to work on the apartment, ironing the linens and stacking them in the reordered closets, scrubbing the kitchen counters and cabinets, and storing snacks out of Dad's reach. As she pulls the apartment back to order, she begins to instill in Dad a sense of both spaciousness and security, and of her own simultaneous authority and tolerance. Unlike Mom, Nilda has nothing else on her mind when she is with him. She is "engrossed."

Neither of them really speaks English—she doesn't understand much of what he says and he doesn't understand her—but their communication is unhampered. He joshes her nonsensically, she giggles. She prepares foods he likes, chicken stews and fresh-orange jello, served at a childlike five-thirty P.M. "Thank you, dear, dear," he says when the plate arrives, and kisses her hand. She seeks out a barber who will cut his hair carefully and takes him every two weeks to have his thick and fungus-crusted toenails pedicured. When the catalogs and the *New Yorker* arrive, she passes them on immediately to him to "read," which he does out loud, getting every sixth or eighth word approximately right and filling in the rest with gibberish, chanted like a cantor. In return, he picks up drop-out subscription cards and carries them decorously to her: "That's for you, dear."

"Thank you, Stanley," says Nilda. "That is veddy nice."

The calm and good cheer spill onto the rest of us. Her schedule more or less fixed, Nilda arrives each morning at eight and stays until five, Monday through Thursday. Fridays she arrives later in the day and stays overnight until Jack comes at nine on Saturday morning; he's with Dad until ten or eleven at night (usually they take a field trip to the park or a ride on the Staten Island ferry), when Mom comes home. Mom is still spending every night in the apartment except Friday and, often by necessity, taking care of other business while she is with Dad. He has not yet begun to allow Nilda to help him shower, so Mom does that, too.

But Mom is also with Sid during almost all of her free time—he's still living in New Jersey but is overseeing the renovation and decoration of a new apartment in the city—and this puts her in an almost gay mood. At her birthday party, she orders a gooey chocolate dessert, something that Crohn's has forced her to avoid like a Hindu shunning beef. "I have a new attitude," she tells me. "My stomach is going to be terrible no matter what, so I might as well enjoy myself."

Living today, Mom is still worried about tomorrow. She calls one afternoon to tell me that the day before, Dad's shower ended up all over the bathroom floor, and "an inch of water" leaked to the apartment of the eighty-year-old woman downstairs, who was "almost killed" slipping on her own bathroom floor, to say nothing of the damage to her ceiling and the wooden tiles in Mom's hall. To prevent further disasters, this morning Mom went into the bathroom with Dad, arranged the shower curtain, gave him the soap and washcloth, and told him to wash himself and pay special attention to his "tush" (which he often doesn't). All these ideas—bathroom, wash, tush—floating in proximity in Dad's brain tumbled out of order. He defecated in the tub. Mom was distraught.

Buoyed by newfound eagerness about the future and weighed down by habitual pessimism that the dreary present will drag on forever, Mom swings between fear that the whole system will crash and cautious hope that it won't. The feelings resolve into resignation that it will crash but might wait until next month instead of doing so this afternoon before supper. One thing she feels sure of: either she or Dad will fall apart, and no matter who goes first, the collapse will send Dad to the nursing home.

I wonder if Mom's support group acts as a Greek chorus singing this scenario, a version of the official Alzheimer's story. In one support group that sociologist Jaber Gubrium observed, for instance, the members narrated the caregiver's plot around a "multiphase chronology reminiscent of Elisabeth Kübler-Ross's stage model of dying." In the first stage, the caregiver adjusts to the patient's needs, embarking on the "thirty-six-hour day," but denies her own needs. The stages of anger, guilt, and depression follow denial, and with struggle, lead finally to acceptance. But acceptance of what? "At this point, the possibility of institutionalization or nursing home placement is discussed for the 'sake of all concerned,' " writes Gubrium. It's a narrative you can read on most any Alzheimer's information Web site.

The caregiver's stages interlock with New York University neurologist Barry Reisberg's now-familiar stages of decline in Alzheimer's disease. As the patient descends the circles of dementia from one to seven, the caregiver moves toward acceptance that he is going, going, gone. Mom organizes and substantiates her own observations of Dad's slide with expert assessments. "They say he's in stage four and a half," she tells me after a visit to the NYU clinic. Or, when the two of them run into Doris Berman, a former social worker turned "care manager," who has known Dad since the mid-nineties, "Doris thinks he looks like a late five." In the heartwarming TV-drama version of this duet, the couple climbs hand in hand to the bottom and kisses good-bye. But Mom and Dad are not walking hand in hand. She does not want him to suffer and has assembled a staff to prevent that happening. But I can't help hearing a grim relief in the reports of Dad's higher (therefore lower) "scores." She wants it to be over—and who can blame her?

I, on the other hand, am resisting both the medical standardization of dementia and for the first time enjoying my father's quirks. So I toss away the chart of stages and notice what is stable in Dad, even flourishing. Yes, he stuffs the toilet with too much paper, but he knows how to use the toilet and is not incontinent. Yes, he is jostled by pedestrians and jangled by traffic, but he's eighty-two years old! He enjoys a walk, likes the flowers in the brownstone gardens, the kids in the playgrounds, and the dogs in the dog run. He is increasingly obstreperous, even violent, at the day program, but he's also the only enthusiastic participant in the room, a veritable party animal.

Is Mom playing Cassandra and I Pollyanna? Each of us is reading a script and casting Dad as a character in it. To her, he's the incredible shrinking man of the Alzheimer's story. When he falls through the cracks in the floor, she will need a place for him to land. I meanwhile am madly looking for plots with happier endings. Reading Oliver Sacks and talking with Damasio about his studies in Iowa, I learn that the brain is a dynamic organ, adaptive to its environment and remarkably capable of compensating for deficit. Many of its areas are highly specialized, but some can pinch hit when others sustain injury. A group of physicians led by Ingvar Karlsson in Sweden have found that high-quality care for demented people even in the last stages of "global deterioration" results in ameliorated emotional outlook and behavior and retarded cognitive decline, and even in recovery of intellectual powers that were considered irretrievable. Recording both psychological and neurochemical improvements, the Swedes hypothesized that a better environment not only improves a person's quality of life, it actually encourages new neurons to grow in his brain. If psychologist David Rothschild suspected that bad experiences could hurt the brain, these researchers are proving that good ones can help it. Kitwood, who has shown similar results at his Bradford clinic, calls learning by people who have supposedly lost the ability to learn "rementia."

Mom and I both consider ourselves realists. Neither believes Dad is "coming back." But she has long been parting from him and is ready to say adieu, and I am just meeting my father. To me, he is still here.

In the meantime, she and I tussle about who is here for whom.

"The best thing for him right now is to stay in the apartment and for me to leave," Mom says one day. I agree. Then, about ten days after the bathtub incident, she reports that she has visited a nursing home in the Bronx, which was cheerful and clean, with an engaged staff and a content, busy-looking group of residents.

"So now you are going to see nursing homes? I thought we talked this summer about going together."

"If we would ever have the time to sit down, we could talk about some of these things."

"So let's sit down."

"Well, you're not available." *Available:* it obviously means more than being willing to pencil her into my datebook.

.   .   .

We meet at La Bergamote, a French patisserie in Chelsea a few blocks from their apartment. When we arrive, I peruse the beautiful pastries. Mom says she doesn't want anything but tea. Deciding that a pastry would appear frivolous, I order two teas, in French. The waitresses, typically French, pretend not to understand me and respond in English.

As we have done before, Mom and I start the conversation reviewing, inconclusively, the rules of Medicare and Medicaid, home care and nursing care, financial "look-back" periods and spousal refusal. I take notes on Dad's pension and Mom's investments, ask delicately and am answered vaguely about Sid's contribution to her finances.

"How's the book going?" Mom asks after a bit. A sensitive subject.

I tell her I am reading cognitive science. "It's the intersection of neurology, philosophy, computer science, and psychology," I begin.

"Really fascinating. It's making me want to ask questions in the book like, 'What is consciousness without memory or language?' Or 'Does a person ever cease to have a self?' "

She listens distractedly, asks no questions. As soon as there's a pause she says, "You know, Judy, you have to look at it from the caregiver's point of view." I have a dark flash: whatever I write is not going to satisfy her. She starts to tell it from the caregiver's point of view. "It's clear that Dad needs twenty-four-hour supervision. He can't bathe or dress himself any longer, and he refuses to let Nilda do it. And Nilda is too old and small to handle him anyway." (So why did you hire her? I ask silently). "He gets up at all hours of the night and walks around." He will need looking after at night soon. "I am running a nursing home at the apartment. You don't know what it takes to hold all this together."

"You have good people now."

"People are unreliable, people quit. Everyone has this experience."

There's no point in debating whether "people are unreliable." The two people in question, Nilda and Jack, have shown themselves to be extraordinarily reliable. "Are you saying you want to put him in a nursing home?" I ask.

"Judy, we're all assuming he won't like it. But he's very social. He likes being with other people, he likes groups. Especially once he can't walk around and go outside, he might do very well at a nursing home, rather than being home with one person. It might even be better for him."

I say I can't imagine it would be better for him. He likes to "go to work" at the center. He likes to be *among* people. But he chafes in a group the minute he feels neglected, and has a tantrum when he doesn't feel duly appreciated as entertainer, leader, and all-around superior fellow. I tell Mom about the social work articles I've been reading that say once people are committed to nursing homes they tend to "decompensate" quickly. What I have not yet learned is that the average number of staff hours devoted daily to each resident in an American nursing home is four, and even the best don't exceed six hours. With a shortage of people to attend to them, about a tenth of nursing home inmates spend their days "in restraints," shackled to their chairs and beds to prevent their falling. "People 'decompensate,'" I say to Mom, crooking my fingers around the jargon. "And then they die."

"We don't know how he'd do," she says.

"No, we don't," I say. "But he can walk around, and he could die before he loses that."

She tells me a story I've heard a number of times, about a friend whose children "wouldn't let her" put her husband in a nursing home. The woman installed a round-the-clock team of private care-givers in their home, at great emotional and financial expense. "I have to think about my quality of my life too, you know." She folds her napkin nervously. "You have no idea what it is like."

"Well, I have a little bit of an idea." She must be thinking a little knowledge is a dangerous thing.

"Ten years without a single real conversation," she says.

"Talking isn't the only way of communicating," I say. "When I'm with Dad, we just walk around, sit by the river, have coffee. We don't talk much." I know I'm treading into hazardous territory, compar-ing my experience with hers, implying that mine is the right way. In fact, I know what she means about the ordeal of lengthy time with Dad. The other night, after making the birthday poster, eating dinner, and dancing, I installed him in front of the TV and turned on an old science-fiction film. Mouth slack, eyes fixed near the center of the screen, he sat nodding along with the rhythm of the moving black-and-white images. I tried to read, but I couldn't. I felt the nullity of his gaze sucking my attention toward him like a vacuum and a nervous unhappiness pouring into the space that was left. I had to get Dad into his pajamas and to bed, out of my sight.

Watching the conversation with Mom deteriorate, I decide to try out my theory of why she and I are at war. "For me, it's easier not to talk," I say. "In fact, his not talking is making it easier for me to get closer to Dad. But you, you're mourning the loss of—"

She interrupts. "Oh, no, no, no, Judy. I finished doing that *long* ago." Her voice is sharp. I wish she would at least hear my sympathy for her, but all she hears is my disapproval. And I wish she would acknowledge that she's sad about what is happening to her and Dad. That is, I want her to *be* sad. She goes on. "For a very long time, there hasn't been much to lose." The irony is, if she loved Dad, his life would be less painful now. But if she loved him, her life would be more painful. Perhaps for the same reason she discarded all those objects that might assume "sentimental value," she has been slowly revising history to excise the love she felt for her husband. It's easier to lose what you no longer want.

Something makes me press on with the monologue I've been reciting to myself for weeks. "I'm not sure what it means to commit yourself to a marriage," I venture, trying to sound as if I'm exploring the idea.

She's no dummy. "You're implying that I'm not fulfilling my *marriage vows?*"

"No-oh, I'm not saying that." I am saying that. "You were married fifty years, and now you're leaving him."

She jabs her spoon into her teacup. "You've been telling me to leave him for years."

"But you didn't. You didn't leave him when he could still fight back."

"I had children, the house—"

"James and I have been gone for twenty-five years."

"You don't know what went on."

"You blame him for everything. No fucked-up marriage is one person's fault." Am I taking my father's side against my mother? I'm trying to take no one's, but clumsily. "You have some control over what happens to you," I say. I'm talking about her marriage, our family, her relationship with Sid.

"I have control over this?" She is glaring at me in rage and disbelief. Her marriage, our family, her relationship with Sid—as usual, it's all blurring together with Dad's Alzheimer's.

Feeling impotent to influence the course of Dad's life, I'm determined not to let Mom represent herself as the victim of circumstance as scripted by the official Alzheimer's story. The implication
of such powerlessness is that the consequences of decisions—to be
with Sid, for instance—are not really her own, either. "You have
some power over how you react to Dad." In my mind I've labeled
this *bad faith*, but I dare not use the term, which is as judgmental as
I feel.

"All I have the power to do is make him angry," Mom says. "And
all he has the power to do is make me angry."

I try to soothe the bludgeoning I have just administered. "I
mean, you had positive reasons to be married to him. You've told me
a million times about the good things in your marriage. It wasn't all
bad."

It's too late. "It was pretty bad."

"You didn't leave him when you would have had to face his pain
and anger."

"I'm facing it. Every day, Judy."

She's asking for mercy, but I am merciless. "He doesn't really
know what's happening. He's at his most vulnerable now. You're
kicking him when he's down."

This conversation is ending as they all seem to these days, with a
peremptory search for her lipstick and a parting declaration. "I have
fulfilled my responsibility for ten years," she says. "And I can't do it
anymore. And I won't do it anymore."

When did I, no paragon of marital fidelity, join Focus on the
Family? When did I become a moralist? Why do I care about this
abstraction, bad faith? Why am I insisting that because she didn't
leave Dad when he was still compos mentis, she signed up for servi-
tude unto death? Am I not kicking her when *she's* down?

Later, I read Gubrium: "If a disease sufferer neither recognized
the caregiver—as, for example, a spouse of half a century—nor
appeared to know who they themselves were, the moral underpin-
nings of the relationship were dramatically put into question.

Could they continue to apply on the basis of the mere memory of historical rights and obligations? Were the mere shells of former selves owed the same attention and consideration as a cognizant wife, husband, or parent?" These are piercing questions, questions that Focus on the Family–like absolutes are too blunt to answer. Dad's not a "mere shell" yet, if he will ever be. But her relationship with him was rich, whereas mine was meager. Watching him shrink is much more harrowing for her. Maybe I'd feel better if she let me know she was grappling with Gubrium's questions—and maybe she is. I have hardly made it safe for her to grapple in front of me. In the end, what rankles me most is her depiction of herself as Dad's victim, both before and since Alzheimer's. But I'm not just defending my father. I am livid that she depicts herself as *my* victim, playing no part in our mutual craziness.

"I have to go. I have an appointment," Mom says. She thrusts her lipstick into her bag and her arms into her coat sleeves.

"Me, too," I say, immediately regretting the unnecessary lie, which will now prevent my lingering over coffee and that coveted pastry. We agree on two dates to visit nursing homes, then stand and hug. We clutch at each other like two climbers sliding over the edge of a ravine, able to pull neither ourselves nor each other to safety.

·   ·   ·

The next time we see each other is at the Goldstein-Levine Thanksgiving. We have temporarily healed our rift, if only by allying ourselves against others. For the sake of convenience and social conviviality, Jill tells me on the phone, she has disinvited Dad and Winnie, another dotty, frail friend of the Goldstein family who has long been a regular guest. I feel bad but say nothing. When I get off the phone, I tell Paul. "Boy, this is a cold bunch," he says. I call Mom. She is hurt, too. We all want Dad there, if only to show a kind of solidarity—"to be a family" is how I put it when I talk to Mom. I promise her I will plead Dad's case. I call Jill back. How much trouble will he be? I ask. And even if he is some trouble, so what? That's fine, no problem, says Jill (Winnie has made the dignified decision to dine with others). She and Gloria just thought the party would discombobulate Dad and his presence would distract Mom from having a good time. It's a mark of our rawness that my mother and I have assumed the worst about the Goldsteins' intentions.

Still, I suspect the real reason for striking Dad and Winnie from the guest list may be to winnow it to near nothing and call the whole thing off. Although our two families have had Thanksgiving together for decades, this year it feels like a chore. No one seems able to host. Gloria's worsening arthritis and asthma disqualify her. Mom can't cook at her apartment with Dad on her tail. Paul's and my Brooklyn place is too small. Alfie and Lisa, the Goldsteins' younger son and his wife, are with Lisa's family in Philadelphia this year. Their daughter and son-in-law, Jill and David, are in the last stages of a divorce after twenty-five years of marriage. Len's death, just around this season, has turned Thanksgiving into a memorial more than a celebration. The pall of September 11 is still on us. And of course, the Levines are engaged in our own terrorist war, with the highly biased reports of each attack broadcast to all.

But it is I who lobby hardest for the dinner. I want us together, especially after September 11. I worry that without the glue of rituals like this, our fractious family will splinter irreparably. I surprise myself with the vehemence of my desire. Jill responds, David consents. They offer to host at their house in Brooklyn.

When Jill comes to the door to let Paul and me in, the ambience is decidedly subdued. Her sons, Tony and Jake, are in their rooms playing video games. David is in the kitchen, lying low. Dad is on one of the couches, feeding cheese and crackers to the two large dogs, whose tails are thumping perilously close to the hors d'oeuvres. David's mother, Rhea, who has just had a stroke, sits in an armchair staring. She tells me when I ask that she is holding it together but struggling with disorientation; she literally does not know whether it is day or night.

I pull up a chair beside Mom. In our customary fashion, we launch directly into Alz-talk. Mom says she had "an encouraging conversation" with Doris Berman, the care manager, who has told her that Medicaid will finance full-time in-home care for someone it deems to be in need.

I don't get this. "Isn't Medicaid for poor people?" I ask. Last time we spoke she told me that the government has started prosecuting people who invoke spousal refusal when the bureaucracy thinks they can afford to pay for care themselves.

"You don't live in reality, Judy," says Mom, her patience already short.

"Ma, I'm trying to understand the reality. You told me Medicaid won't pay because you have too much money. Now you're saying it will pay for everything."

"Judy, I've told you a million times."

"What did you tell me? Weren't we just talking about all these people who put their family members in nursing homes even when they don't want to, because Medicaid won't pay for home care?"

"I'm not going to spend all my principal on this. That's what I live off!"

"I know you live off that. I know you don't want to spend all your money. But does Medicaid see it that way? Does the government give money to people who have half a million dollars?"

"That is all the money I have. Dad's pension will only pay for some of the care." Her body is tense, her face flushed. She is inching away from me on her chair.

"Don't get angry, Ma. I am just trying to understand this."

"That is all the money I have," she repeats.

"Mom, I know this is the money you have. I'm asking you about Medicare and Medicaid. It's complicated. I don't understand it."

We go back and forth on this question a few more times. Finally, she says, "I just don't understand why you are so angry that I should have a happy life."

Like the blast from a fire hose, this sentence pushes me backward to infantile rage. "What the fuck are you talking about? You are crazy! " I scream. "You are fucking out of your mind!"

The room stirs in astonishment. *What's going on? What just happened?* Rhea is shrinking into her chair. Tony and Jake, who have just moseyed into the living room, are practiced in dodging bullets after a lifetime of parental strife. They mosey out of the living room toward the kitchen.

Gloria follows me to the foyer, where I am tossing bags and jackets around in search of my own. "It's not fair for you to leave, Judy, after we have all worked so hard to have this happen."

Now Mom is bustling into the foyer, too. "You don't have to leave," she declares, "because *I'm* leaving." Gloria tries to guide her back into the living room. She breaks loose and stomps up the stairs. I tear out the front door. David and Jill scurry into the kitchen with their kids and slide the door closed.

Paul grabs the coat I've dropped in my escape and follows me down the brownstone stoop to the sidewalk, where I am trembling with cold and frustration. He wraps the coat around my shoulders and his arms around the coat. "Judith, Judith, what is going on?" he asks. "Why are you so angry?"

"Because she never listens to me," I say between sobs. "She refuses to see me beyond her fantasies of who I am. Now I'm the person who hates her boyfriend. So whatever I say, she just uses it to prove that I won't let her be with him." I quickly rehearse the conversation. "I'm talking to her about Medicaid and she acts as if it's me, not Medicaid, that wants to take her money away."

"That's exactly the same thing she says about you," he answers. "That you don't listen, that you don't see her. That you use everything she says to build a case against her."

I'm in no mood to draw up a peace plan. "Then we're at an impasse," I say. "We should just stop talking to each other."

Paul and I stand on the sidewalk in the gray afternoon light. He strokes my hair. "Will you come back in?" he asks, taking my hand. I shake my head no. I am still crying, drily now. "Come on in." He starts to climb the stairs. "C'mon up, c'mon up," he coaxes, using the phrase we've taught Julius to get him onto the table for his shot. I laugh feebly but follow him up the steps. "I'm going to go up and talk to your mother," he says. "Okay?"

"Good, you talk to her."

From the step above me, he kisses me on the head.

When I open the door, Gloria is waiting in the hall. She clasps me to her. I feel her belly, hardened inside a girdle, against mine. She is crying. "Oh, Judy, Judy . . ." She won't let me go. "There is no one your mother loves more than you. But the two of you just . . . just . . . *pass* each other." I start to stammer my arguments. "Shh, shh," she coos, her face close to mine. "Don't talk." She keeps looking into my eyes and holding me in the kind of embrace I cannot remember from a member of my family. "I love you both," Gloria says. "I know how painful it is for both of you."

Dad has arrived in the foyer. His limbs hang limp at his side, looking as vestigial as he is right now. He watches, almost panicked, like a child witnessing a violent fight between his parents. Does he worry, as children do, that it is his fault? I do not move as he steps toward me and takes both my hands. "I won't leave you," he says.

"I know you won't, Dad," I say. But rather than comfort me, the statement fills me with dread—just as it does Mom. And just as it does Mom, his next comment fills me with more dread: "I need you."

"Don't worry, Dad," I say automatically, trying to shake myself from his grasp without his noticing. "I won't leave you, either."

We are called to dinner. As I walk toward the table I enumerate my feelings to myself: "One: I am an orphan; I have no parents. Two: I wish my parents would die and leave me orphaned."

Mom and Paul are upstairs. The food is passed around. Being a vegetarian already makes Thanksgiving dull for me. And with Alfie and Lisa absent, the table is bare of the buttery, fussed-over dishes they always bring. Jill's diet consciousness rules. I consume dutifully, feeling guilty that I've ruined an already underwhelming party. Mom comes downstairs with Paul and they each put a small amount of food on their plates. Conversation is spotty. David, whose father got Alzheimer's in his fifties and lived with it for more than twenty years, leans in and whispers in my ear, "I really know what you're going through. When my father was sick, it tore my family apart."

After dinner, while David and the boys do the dishes, Jill and I sit alone at the table. She tells me that sequestered in the kitchen, she and David shared a moment of pre-divorce camaraderie. "At least it's not us this time," she'd said to him. They'd wiped tears of stifled, guilty laughter from their cheeks.

I tell Jill about my epiphany during the conversation at La Bergamote, which I have just experienced again: "Whatever I write in this book, my mother is going to hate. It's actually a little liberating. If she stops talking to me, so be it."

Ever the realist, Jill says, "Forget it, Jude, you won't be so lucky."

Shortly after seven, Rhea is ready to go home. Mom stands up from where she is sitting with Gloria on the couch and announces that she and Dad are ready, too. They will take a cab to Manhattan. Paul and I have offered to drive them, and now we insist. We say our good-byes quickly. There are not enough leftovers to bother with, and besides, I don't want any reminders of this day in the house.

I help Dad climb into the back of the Honda. Before getting in beside him, Mom seizes me fiercely and pulls my face down to hers. "I love you, Judy. You know that."

"I love you too, Ma."

The next day I call Jill. "Thanks for putting up with me," I say.

"Hey, what are families for?"

"Good question," I say. "What the hell *are* they for?"

Families, apparently, are for turning pathos into bathos—and then to absurdity. Jill can't wait to recount the phone conversation she has just had with Rhea, who witnessed the fray through the lens of her own dementia. "So Rhea tells me—" Jill, already giggling, shifts into her mother-in-law's Queens accent, "'When all that screaming and crying between Judy and Lillian was going on, at first

I was very upset. Of course.'" Jill's voice starts to break again into laughter. "Then she says, 'But then I realized—it was only a play!'"

．　　　．　　　．

Over the next month, I attempt to revise the last act of the play. I try to help Mom and Dad at the same time, not taking sides. I spend more time with him, which also relieves her. I discuss nursing homes with her; I try not to argue or dissuade her, but hope that the reliably upbeat reports from Nilda will reassure her that things are working out at home. I even inquire about the progress of Sid's renovation. Although she lets slip the occasional disparagement of his art collection and quips about the interior decorator (or "drekorator," as she calls her), Mom is uncharacteristically blasé about the decisions being made. She doesn't really care what the place looks like, she says, as long as it's comfortable. And if Sid is in it, I have the feeling it will be comfortable for her.

We're all holding our breaths. Mom is waiting for the day she can move in with Sid. I am waiting for a commitment from Mom that she will not move Dad into an institution. Paul is waiting (without much hope) for Mom and me to stop yelling at each other. And we are all waiting for the next crisis.

Except Dad. Dad is not anticipating a crisis or anything else. His focus is tapering to the here and now, to the buttered toast on a plate on the table, the look on the face of a fellow care-group participant, the roar of a ferryboat past Chelsea Piers. His emotional life is focusing in, too. Less and less is he aroused by his relationship with Mom, who comes and goes stirring memories of desire and discord. Now he is settling into the dulcet atmosphere of Nilda, who arrives each morning glad to see him, to speak to him, to serve him. Of all of us, only Dad is breathing easy.

．　　　．　　　．

On Christmas Day, the crisis comes.

Paul and I arrive at Twenty-fourth Street for brunch at eleven.

Mom, who prided herself in donning the same jeans every non-working day of her life, is wearing a new soft-blue sweater and chic black slacks. The clothes are another aspect of the person she is becoming in her relationship with Sid. They dine at expensive restaurants, go to the theater frequently and sit in the best seats. She tells me Sid is buying her a Steinway baby grand piano for the new apartment. I don't know if he buys her things or encourages her to buy them, but the woman who has forever maligned her wealthy friends for their materialism is now enjoying her own. She looks pretty in the blue sweater.

We've brought Dad a Christmas present, which he unwraps clumsily but effectively. It's a wall calendar of photos of sailboats on the Seven Seas, each boat and each sea more exquisite than the one before. The lower pages of the calendar, the days of the months, are printed on nautical charts of the region where the photos are taken. He used to love charts, and several were hung on the walls of the Maine house. Now this graphic subtlety, as well as the technique of turning the pages vertically instead of horizontally, is lost on him. But he likes the pictures, and as I turn the pages he touches them and strokes the boats. "It's mine," he says of one.

When he's halfway through, Mom announces we have to eat.

"Why?" Paul teases. "Is the lox getting cold?" He knows she's eager to leave for Sid's.

Dad scoops huge dollops of cream cheese and whitefish salad onto his plate and jams the slimy cheese under his index fingernail trying to cut the bagel with his spoon. "Tough to eat," I comment to Dad and reach over to cut his bulging sandwich. He doesn't resist. Mom starts clearing the table while he and Paul are still eating. I load the dishwasher while she shows Paul some repairs she wants done. When she leaves, I take Dad out for a walk and Paul sets about the chores. We're to stay with Dad until Nilda's arrival, at two.

When Dad and I get home a little before two, Paul is putting away his tools. Nilda has not arrived. Two comes, no Nilda—unprecedented. The phone rings at two-ten. I think it's she, but it's

Sid. "Hi Judy, this is Sidney Simon. Your mother has had what looks like a ministroke, and we're on the way to the ER at Columbia Presbyterian," his hospital, not hers. I stammer a few questions. "Okay, I'll see you there," he says.

"Wait," I shout. "Where's the ER?" But he's gone. I don't have his cell phone number.

I call James in California. He says he'll fly in if need be. I call Columbia Presbyterian and find out there are two campuses and two emergency rooms. Neither has admitted Mom yet. I decide on the one further uptown, where I imagine they'll go from Sid's apartment in northern New Jersey. I jump onto the C train and take it to Fifty-ninth Street. Just as I'm about to change to the local, I stop and phone the ER that's closer. The triage nurse has just seen Mom. I rush back to the A train, and just before the doors close, notice my purse is gone. I duck out and pluck it from the platform under the disparaging gaze of the train conductor. "So shoot me, I'm an irresponsible fuckup," I mumble. It is cold on the platform and I am sweating. It strikes me that Mom might die before Dad.

I arrive at the hospital and call Paul immediately. Still no Nilda, but Dad is fine, unaware. The cop in the ER helps me find Mom, on a bed in a curtained alcove. Her tiny feet are peeking out the bottom of the sheet, and the ER doctor is poking them. I kiss her.

"I'm going to live," she says, a little doubtfully. "Where's Paul?"

"He's still at the apartment. Nilda hasn't arrived." Sid doesn't look up or say hello. I reach across Mom and offer him my hand. He shakes it limply.

"What do you mean?" Mom asks, practically bolting up. "She was supposed to be there at two!"

"Don't worry, Mom. Paul is with Dad."

Sid glances angrily at me. "Don't you worry about that, Lillian. There's nothing you can do about it. Don't worry." When the doctor leaves, Mom explains that on the bus to Sid's she felt a tingling on the right side of her face and in her right hand. When she stepped off in front of his building, she could not control her foot, and stumbled. The doorman helped her upstairs, they got her into a wheelchair left by Sid's wife, into a cab, and to the hospital. Sid says Mom has had a stroke and he is certain it was caused by stress. He says she has been crying all week. I feel vaguely accused.

I call Paul, who is trying to locate Nilda, but he doesn't have her phone number or even know her last name. I come back and start to ask Mom for this information.

Sid flies in to intercept. "Don't you—" He moves closer to her bed, her bodyguard.

"I'm sorry, Sid," I say. "But I have to talk to my mother about this."

Several calls later, I learn that Paul has located Nilda at her cousin's house. She says Mom changed the hour several times and she was sure she was on duty at six thirty. When I come back, I report that there had been a confusion about the schedule, but Nilda is on the way. Mom is angry at Nilda. Sid says to Mom, "You never change the times!" He is angry at me, and I'm angry at him.

By six, Mom still hasn't been admitted to her own room. While another doctor asks us to leave the cubicle to perform some procedure on Mom, the woman who arranges the rooms comes by and asks, "Who is the family?" I raise my hand, Sid steps forward. He wants her in the exclusive hotel-like pavilion across the street, which insurance doesn't pay for. The woman asks if we want the standard room or the exclusive.

"What's the difference?" I ask.

"Not much. Both are private rooms. The food is the same, the nurses are the same. The standard is $400, and the exclusive is $425."

"Well, I guess the standard is fine," I say. Mom has never gone in for the deluxe model of anything.

The administrator walks to the nurses' station to request the standard room. Sid follows her. "Do the exclusive rooms have a river view?" Yes, she answers. "Then she'll have an exclusive room." He's paying. I, the cheapskate, am overruled.

At about six forty-five Sid goes over to the pavilion to talk to the "concierge" about expediting Mom's transfer. Alone with her for the first time, I ask if she has felt odd or sick before this episode. Not really, she says, but tells me again that she's been under lots of stress. She looks at me meaningfully, almost sharply.

"I know I've been part of your stress," I say.

"Yes, Judy, you have been."

At that moment, a burly male nurse comes in and introduces himself as "Lenny, just call me Lenny." As he searches through his tray of needles and lances for a Teflon catheter to insert in her arm, he keeps up a continual patter. "Aw, if you weren't here, you'd probably just be off having fun—so you might as well be here." He invites her to take out her frustration on him. ("No need," I want to say. "She's already got someone for that.") He keeps trying to insert the catheter, and her old veins keep collapsing. I feel both afraid for her and afraid of her.

"Mom," I say when Lenny leaves, "this is a hard time. We're not always going to agree. There's going to be conflict. But we need to be able to talk to each other."

"That's true," she says.

I take a breath. Then I propose what Paul has suggested and I have resisted, that the two of us go together to talk with her counselor, Carole.

"That would be a good idea," she says. The sentence is like a raisin in a stale, flavorless bun. My outlook sweetens for a moment.

We sit quietly. Sid storms in. "It's Catch-22 here. Over there, they told me they can't admit you until the ER reports you, and here they told me to go over there."

Lenny, walking by, addresses Mom. "I doubt anyone told him to go over there," he says. Then to Sid, "They're just humoring you. There's a shift change between seven and eight, so the nurses won't take her over there until eight anyway."

Finally, the attending physician, still in crisp Christmas brunch attire, starts his shift by ordering one of the nurses to wheel Mom to the other pavilion across the hospital's internal bridges. Sid and I walk outside to meet her. On the way, we stop at a deli to get a snack and he pays for my banana. In the street, he tells me what a wonderful woman my mother is. I'm getting tired of hearing this.

All afternoon, I have been calling Paul and trying to figure out how to cover Dad's care. I am scheduled to work at a magazine copy desk this week, three double shifts in three days, from ten in the morning until one in the morning. I need the money. Tomorrow, friends are arriving from the Netherlands to take over my apartment for two weeks. I am staying at some other friends' house while I work at the magazine, and Paul is driving with Julius to Vermont, where he has work meetings lined up from the day he arrives. If he cancels his meetings, there's still the problem of Julius, who can't stay at our apartment because one of our guests is allergic to cats and can't stay where I'm staying because their children torture him.

The doctor says Mom has to stay overnight for tests, even though she feels okay, and I ask if she will be home the following day. "Absolutely not!" declares Sid. "You're coming home with me."

Two days later, she does. By then Paul and I have arranged Dad's care. We've spelled Nilda and Jack in the hours they could not be with Dad, and they've committed themselves to stay with Dad until Mom gets back. Both have called her with their condolences and assurances. I leave for Vermont.

I'm home!" Mom trills when I pick up the phone in Vermont on Saturday. She's at Sid's. "And I have a most *excellent* nurse." I hear Sid laughing in the background. The tests have come up with no stroke, no neurological damage, no clue. "Another crisis averted," says Mom, who views such fortuitous outcomes as glitches in the ordinary catastrophic course of events.

But I'm no more of an optimist than she (I keep a file of studies showing that we pessimists are more intelligent, educated, and realistic), and it is clear to me that Dad is living in a house of cards, held up by Mom alone. It seems impossible even to share the load with her. She doesn't trust me to assume responsibility for any part of it, and Sid appears to be encouraging this mistrust. I get angry at both of them, which only increases her resentment and diminishes her willingness to cooperate with me. Yet if I don't share, even seize, some of the caretaking duties for Dad, the next crisis or the next will not be averted. The house will tumble, and there will be no place for him to live but an institution.

December 31, 2001

Paul and I pick up James at the Burlington airport. He has come from California to look at a house he and his girlfriend are thinking of buying and moving to in the next few years. After a few days with us, he'll go to New York to see Mom and Dad and meet Sid.

The next day, Paul and James drive to the food co-op and I stay home. I listen to yesterday's messages on my phone machine, which I didn't pick up when we returned from fetching James. "I'm calling you because you didn't call me." It's Mom. She had called my machine the day before yesterday and Paul's machine right after that, and he had called her back for the two of us. Unenthusiastically, I dial her number at Twenty-fourth Street.

"Frankly, Judy, I was *shocked* to hear Paul's voice on the phone instead of yours," she says.

"You were shocked?" I try to keep in mind what Paul always says: When she's with Sid, she's happy. When she's with Dad, she's angry.

"And James didn't call either."

"James got up at three a.m. yesterday, then he was on a plane all day, then we picked him up at four in the afternoon, then we went directly to someone's house for dinner, then we got home at ten o'clock. That's why James didn't call you."

"All right," she says tersely. "So how are you?" It sounds like a dare.

"I haven't slept much since you were in the hospital," I say, seizing the opportunity to gain a point in the suffering contest. "We've been talking about Dad twenty-four hours a day." I pause to let this sink in. "And I don't exactly appreciate that you didn't inform me you were starting the process of applying to nursing homes."

"I told you I was."

"No, you did not. I talked to Jill yesterday and she told me that Gloria told her."

"Judy, I discussed this with you."

"I heard it from Jill and then from James."

"Well, you weren't here."

"What, I don't have a telephone in Vermont?"

"What?"

"You can't call me on the phone?"

"I can't talk to you about this on the phone."

"And you don't think I would come back to talk with you about something as important as this?"

"You know, Judy, yesterday I felt just terrible. And I'm here all alone, and if something happens to me there is no one, *no one*, who can take care of me or Stan."

Knowing this conversation is going nowhere, I try to reroute it by asking the details of her symptoms. She says she had the same nausea and malaise she used to feel before she went on blood pressure medicine. "But I diagnosed myself." We engage in a little doctor talk. Whatshisname, the Most Famous Neurologist in the World, the Top Guy, had told her to stop taking the blood pressure medicine until she got to talk with Dr. Frankel, her physician, who specializes in geriatrics.

"So did you speak with Dr. Frankel?"

"I can't speak to Dr. Frankel because every time I call him I just get his answering machine."

"So leave a message."

"So I called back the other neurologist—"

"The resident?"

"The other guy from Columbia Presbyterian—yes, the resident— and he said to go back immediately on the blood pressure medicine."

"So did you?"

"I already *knew* I should go back on the blood pressure medicine."

"So you did."

"Yes, I did!"

"And?"

"And I felt better immediately . . . But Doctor Mayles—"

"The Top Guy?" I laugh faintly. We used to joke about the Top Guy, a typically Jewish term of respect, but Sid takes Top Guy-ness seriously. The joke flops.

"Yes! Dr. Mayles said it wasn't a stroke. It was a neurological thing."

"So there's no blockage? I thought you said there was a blockage."

"There probably is a blockage somewhere."

"So then it is a circulatory thing, if there's a blockage."

"JUDY!" She's about to pop. "They don't have any idea what it was. And this is not the only time—" She tells me there were other times—"many times"—that she should have gone to the hospital but did not because she was all alone with Dad.

"So, do you want me to come home and look after Dad? Because I can come home if you need me to."

"No. I already worked it out. Jack is coming later, and then Nilda is coming in the afternoon tomorrow"—New Year's Day, her day off. She tells me she has decided to hire a caregiver for three nights a week and weekends.

I offer to interview people. I tell her Paul and I have been talking about what tasks we can take over.

"No," she answers. "I don't want you to interview people because I already have someone I want to interview." It's the man who takes care of her piano teacher's husband at night and now wants week-end work. "Anyway, Judy, you're up there."

"I just said I would come down. I don't have to be here."

"I'm less busy than you are," she says. Is this a neutral fact, a polite no-thank-you, or a complaint?

"You seem busy," I say. "Every time I try to talk to you, you say 'I can't talk about this now.' "

"That's not true. It's you who's never able to talk." This is a weird argument. We are both chastising the other for not talking, but neither of us really wants to talk. "When you started your book, I thought we would have lunch and talk," she says. "You've interviewed everyone else."

"I don't need to interview you, Ma. We talk all the time. We're in the same life."

"I have never had a chance to express my feelings to you." So it's not that she wants to talk more. She wants me to hear her.

"I know we've had a really hard time talking, Mom. That's why I thought we should go see someone together." A long silence on her end. "Hello?"

"I'm here."

"So?" More silence. "Remember that? Remember that I suggested we talk to Carole?"

"What?"

"Don't you remember this? When you were in the ER, I said we might go to see Carole and you said you thought that was a good idea."

"I couldn't focus on anything at that moment, Judy," she says. "And I have to say, that was a completely inappropriate time for you to be bringing that up." I hear Sid's voice in the word *inappropriate*. We've got a lot of unspoken rules in our family, but being appropriate is not one of them. My spirits slump. I had honestly thought I was offering a way forward, even a kind of surrender, by suggesting we go to her therapist. I say nothing. She adds: "And I don't even know if Carole would agree to that."

"Then maybe she can recommend someone else."

Another long pause. "I don't know. I'll have to ask her when I see her. I'm not sure when that will be." She makes no commitment to call the therapist. A weight lowers on my chest.

When he gets home, Paul encourages me to come skiing with

him. This turns out to be a fine idea. As I kick and glide along in the silent powder, I feel my concentration move to the cadence and placement of my stride, the cold on my face, the sweat on my back, the soreness of the hip muscles that indicates my technique is improving. It's nice to do something in which pain actually brings gain.

Back at home, I go to our bedroom for a nap. Julius nuzzles into my stomach and purrs as I roll over on top of him. I hear Paul and James discussing me at the kitchen table. Both agree I have to work on my feelings in one place (not with Mom) and strategize the practicalities of Dad's care in another (with Mom). I feel about James the way Mom feels about me: he's a carpetbagger who arrives once a year and grabs a role in the government. As far as I'm concerned, he doesn't get a vote. I look out the window and think of Wallace Stevens: "It was evening all afternoon./It was snowing/ And it was going to snow." The weight I felt during my conversation with Mom lowers again. Now I can name it: despair.

Paul comes upstairs and we lie on our backs looking at the fly-specked ceiling. Downstairs, James is doing laundry. "Jesus!" he cries suddenly, as our geriatric washing machine starts to scrape and clatter and march like a monster across the bathroom floor. It's a deafening noise Paul and I hardly hear, we're so used to it. James shouts, "What the hell is that? The mangle cycle?" It feels good to laugh.

Paul goes to a New Year's Eve party and James stays home with me to "celebrate." I make us peanut butter and jam sandwiches.

"Got any champagne?" he asks.

"I'm too bummed for champagne. How about beer?"

"Beer, the beverage of bummers," says James, and we clink bottles.

That night I dream that Mom is in a bed, dying. It is certain that she will go within the next few days. I am lying in another bed in another room with another Mom, who is alive and healthy but (I understand) just around temporarily, to work a few things out. I am crying on and off. Temporary Mom is comforting but not intrusive.

Her body is warm beside me. Suddenly, I realize that once Real Mom dies there will be a funeral and lots to do—put the apartment on the market, deal with her papers, sell the furniture, pay the bills. Who will take care of Dad? Someone will be needed to watch him every minute. I turn to Temporary Mom, who has now merged with Real Mom. "When you die, Paul and I will have to put Dad in a nursing home," I say.

She says, "That's okay, honey. Whatever you decide to do is fine."

If dreams are wish fulfillment, what am I wishing for? A catastrophe that will resolve the nursing home question once and for all? Dad's incarceration and the end of my responsibility? My mother's death? Or nothing more than her blessing?

New Year's Day

I call Twenty-fourth Street. Jack picks up the phone.

"How was your New Year's Eve?" I ask.

"Oh great, it was grrreat!" says Jack, joyful as always.

"Did you and Stan celebrate?"

"Oh, yes." He laughs. "I brought Stanley up to the church and showed him my art. He gave me a few pointers."

"I bet he did."

He gives me Dad.

"Happy New Year, Dad."

"Yes, it's a new world, a new for us, a new day, and we will all this day, we are here together, and it will be that—"

"Yes, it's a new year," I say.

Around nine, Mom calls. "Happy New Year," she says.

"Happy New Year to you, too. Did you have a happy new year?"

"Oh yes, very happy." She and Sid attended a gala performance by the New York Philharmonic Orchestra and Chorus of the "Ode to Joy." "It was thrilling," she says. She asks what we did for New Year's Eve.

"I was too depressed to go out, so James and I stayed in and Paul went to a party." She says something general about what a bad year it's been, to which I agree with anemic heartiness. I return to Beethoven, a safe subject, and tell her what Jack said about Dad's art criticism. She laughs—she's in a mood to appreciate him from a distance.

She says, "Even though the world is so awful and people are doing such horrible things to each other, when you hear music like that, created by a person, you have to have hope."

A wave of love for her passes over me and then, immediately, shame for the months of condemnation I've subjected her to. I remember the two of us standing on the deck in Maine twenty-five years earlier, looking toward the moonlit ocean. On the old stereo propped up on a weathered board across two cinder blocks, Horowitz was playing a Chopin nocturne. Mom spread her arms to embrace the music, the night, the sea—"the whole gestalt," as she called it. "Why do I love this so much?" she asked. "What is it about this music that moves you every time, no matter how many times you hear it?"

"Three things," I said. "It's ineffable, it's immortal, and it's got a tune you can whistle."

For some reason, this struck both of us as ineffably, mortally funny, and we collapsed on the deck chairs, weeping with laughter. "Oh my god!" Mom shrieked, grasping her crotch and running into the house—peeing in her pants. I sat on the deck chuckling until she came back, and we began to laugh again sporadically, while Horowitz swept the night into Chopin's arpeggios.

Now, as Mom talks about Beethoven's inspiration of hope, I refrain from wisecracking, "Excuse me, to whom am I speaking?" Remembering our shared hilarity, a small space opens in me. If Sid can bring hope and happiness to a woman whose pessimism is second only to Friedrich Nietzsche's, I think, then God bless Sid. A not-insignificant by-product of his presence: I don't have to worry about her, because he's doing that for me. Again, God bless Sid.

The next day I receive an e-mail from Sylvia Tiger, a therapist friend, in reply to one I must have sent off in a fit of self-pity.

SUBJECT: Your mother doesn't hate you

Take it easy. Your mother cannot do all this without you and your brother, and now that she's sick her-self she really needs you. Even if her behavior seems to indicate the exact opposite. Thus is life. I'm most bitchy when I'm most unhappy, that's for sure. Go out and chop wood. I have a swell photo of you holding latkes in your apartment. Think latkes.

Love, Syl.

January 4

James calls from New York. Mom has taken him to see one of the nursing homes she likes. He describes the place with enthusiasm. He says she's asking all the right questions. Although he hasn't seen Dad yet, he is convinced that it's the best place for him.

My hope is faltering. James wants to be supportive of Mom. He feels no loyalty to Dad—in fact, he harbors nothing but hostility toward him. If I'm taking my father's side, he is taking our mother's. Whereas last time James visited, Mom complained that he "didn't have the compassion" to pretend to like his father for a day, she now praises her son for his maturity and warmth. Even Paul is agnostic about the nursing home these days, and when he suggests that Dad might do well there, it sounds reasonable. It has even occurred to me that if Dad lived in a nursing home, I could drop by whenever I wanted, eliminating Mom as the go-between. I'm not against insti-tutions on principle—if they could offer sufficient care to residents and create real communities within their walls. But that's a big "if." Institutions being what they are, I fear that Dad won't get enough privacy or attention, that he will be angry and "act out," and then be "managed." Nilda agrees with me. He still loves his home, she says, and his "little things." But she isn't putting up any resistance; that's not her job. She has reassured Mom that if he goes, she will help Dad make the transition by working with him at the nursing home part time.

After the nursing home visit, Mom took James on the ferry to New Jersey. Sid picked them up and took them to lunch at a restaurant, then returned to his apartment. James describes the place, its size, its view, and its furnishings with a mixture of awe and derision. He says Sid told him he's been encouraging Mom to bring her things to the new apartment when he moves to Manhattan. "But I just can't imagine her little antique chairs next to that stuff," James says. The chairs are beside the point, I say to myself; it's the double bed that's disturbing him. Then he moves on to the real purpose of the call. "We discussed the situation," he says. The situation between Mom and me.

I'm instantly paranoid, imagining the three of them hunched around a small table, cigarette smoke curling into an overhead lamp. "If Sid has complaints about me, he can talk to me."

"It's not about Sid," James says. "This is between you and Mom." Then he begins to lecture. "You know, and I told Mom too, you and Mom, you're both the same. You are both very, very opinionated and defensive. Neither of you listens to anyone else. You are just going to have to work things out between the two of you. I'm not going to take sides." He continues on this tack.

I am trying not to say anything, but not trying hard enough. "You haven't been here for years," I snap, "and now you come in and tell us what to do. How do you know what's going on?"

"I just know, Judy, that you have very, very strong opinions." He's got a point. "And it's almost impossible to talk to you."

"And you don't have strong opinions? And it's easy to talk to you?"

"You see, Judy, this is *exactly* what I'm talking about." He's got another point. He should rest his case, but he doesn't. "You know, the thing I fear most about moving east—I mean, I'm leaving behind my whole life, my career of thirty-five fucking years, and the city, and my friends, and everything else—but the *biggest fear* I have is how it's going to be with you, and whether I'm going to be able to get along with you."

I doubt it's his biggest fear. He's worried about something far closer to home: he wants to move to the country, and his girlfriend doesn't. I should get off the phone right now and not dig us in any deeper. After a lifetime of fighting, my brother and I have become friends in the last decade. We like each other, we support each other, we even say "I love you" to each other. But the way we've managed this is tacitly to agree to avoid the issues on which we will never agree. Now he says, "You know, there are *hundreds* of things I never even talk to you about, because I know you're going to give me shit. It's always extremely tense with you." He says it again, this time with feeling: *"Extremely tense."*

"I thought we had a good time together," I say in a small voice. I had imagined James arriving early at our house with his tool belt to help Paul shingle the roof, or Paul and me driving to their place with a pie and a bottle of wine on the back seat of the car. "I was looking forward to your moving here."

"Well, I don't know," he says, backing down only a little.

All right, then, shithead, don't move here, I grumble to myself. *See if I care.* But of course I do.

9. *Decisions*

IN THE TWO WEEKS before Christmas, Mom and I tour nursing homes.

The first one we visit, in the Bronx, is on a nineteen-acre estate graced by guarded gates, spacious red-brick buildings, dappled lawns, and aged trees, commanding views of the Hudson that Thomas Cole would envy. It is the crème de la crème of New York elder care, from its extensive collection of American art to its programs for "enhancing the quality of life in mind, body and spirit," which range from horticulture to tai chi to pet therapy. Its award-winning Alzheimer's program features such innovations as shortened religious services using "soft-toy Torahs" and a policy called "Freedom of Sexual Expression: Dementia and Resident Rights in Long-Term Care Facilities," which is revolutionary in recognizing that the demented have a right to sexual expression at all. The home even offers several choices of places to die, with different kinds of care in each.

We learn all this as we stroll through the ground floor past the Warhols and Lichtensteins and little niches filled with dioramas of Lower East Side tenement life and model trains. I ask our guide if the demented residents get to go outside onto the gorgeous grounds every day. Only if they have their own private aides, she says. The staff doesn't have enough time.

The floors where the demented residents live are different. They are unmistakably hospital wards, decorated so blandly that they'd narcotize Hannibal Lecter. Outside the dining room I watch a woman standing and calling out, "Somebody! Give me a glass of water!" She sits, stands again. "Somebody! Give me a glass of water!" Sits, stands, calls. Sits, stands, calls.

When we leave, walking to the downtown bus to the subway, I say to Mom, "That first floor, with all the paintings and stuff, is more for the families than for the residents themselves." She agrees that the place is beautiful and seems to "have everything." But like me, she's unsure how much of that "everything" would benefit Dad, or whether he'd get those things that might benefit him, like a walk in the gardens.

The next residence, on the Upper West Side of Manhattan, also is reputed far above the average New York nursing home. Yet its halls are noisy and its rooms untidy, and after a cursory walk-around with an ill-informed worker, Mom is antsy to leave, and so am I. What I remember of our tour is the "sun room" we pass on leaving, a bank of ground-floor windows where the residents doze in their wheelchairs while beside them their aides, almost all black and brown women, chat in French and Spanish. The floor of the room, like the sidewalk outside, is littered with Styrofoam coffee cups. From the street, it's a grim parody of an animated display in Macy's window: "Christmas Future."

Neither of these homes keeps residents in restraints. All permit the patients to wander within the confines of the ward. But in both, those who cannot wander loll in wheelchairs, uncommunicative and, at least when we were there, uncommunicated with. In Manhattan, I hear a nurse scolding a woman for trying to stand up from her wheelchair. "You're gonna fall," she warns from across the room. In the Bronx, the guide explains that because lunch is about to be served, the aides are otherwise engaged and there are no programs in progress. When no one responds to the thirsty woman, I hand her a paper cup of water from a nearby cart. Too bad for her, life isn't a program. It's what happens while you're waiting for lunch.

The week before Mom's Christmas Day emergency, Paul and I walk through the streets of my Brooklyn neighborhood to meet her at a home I'll call the Gardens Eldercare Center. Like the other two we've visited, the Alzheimer's unit here has won its share of accolades. Our appointment with Kitty Henderson, the head of the program, is scheduled to start at ten. Paul and I arrive precisely at ten, but Mom is already in Kitty's cubicle, leaning in close, describing Dad's life, her life, their needs. Later, as we walk through the home, she stays close to Kitty, and the two address each other. Paul and I trail in their wake.

To me, the home feels better than the others. It's busy and unfancy, the staff involved and seemingly happy. Housed in a friendly brownstone fortress built at the turn of the century as a Catholic hospital, the residence is undergoing one of an apparent series of renovations, this one in the style of the neighborhood, an upwardly striving community of Italian American tradesmen and their families, which has only recently begun to gentrify. No Warhols here. The main dining room is a cross between a 1980s discotheque and a Victorian front parlor, trimmed with Home Depot carpenter's gingerbread. Upstairs on the wards, the accommodations are spartan; most bedrooms sleep four.

The clientele are a mixture of working-class Latinos (or Latinas mostly) and Italians from the neighborhood, and in the Alzheimer's unit people from Manhattan and other parts of the city as well. Residents are not forced into wheelchairs if they don't need to be, and the policy, says Kitty, is to "undermedicate" them even if they tend toward agitation. Being drugged into compliance benefits neither residents nor staff, who can care more easily for people who are alert.

Kitty personifies the professional but gemütlich, democratic quality of the place. She greets everyone by name, treats residents and workers alike with affection and respect. As we pass the kitchen,

I ask her how the food is and she points to her own comfortable hips. "The residents and the staff eat the same food," she says. "You can see I'm not starving." She says she loves her job.

When we return to her office, I want answers to the questions that are troubling me more than the quality of the food. "Who decides whether a person will be committed to the home?" I ask.

"That decision always has to be fifty-fifty," she answers, having heard Mom's and many other family sagas. "Fifty percent the resident's need, fifty percent the caregiver's."

Do they tell the resident he is moving in and not moving out? "I guess I'm asking you—I mean, we've had some disagreement about this—should we tell my father the truth that he's moving here?" The suggestion has been made to acclimate him by installing him in one of the homes for a week or two of respite care and bring him back later for a permanent stay, even then carrying only an overnight bag so he believes he won't be staying long. "What if he keeps asking, 'When am I going home?' "

"You should answer, 'I don't know,' " she says.

"So you should lie?"

"The word 'lie' doesn't have that much meaning in the Alzheimer's field," she answers. "We prefer to think of it as 'creative expression.' " But she does state that the person should be told as accurately as possible that he is going to another place. And when he needs an explanation as to why that is happening? "Tell him, 'I can't take care of you anymore.' "

Mom is uncomfortable with this line of questioning and brings the conversation back to more immediate matters. How many beds are available and when? What kind of applications need to be filled out, what about Medicaid?

But I have more questions for Kitty. "What about other things, like if the resident is a Jew but he wants to go to Catholic mass, or he's married but he wants to move in with a girlfriend in the home?"

Mostly, things are pretty laissez-faire, she says. But with more sensitive issues, "we discuss it with the family as well."

And then there's the ultimate decision. "If the demented person is dying, who decides whether to withdraw life support?"

"In the absence of an advance directive"—the document in which a person spells out her wishes about end-of-life decisions—"we rely on the family."

.   .   .

The nursing homes we visit win awards. They devise their policies from up-to-date research on dementia, train their staffs and evaluate the "outcomes" of their programs conscientiously. They do their best to integrate the lives of their residents with those of others in the community, including children and even specially trained visitor animals. Their funding is always inadequate, and in a society that neglects its sick and indigent elderly, they are among the few who are dedicated to lobbying for more dollars for care. Although tainted by the shysters who collect Medicaid checks for warehousing the elderly and mentally ill in vermin-ridden flophouses, the doctors and nurses, social workers, physical and occupational therapists, home health aides, and companions who labor in this underappreciated field do so with the best interests of the demented elderly in mind.

But who is to say what those interests are? "Dad may do better here than at home," Mom says as we exit the Gardens. What if he doesn't want to? And even if he *would* do better but does not want to, under what circumstances should his desires be subordinated and the judgments of others prevail? "The ethical goals of care are to assure that patients' choices are respected and that patients' best interests are protected," writes Leslie Francis, a professor of philosophy and law at the University of Utah. "These goals may not always recommend the same decisions about care, however, and there is controversy about how they should be balanced when they conflict." There is controversy, all right. "I don't think he'll do better here," I answer Mom. And I really like this place.

Bioethical decision making is shaped by three principles: autonomy, beneficence, and justice. All start with autonomy. Autonomy is a legal and moral right of personhood, but to earn the right of autonomy, you have to demonstrate that you have the capacity for it. "To talk of universal, natural, or human rights is to connect respect for human life and integrity with the notion of autonomy," writes philosopher Charles Taylor in *Sources of the Self.* "It is to conceive people as active cooperators in establishing and ensuring the respect which is due them." The demented person sometimes seems bent on ensuring his own disrespect and establishing himself as the worst guardian of his own interests—for instance, when Dad asserts his autonomy by standing in the middle of Ninth Avenue in traffic. Unfortunately, he doesn't get to be an "active cooperator" on a case-by-case basis: *Doesn't know best interests when standing in traffic; knows best interests when refusing to go to a nursing home.* We aren't endowed by our creator with inalienable rights. We either use them, with consistent competence, or lose them.

When a person's autonomy is gone, our response to him is ruled by the second ethical principle, beneficence, which compels the competent to act in the best interests of the incompetent. Beneficence is altruistic by definition. To "rely on the family" is to assume the family will do the right thing for the patient, out of love. "He's very social. He likes being with other people, he likes groups," Mom said to me at La Bergamote, listing Dad's best interests, as she perceives them, in living in a nursing home rather than his own apartment with Nilda.

Beneficence is empathic: you do unto others as you'd have them do unto you. But the Cartesian veneration of reason undermines that empathy, because it renders the feelings and desires of the demented virtually unimaginable to the cognitively intact. And "the harder it is for us to imagine life as tolerable in such circumstances," says the Hastings Center bioethicist Daniel Callahan, "the harder it will be to determine what is beneficial for the patient." Add to this failure of imagination the pressing, often competing, needs of the caregiver, and in spite of the loftiest intentions, the guardians of the demented may find themselves doing unto others, for their own good, what they might not want others to do unto them. In the above-quoted article, for instance, Callahan is examining the best-interest argument for withdrawing medical treatment from the physically ill demented.

.   .   .

After visiting the Gardens, Paul, Mom, and I walk a couple of blocks to one of the Yuppie lunch places that have sprung up in the neighborhood over the last few years. Paul has a cup of coffee and a bran muffin and takes off for a meeting in Manhattan.

Mom orders her standard Crohn's-proof lunch: turkey, lettuce, and tomato on toast, no mayo, and tea. But she eats without relish. She's harboring anger over my questions to Kitty. She is not going to tell Dad he is going to a nursing home, because if she does he will refuse to go, she says. She has given him the last ten years of her life, and ten years are enough.

Her life is being devoured. "I never have time to practice the piano anymore. Dad is always there, standing right next to me."

I have the option of arguing or not. "Why don't you practice during the hours from nine to three when he's at his program? Or Monday and Friday for an hour. Couldn't Nilda take him out for an hour or so?"

"Well, I have other things I have to do then." She enumerates: "The support group is for him. The therapy is for him, because I wouldn't need it if it weren't for this—"

"Well, I wouldn't say—"

"His doctors' appointments, Nilda—"

What about her peace group, the gardens? I prod. "You have other things you want to do more than play the piano. Including spending time with Sid. Piano isn't your highest priority right now."

"I only have dinner with Sid," she says. "And sometimes lunch, which I'd be having with someone anyway."

"Unless you were practicing the piano." She is telling me she needs to have a little fun, and her constant consciousness of Dad makes fun tough to have. So she's going to grab it any way she can.

Fair enough, but I can't stop myself from insisting that Dad is not the cause of everything wrong with her life.

This provides her with a perfect segue. As a matter of fact, Dad is not the only cause of what's wrong with her life. "You know, my therapist told me yesterday that in all the studies of what makes the difference for caregivers, one, in taking care of the person, and two, in their own survival—and there have been hundreds and hundreds of studies—the number one thing that makes the difference is family support."

A beat. "Yeah. So what's your point?"

"Well, with your lifestyle . . . it's not that you don't want to, but you just can't, you have to work. And besides, it's not just your lifestyle, it's your relationship with Paul in Vermont—" She adds a few softening disclaimers, then socks it to me: "You're not reliable, Judy. You're just not reliable."

I feel duly socked, but I'm not on the ropes yet. "Mom, I make appointments all the time. I keep appointments, including with you. Including with Dad. If you want something from me, you have to tell me. I'll do it. But I don't know you want it if you don't tell me."

She doesn't want to discuss whether or not she lets me know what she wants. Perhaps she feels that her needs should be obvious. She repeats that she is all alone—that's just how it is, she holds no grudge—but because she is all alone, she will make decisions alone.

·   ·   ·

"Fifty-fifty," says Kitty Henderson." We rely on the family." Beneficence assumes a unanimity of interests within families. What's good for the patient is good for the caregiver, what's good for the caregiver is good for the rest of the family. And all agree on what's good. Beneficence is supposed to dovetail with the third principle of ethical decision making, justice. Fifty-fifty, win-win. Justice for all.

Except that in our family, as in others, it's often justice for none. Mom feels the big injustice of shouldering Dad alone and the small injustices of everyday life with him: "He can do everything he wants, and I have no civil rights." I feel the injustice of James's distance not only from Dad's care but from Mom's resentment, which falls exclusively on me. As for Dad, one of the strongest surviving parts of his personality is his honed sense of being wronged. "She has all the money!" "Why don't you put on *your* pajamas?" Win-win? Before Dad got sick, I had no idea how many permutations of lose-lose you could wring out of a family of four.

I pick at my tuna salad as Mom pulls out her compact and her lipstick, smears some bright red on her upper lip and presses her lips together, leaving half the lower lip naked. In sixty years of applying makeup, my mother has not quite mastered the technique, which endears her to me even now. "I have to run," she says, having dropped her little smart bomb. She calls Sid on her cell phone and giggles at something he says.

I watch her through the restaurant window, hurrying toward the subway. Lingering over a second cup of tea, I feel angry with one sip, guilty with the next. So she's telling me that my neglect is the reason for her fatigue and therefore the real reason Dad is going to the nursing home. I shouldn't complain about his commitment, because it's my fault. So now she's not even making the decision to commit him; this is happening to her too. How dare she? I rant silently into the cup. How dare she blame me? I'm doing the best I can! I am reliable, damn her!

On alternate sips, though, I feel guilty. Maybe I am unreliable, unworthy of voicing an opinion in the matter of Dad. Love is an act—toward my mother as toward my father. I should put my money where my mouth is.

      •   •   •

As far as the administration of the Gardens Eldercare Center is concerned, Dad is ready to enter the home as soon as a bed becomes available, which could be any day. One male Alzheimer's patient has fallen ill and been transferred to the hospital. It's unlikely he will return.

So during the first week of January, while Paul and I are in

Vermont, Mom readies the financial application for Medicaid and invites a nurse to their apartment to conduct the evaluation of Dad—the PIA, or Patient Intake Assessment—that the nursing home uses to decide whether to admit a resident. Dad refuses to talk to the nurse and orders her out of his house. She suggests to Mom that Nilda take him outside, and so the two of them repair to Nilda's apartment a few blocks away, where she makes a snack and they watch *Murder, She Wrote*. Dad likes Angela Lansbury.

Mom talks for two hours with the nurse, who will use this conversation plus her five minutes' observation of Dad as the basis of her report. It strikes me that the emphasis is on intake more than assessment—to get the patient into a nursing home, not to decide whether he needs to go. The nurse informs Mom that, in her experience, the first month of residency is almost always "hell," though a few people adjust more quickly. It's a mark of Mom's desperation that she blots out the first half of this warning, which is consistent with her usual pessimism, and hears the second.

Getting the papers together for Medicaid takes a whole day; it requires an accounting of every check over $500 written in the last three years to prove the applicant hasn't been sequestering her money somewhere. Both it and the PIA will be submitted to the Gardens on Monday. At the same time, Mom is interviewing a male caregiver named Ernesto Cabrero who works in a hospital, possibly to hire him to stay with Dad at night. She says that if a bed comes empty at the Gardens, she will let him go and put Nilda on a part-time schedule, helping Dad make the transition.

"I'm not quite ready for this," Mom says on the phone, filling in the details of the accelerated nursing-home application, after I hear about it on the Levine-Goldstein grapevine. The stress is overwhelming, she says. "I've been crying in inappropriate places."

"Stress" is a roomy category, in which other feelings can lurk. I ask Mom if she feels homeless—displaced from her own apartment by Dad, yet not quite eager to move in with Sid. This is Paul's theory.

"Oh, but I am eager!" she exclaims. She clarifies that when she said she isn't quite ready she meant that Sid's *apartment* is not quite ready for occupancy. One thing she knows, though: "If I did not have this alternative, I would be putting Dad in the nursing home, without question."

This seems the moment to get a straight answer. "But now that you do have the alternative, do you want to try the at-home full-time care and keep sending Dad to the day care program?"

Her answer isn't straight. Yes, she wants to keep looking for a nighttime caregiver to stay with Dad.

"Indefinitely?"

"Well, until a nursing home bed becomes available."

This seems unfair to the caregiver, I say, who might take the job only to be fired a month later. "Even if it's just, say, four weeks or even eight weeks?" I ask.

"Four weeks is a long time," Mom says. She is at the end of her rope, which may feel even shorter now that rescue is in sight.

When I get off the phone, I storm into the living room, where Paul is reading. "She's doing it. She's putting him in the nursing home. She told everyone but me." While I rant, he keeps trying to focus on the page.

Finally, he interrupts. "Stop it. Just stop it. You have to let her be. You have to get over this anger. It's not getting you anywhere."

"But she—"

"Fighting with her is only going to marginalize you more."

This is more convincing than the Nike-like injunction to "just stop it." I say doubtfully, "I guess you're right."

"Nothing has happened yet. You don't know what is going to happen. She's obviously ambivalent about this, probably more ambivalent than she's saying. Haranguing her isn't going to do her or your father any good."

Sheepishly: "Yeah."

"And it's making her miserable."

"Yeah."

"And it's making you miserable."

"It is."

"And it's driving me crazy," he says, though gently.

"Sorry."

A few days later, Mom and I discuss the Gardens again. I ask a few questions, just clarifications. We don't fight.

·   ·   ·

"Now what?" reads the subject line of the e-mail I send my friend Adrienne Asch on January 4, 2002. I first met Adrienne around 1973, when she sang beside me in the alto section of a New York chamber chorus, reading her music in Braille, and we've kept in touch on and off. Now she is a prominent feminist ethicist and disability rights activist, and the Henry R. Luce Professor in Biology, Ethics and the Politics of Human Reproduction at Wellesley College. Last time we spoke, I told her about my family. She told me that her mother, with whom she has had a troubled relationship, was dying. I bring Adrienne up to date on the high-speed moves in the direction of the nursing home and on the rational family conferences that should, but decidedly are not, taking place over this momentous decision:

> Everyone but me is convinced Dad will be better off at the Gardens Eldercare Center in Brooklyn, and who am I to say he won't be? Nobody is asking his opinion; they presume he won't understand what they're talking about or will resist if he does. And since they aren't going to consider his wishes anyway, why ask?
>
> And me, I am keeping my mouth shut for the time being. I gaze at my navel and read about the rights of people with dementia. I wonder if commitment to a nursing home can be considered involuntary confinement. I feel impotent, immoral, frustrated, confused, angry, defeated, and cowardly.

I ask after her mother and her family and sign off with a big hug. I hit Send, hoping for a comforting—or even better, instructive—reply from someone who's thought about these issues far harder and longer than I.

Adrienne calls me the next day from her mother's. She says she can't talk long; her mother is worse. Still, she commiserates. It's hard to be in conflict with your mother, she says. But "your father is lucky to have you as an advocate. He needs an advocate." Her clear sympathy, both political and personal, is a tonic. And I have to admit, having her on my side, questioning the nursing-home commitment, makes me feel righteous. *Mom, listen to her! She's disabled! She's an ethicist!* Adrienne recommends I call her friend and colleague Leslie Francis, whose *Georgia Law Review* piece I have in my files. She tells me Leslie specializes in navigating the labyrinth of rights and interests, autonomy and beneficence that my family finds itself lost in. "Well, Judith," Adrienne says before hanging up, "you're in the middle of a bioethical, family psychological dilemma."

I laugh at how everyday conversation with the fearsomely smart Adrienne can sometimes sound like a journal article. I reply, "You ain't shittin' nickels, A."

Within five minutes of saying hello to Leslie Francis, I understand that this labyrinth has even more twists and turns than I'd mapped. The conflicts of interest in making decisions for "incapacitated" people like Dad do not end with the clash between the interests of the family or nursing home and those of the person being cared for. The interests of the demented person himself can also be at odds.

Like all of us, people with dementia have at least two species of interests: the pains and pleasures, desires and aversions they perceive in the present, or "experiential interests"; and what the legal theorist Ronald Dworkin calls "critical interests" and Francis loosely classes as "values," the more abstract personal goals and principles that give a life meaning and coherence.

"Critical interests," or values, are easiest to articulate when you are still of "sound mind," and in fact they're the interests you set down when you are, in the documents called "advance directives" for future medical care—the living will and the more detailed health care proxy, which specify the kinds of treatment you want (or do not want) when you are in various conditions of health and conscious-ness. Advance directives are a way of codifying what you care most about. One person might consider "pulling the plug" a kind of assisted suicide and thus immoral, while another might have no moral qualms about suicide and even believe that extraordinary medical measures at the last minute are an immoral waste of scarce health care resources, not to mention a cruel trial for the patient and those who love him. Some people may want to eke out every second of life no matter how torturous, while others want the ordeal over as fast as possible.

Mom and Dad filled out detailed health care proxies in 1995, two years after Dad consulted the first psychiatrist for memory tests and a couple of months before he enrolled as a subject at NYU. They did them together and their forms are identical. As a pair, they are hard core: they refuse all medical measures, including blood trans-fusions and antibiotics, and allow only diagnostic tests and painkillers whether they are in a persistent vegetative state with no hope of recovery or they "develop a life-threatening but reversible illness" when still in "my current state of health," which they both described as good. The proxy is not legally binding, but it acts as a crucial guide for the special power of attorney, the surrogate charged with making decisions for the signer if she can't make them herself. The person in charge of Dad is Mom, and I'm her surrogate and, if she's unable or deceased, Dad's too.

I call Mom and ask her if she and Dad discussed each option when they signed their proxies. Yes, they did, she says. Did they always agree? "Of course!" Then, anticipating some challenge from me, she adds firmly, "There is only one way to make these decisions. That is the desires of the person expressed at the very last moment that they are compos mentis." For Dad, she says, 1995 was that moment.

Unfortunately, her certainty is misapprehended. The myriad interests of the person in the bed (or at the threshold of the nursing home) can be dissonant, multiplying the ways to make these decisions. This fact becomes disturbingly clear when I read Dad's health care proxy. In 1995, he declared that "if I am aware but have brain damage that makes me unable to recognize people, to speak meaningfully, or to live independently, and I do not have a terminal illness," he would reject all medical interventions, even diagnostic tests, and welcome only painkillers. Nineteen-ninety-five may have been the zenith of Dad's terror about his impending dementia. But the combination of limited cognition, extreme dependency, and a number of chronic but not fatal maladies describes precisely the condition he is in today. The difference is, now he's not terrified. And he appears in no hurry to leave this world. Nilda tells me that one night while she was tucking him in, he turned suddenly melancholy and said, "I'm going to die."

When making decisions about the care of the demented, "the real conflicts . . . lie between prior choice and present interests," writes Francis. Where you end up rests largely on how much moral weight you assign each.

You can put the weight where Mom does, contending that the "only way" to decide, the only authoritative statement of the person's wishes, is the advance directive written when the person is competent. Dworkin agrees with her, saying that the demented person cannot hold current values, since he can't do the rational work to consult a personal sense of right living. Or you can take the position that the demented person's life is circumscribed by his pains and pleasures in the here and now. To the philosopher Rebecca Dresser, the demented person is a "different person" from the one who signed the living will and has only "experiential" interests.

Yet even this distinction does not set the scales on even ground. For if you are to be guided by the demented person's desires, how do you know what they are? A nursing home patient tries to yank out her feeding tube. Her message is obvious: *get this monster out of me!* But does she want it out right now because it is hurting her (her experiential interest)? Or does she want it removed for good because she is ready to die (her critical interests)? What if she wants it out but has expressed, either before her dementia or since, that she doesn't want to die? The logical capacity to entertain two conflicting ideas or feelings at the same time—to understand the need for a procedure and also hate it because it hurts—is beyond a person with severe dementia, for whom medical treatments can feel like nothing but torture. Satisfying this woman's experiential interests in relief from present pain could negate the critical interests she may have codified in a health care proxy to be kept alive by technological means.

Or it might go the other way: a person who has expressed what Dad has—no extraordinary measures—may struggle for life. Such a struggle could be read, and dismissed, as the organism's primitive fight for survival. But if he could articulate his wishes, would the person ask to be saved? Would the doctors try to save him?

The decisions often aren't life and death. "Here's a wonderful example," says the engaging Francis, who consults with nursing home staffs and families to resolve the ethical dilemmas of care. "A man develops a committed relationship and wants to live with the woman in the Alzheimer's unit. His children are appalled. They think this dishonors the memory of their mother. They put the kibosh on the relationship. It presented [itself] as an ethical question. The children say, 'Look, he's incompetent. If he knew what was really going on, he wouldn't want to do this.' On one level, it might be true; he was a loyal husband. But what's also going on is the woman is very much like his wife. You can see him continuing to value the same kind of things as what he initially valued."

"You seem to be saying that the caregivers may not only have interests that conflict with the patient's, but emotions too," I comment, reflecting on a story that hits rather close to home. "I mean, these children might be projecting their own feelings of betrayal onto their mother and calling them their father's values." She agrees that everyone's feelings are mixed into the heap of ethical issues on the table.

Who is my father? Is he the signer of the health care proxy, terrified of dementia yet relatively rational, or the seemingly content senile fellow who sings and dances and makes stupid jokes, but is overwhelmed when given the choice to turn right or cross the street? "Dresser takes the position that you take the person now on his or her own terms. You don't look for links to the past," Francis says. "I take the position that I have an interest in the shape of my decline [and] a right to take control of the shape of the rest of my life. So part of what we need to factor in are earlier desires. I don't want to be remembered as an aggressive person, so medicate me. I value science now, so I'd like to participate in experiments should I become demented. [In demented people] I think you see pleasures foregrounded, but you also see flickers and glimmers of earlier ways of being. When you are making decisions with (and I like to say 'with,' not 'for,' and not 'by,' because that's not quite right either) patients with dementia, you need to think through all these things. You try to figure out as much as you can what the person wanted, what the person now values, and follow as much as you can their present interests, unless those desires would result in pain, abuse, or impoverishment. That's my bottom line."

Francis calls the complex of desires and values in the past and the present the "then-self" and the "now-self." What she does not seem to doubt is that even far into the depths of forgetting, the patient has a self.

.   .   .

January 13, 2002

For Sunday breakfast on his birthday weekend, I cook Paul eggs, toast, and "soysage." Smoked meat is his only persistent carnivorous desire since our conversion to vegetarianism last year. The compromise is "soysage," a perfect simulacrum in color and texture of cat puke. Paul insists it improves when fried. I'm happy with eggs and toast.

It is already noon by the time we eat, and snowing too hard to ski. I bring up, for the hundredth time, The Question: "Could I—we—manage full-time care for Dad?" Where would we do it? We live in two states, have two careers, two political lives, two circles of friends. We have two homes, one belonging to each of us, three hundred and fifty miles apart. Both are small, neither has a guest room or second bath. Mine is a fourth-floor walk-up apartment, Paul's is on a dirt road two and a half miles from town. Mom calls this our "lifestyle," as if it were a sort of consumer choice easily traded in for another. But we met each other when we were already adults, and for ten years since, neither of us has been able, or maybe willing, to sever the ties established in the previous thirty-nine years. How could Dad fit into this life? Could he fit in?

"I guess we could bring him here," I say. "Build an extra room. Hire someone to be with him for part of the day. His pension would pay for it, and it would probably cost a lot less than in New York." Paul has wanted to put an addition on his house anyway.

"And you'd move here?"

"I could rent my apartment." I feel trapped even thinking about it. And my stomach lurches when I think of Dad hovering, needing, just feet from the kitchen, from our bedroom, from my office. My stomach reminds me of how Mom feels. "Or I could stay in New York and Dad could stay living in his apartment."

"And where would I be?" Paul's work and political life require him to be in Vermont more than half the time, which is why I come here more than he goes to New York.

"You'd be there as much as possible, and I'd be here for a month in the summer"—instead of four. "Or maybe Mom would take over in the summer. If she'd even be willing to let us take over."

"Or willing to take over from us in the summer," he says. We regard each other gloomily. Both take-charge types, Paul and I understand her dilemma perfectly. She doesn't like doing it, but she doesn't want anyone else to do it either. "I think if you were really serious about it, you could convince her you were going to do it one hundred percent, and then she'd probably say yes."

"It would put a real crimp in our lives," I say.

He looks at his plate, then up at me. "Let's face it. He's inconvenient. He's inconvenient for all of us."

"Not to mention our work. How would we get any work done with him around?" We both work at home.

"Good question." We hash that one out for a while. If I lived in Vermont, I might not have to make as much money. I wouldn't have to work as much. We agree: if we decided to take care of Dad, it could be done.

I get up to grind more coffee. We talk about other things—where to ski if the snow stops, what to make for Paul's birthday dinner. Then we return to the matter at hand, always at hand.

"The question is not can you, or we, manage his care," Paul says. "It's will we?" He will participate fully in whatever care we take on. "The question is, do you want to?"

"Do I want to give up our life for who knows how many years, so that he can keep living the life he wants to live?" I talk about how I've been loving skiing so much that every time I'm on the trails I scheme about how I could live here three months in the winter to do it. Not that I'd give up New York. I've been trying to figure out how to respect Dad's remaining selfhood by engaging him in decisions about his own life, I say. Yet when it comes to thinking about incorporating him into my life, that respect feels like an abstraction. I have moved close enough to him to feel affection, tenderness, ease, tolerance, even love. But do I feel enough for him that I want to reorder my life completely to keep order in his? I've been accusing Mom of using his "best interests" as a rationale to put him in a nursing home, when in fact the move would serve her interests and now Sid's. "The difference between me and Mom, really, is that I think the nursing home will be horrible for Dad and she probably really believes it might be good."

"And it might be."

"But the point is, I'm acting in my best interests too."

"You know, Jude, however you slice it, somebody loses." A policy wonk and business manager, Paul outlines the possibilities: "If he doesn't go to a home and we take care of him, we lose. If your mother takes care of him, she loses. If he goes into the home, he loses." To distract myself from the hardness of this fact, I stare at Paul as he devours another greasy beige lump. He laughs at my disapproving face and pops an extra-large piece into his mouth. "Yummy!"

Julius pads in from upstairs and gives us a look that is the feline equivalent of tapping his foot and pointing to his watch. He's ready for breakfast. I pick him up and induce him to lie in my lap for a few minutes by scratching him under the chin. "Don't worry, Poo," I say. "Soon." He's a high-maintenance cat. We can't go away overnight without finding a catsitter to give him his shots. But his care never feels onerous.

After a while, Paul says, "You know, honey, your father has his own responsibility in this. There is a reason no one in his family wants to take care of him. He lived his life without figuring out how to love anybody else. So now, nobody loves him enough to want to give back to him."

I interpret: "He may be helpless now, but he wasn't always helpless."

"Yeah. I mean, there's got to be a reason you have no fond memories of him. Coming out of the bathroom and him whacking you—that's your big memory. This may sound cold, but you reap what you sow. If your father had been a different kind of father and a different kind of husband, you and your mother would probably feel different now."

"He's got his own karma," I say, scraping up the last of my eggs with seven-grain bread. "But I've got karma too. He was fucked up. But no matter how he fucked up he was, maybe I have more responsibility to him now than I had then. *Because* he's helpless."

"You mean he deserves more now?"

"It's not a matter of deserving. Just a fact: helpless people need help. I'm his daughter. Shouldn't I help him because he needs help and I'm his daughter?"

He considers this. "That's a question." I like this about Paul. He doesn't venture an answer when he doesn't know what it is.

"I also have some responsibility in this," I continue. "I've been an adult for thirty years, and I could have changed things between us—"

"That's true."

"—but I didn't. I tried a few times, but as soon as it got hard, I gave up. I just wanted to get away from him."

"I'm sure you could have. But the question is, what's going to make you do it differently now? If you don't love a person and don't expect any reconciliation, how far can you go in trying to mend things?"

"I'm not going to mend things."

"Okay, so then what are you willing to do even if things aren't mended?" How much am I willing to give when there's no guarantee of getting anything back?

Paul reminds me that in the early nineties, shortly after we met, he suggested I try to work things out with Dad. He said I might feel sorry I hadn't done so after Dad died. I'd told him I could not and did not want to work things out.

Paul tried to work things out with his own father, who was critical and violent toward his cooperative, studious, and pious youngest son. "You didn't have to hit me. I was always good," Paul told his father when he was in his teens. His father replied, "I never hit you." Talking about it for the umpteenth time, Paul displays his perennial incredulity. "He just completely denied it. Or forgot," says Paul. "It didn't mean anything to him. We kids weren't really people to him." Hearing about Paul's childhood always puts mine in perspective. Dad tried to see us as people. He just couldn't move enough out of his own way to get a decent view.

"I went as far as I could with Dad," Paul says. "I felt all right about it." But he's also said he feels he "dodged a bullet" because his sister cared for their father until he died. "I would have done it, if Sarah wasn't there," Paul says. "But I would have resented the hell out of it."

"Sarah resented it, even if she never says so," I point out.

"Your mother resents taking care of your father."

"Yeah, and I would *really* resent it," I say. "I think." I pause and think some more. "Though maybe if I actually chose it, I wouldn't resent it. Mom didn't decide—beyond marrying him in the first place."

The question of motivation keeps returning. I couldn't believe in a god-given duty, but I was surprised to encounter that feeling when it arose, firm and clear. Now, I am not surprised that the sense of duty is failing me. It seems a weightless whim in comparison to the density and gravity of the work its fulfillment would require.

"Nobody's making you do anything," Paul says.

"I wish someone would," I say, laughing, and start to carry the dishes to the sink.

Paul says, "You get to decide. We get to decide."

.   .   .

Back in New York at the end of January, the weather is springlike, though it's hard to say if this is the end of the no-winter winter or a preternaturally early beginning of spring. The plants are as confused as the people. Forsythia are blooming on the block and the crocuses are starting to poke through the ground. I pick Dad up at his program as usual. He is holding his jacket, ready to be helped into it. "Can we go home now?" he asks, and I feel a pang. *Not your home for long,* I think. Before we leave, he kisses Ewa twice on the lips and once on the hand.

Dad is in a lighthearted mood. I warn him to avoid a patch of dog shit on the sidewalk, and he does a sprightly dance around it, which makes me laugh. We walk around the exhibit at Max Protech gallery of proposals for a memorial at Ground Zero. It is busy with people circulating among dozens of slick maquettes and drawings, jargon-filled text, and CAD images morphing on laptop screens. An elderly European man peers closely at the text beside drawings of a rainbow-colored undulating metal sheet taller than the original towers. "Utopian," he spits disgustedly at Dad, who is crowding him to the wall. "Useless."

I shrug and smile. "Dreams," I say to him, as I guide Dad out of his way. "Dreaming is good."

As we leave the gallery, Dad pronounces his critique: "Cute."

Paul meets us at the apartment, where he has offered to move the white Tiffany lamp hanging near the wall to illuminate the table, which Nilda has moved to the middle of the room. Dad likes to be at the center of traffic when he eats, "reads," draws, or arranges, over and over, a box of geometrically shaped colored wooden blocks I bought him. Dad helps Paul rewire the lamp, holding a screw or throwing away a cardboard package. I comment to Nilda that everything seems to be going well. She smiles indulgently at her charge. "He's happy," she says. He's happy because he feels secure in her love and is growing to love her.

We ride the subway back to Brooklyn, neither Paul nor I speaking for several stops. "My mother probably thinks I trust Dad to make his own decisions," I say, looking up from *The New York Times Book Review*. "But I just want her to see him as a person, who has preferences and desires. And relationships. And feelings."

Paul has been watching a homeless woman, somewhere between the ages of forty and eighty, clawing through her stash of overstuffed I ♥ NY bags. He turns from the woman to me. "Your father is in good hands," he says.

"He is," I reply, thinking of Nilda.

But he's talking about Mom. "When your mother said your father isn't human, she didn't mean he was not human. She was telling us she would take care of him, but she would not be forced to love him."

"Hmm," I say, neither in assent nor dissent, and go back to reading about books.

In the next couple of weeks, Mom doesn't call much and I don't call her much. She spends more time with Sid.

When we do talk, our conversations are more reasonable. I ask after Sid. She praises James, who has been calling regularly, for his even-keeled consideration and warm support. We talk about the application process for the nursing home. On Paul's advice, I tell her I will help with whatever she needs me to do. Finally, she asks me to do something: help her find a nighttime caregiver.

Subj: caregiver needed
Date: 1/20/02 12:32:00 PM Eastern Standard Time
From: JudeBklyn

Dear Friend,
I turn to you to help my mother and me in the next step of the care of my father, who has Alzheimer's. My mother and I would like to forestall Dad's placement in a nursing home. We are seeking a nighttime caregiver to stay over at their apartment on W. 24th St. in Manhattan, three or four nights a week (on a fold-out couch in the living room), then help Dad dress and toilet in the morning, until his other caregiver arrives at 9 a.m.

Dad goes to a day care program he likes and has a couple of wonderful caregivers during the days, one of whom occasionally stays overnight. He is, for the moment, content and cooperative. Although his language and cognitive faculties are on the wane, he still has lots of feelings and enjoys music, movies and TV, food, art, dancing, walking, and goofing around. He needs help with just about everything: dressing, bathing, shaving, crossing streets, etc. He has to be watched virtually all the time (the hallway door is locked with a key while he's inside, so he can't get out unaccompanied). He is in good physical health and

still largely continent, though he has had two or
three accidents.

The caregiver should be male; Dad is still
modest about letting any women but his wife perform intimate duties on his body. He should be
kind, good-humored, patient, intelligent, resource-
ful, respectful, and reliable. Experience with
people with dementia would be a help but is not
absolutely necessary. Most of the hours of work
would be spent sleeping, but the person would have
full responsibility for Dad during these hours.

If you are on e-mail lists through your work,
art, political, or spiritual communities, I'd appreciate your posting this notice there, but please
be selective. For obvious reasons, the person must
have excellent references, including from you.

With warm regards and thanks, Judith

When I send Mom the message for editing before I post it, she makes a few minor changes. Take out the part about the sleeper couch; she hasn't bought one yet. Other than that, she asks that only one whole sentence be deleted: "My mother and I would like to forestall Dad's placement in a nursing home."

I swallow my irritation and remind myself that she is indeed arranging for full-time home care. It's okay if she wants to keep her options open. Sid's apartment is nearing completion, and I am silently rooting for the interior drekorator to get the carpets down before Mom finds a night caregiver. Maybe my mother's liberation will inspire her to suspend my father's incarceration.

In the meantime, I undertake to lobby for small things. First, no lying. No suggestion to Dad that his stay at the nursing home is temporary, lest he keep expecting to return home. No "respite care" at the home, because a forced return to a place where he's had a painful experience will only be more disturbing and frightening.

And no abrupt final decisions. Keep exploring alternatives to the nursing home (Paul has offered to work through the finances with Mom again) and retain those alternatives even if Dad does move to the Gardens. If he is inconsolable there, don't insist that he stay.

Sending the e-mail brings unforeseen gratification. I like having the opportunity to use my talents and contacts to help Mom. And I like portraying my father in public as a person with tastes and interests, abilities, needs, and feelings. As a person.

.   .   .

Mom seems to be coming around to agreeing to my requests when I arrive at their apartment and she tells me in a whisper that there will probably be a bed at the nursing home in mid-February. The board there reviewed Dad's application, including the PIA, and feels "he will be just right," she says. Just like a college admission, I think, or an exclusive nursery school. He's the perfect applicant: male, ambulatory, and married to an intelligent, involved woman.

"But how do they know?" I ask. "The woman who did the PIA didn't speak to Dad."

"She spoke to me."

When I get home I have an e-mail from Adrienne that her mother has died and a phone message from my agent's office that her mother has died, too. I call Paul. "She's putting him in the nursing home. For real." I tell him about my friends' parents' deaths. "If he's lucky, he'll die before they lock him up."

"Don't be melodramatic. You don't know how he'll do there," Paul says. He adds: "It's your mother who feels like she's dying."

"Oh fuck," I whine. "Are we going to have to take him?"

Paul doesn't answer this, since we both know the answer. Then he chuckles, recalling a phone conversation he had with James the night before. "Your brother told me, 'I had a thought the other day that my mother will die and my father will die, and Sid will move in with me.'"

Feeling things spinning out of control, I take the subway the next day to the New York Public Library, where I think I'll be able to think. Coming in from the gray and trudging up the marble steps, I stop in the anteroom of the renovated Rose Main Reading Room and write out my book request for Eva Feder Kittay's *Labor of Love*. The clerk rolls the little slip of paper into a metal capsule and inserts it into a pneumatic tube that spirits it to the stacks. In the reading room, as I wait for my number to appear on the LED screen above the circulation window, I lean back to gaze at the blue skies and sorbet-scoop clouds of the restored Beaux Arts mural overhead. The painting makes me almost dizzy with cheer. The guardians of Truth and Knowledge are smiling on me. Here, I am confident, I will figure it all out.

When I get my book, I settle down to reread the story of the author's profoundly disabled daughter. Sesha has "no measurable IQ" at the age of twenty-seven; she can neither speak nor walk and still wears diapers. But what Sesha has in abundance, according to her mother, is the capacity to love and to feel joy. This, says Kittay, is what makes her human; it is what makes sui generis, not a Disabled Child, but Sesha. When Sesha was an infant, Kittay's mother urged her to institutionalize the child, even though Kittay had a supportive partner and son, a flexible job, and enough money to hire a professional team of caregivers to execute what she calls the "distributed mothering" of raising the needy little girl. What Kittay also had was enormous love for her daughter.

Time with Dad has grown easier, even fun sometimes. Visiting him when Nilda is with him and Mom is not has eliminated the split loyalties of our family get-togethers. I know that whatever I decide to do in the future, Paul will be beside me. These thoughts drift through my head as I read about Sesha and the ethics of care.

Then a sentence marches into my head: *Unlike Eva Kittay, I am not willing to sacrifice my life, or even a substantial part of it, for my father*. It is as plain as the clacking heels on the wood floor around me. I have been guilt-tripping Mom with the contention that she chose to marry Dad and is now abdicating the vows she freely took. But I am abdicating, if not vows freely taken, then obligations universally understood. Do adult children owe their parents? Yes, they do. Marital and filial obligation, in our culture and era, are not the same. But in the end, just like Mom, I am choosing my life—my seasons with Paul in Vermont, my work, my time to read, do politics, ski and swim, go to the movies and see friends, and, most important, to gaze at the library's clouds, to wander in my thoughts. I am choosing my needs over the needs of my father, who can no longer satisfy them himself.

Like Mom, I am making a choice in the context of real exigencies. I have no permanent job, no paid health insurance, family leave, or pension. I'm in a relationship that thrives on travel, a supple schedule, and a dearth of serious encumbrances. Still, if Mom is parceling out what she gives her husband emotionally, I am rationing my practical contribution, and this affects both my parents.

I look around the shelves of books. No less a great "renewable resource" than the Colorado River roaring in spring, the New York Public Library exhilarates me each time I visit with its promise of pleasure, excitement, and personal expansion. I learned to love this place from my mother and father. Now I think about my father, his diminishing life and the impending separation from the last things that offer him challenge and happiness. And I find myself crying.

Am I crying because I can imagine his pain or because I feel guilty? Am I crying for his loss or my own—the loss of an idea of the person I am? Am I crying because I do not love my father—or because I do?

Finally, I can say I love him. But I do not love him enough. Like my friend Rachel, I feel the limits of my love. And in this huge room designed to lift a visitor's spirits beyond its painted heavens, my limits are stifling.

January 24

I meet Mom at three in the lobby of her building. She hurries around the corner from the elevators in a big, blue, puffy down jacket from the pre-Sid era. I like how she looks, practical and prettily unfashionable. But she is shaking her head vigorously from side to side and she has a don't-fuck-with-me expression on her face. "I'm having a very hard time right now. It's a very, very hard time for me," she says, as if to fend off any guff.

For once I don't give her any. "I know," is all I say.

She's just come from seeing her therapist, who has helped her understand why she is so upset. It's not just that she's about to put her husband of fifty-nine years in a nursing home. "It's the juxtaposition of everything that's happening," she says. "Of where Stanley is going and where I'm going"—to Sid's luxury co-op, with its three bathrooms and river view, its housekeeper and cook. "It's just too hard to take. I can't take it." The don't-fuck-with-me tone softens a little. We are walking down Ninth Avenue, the buses and trucks rumbling over the potholes. She doesn't look at me as she talks, bustling forward at a New York pace. I feel like I did as a child, trotting to keep up with her. I can hear her only in spurts, but she keeps talking. It's as if this urgent information cannot wait the five minutes it will take to get to the café.

We arrive at La Bergamote, scene of my last crime, when I informed my mother she was falling short of her marital vows. Today she says she doesn't want anything to eat or drink, not even tea. Again, I've been looking forward to a French pastry, but it feels even more frivolous than the last time. Again, I listen to the waitresses chatting in French and place my order in my own, good French. And like the last time, they pretend not to understand me and inquire in heavily accented English as to what I want.

When I sit down, Mom says again, "This is a very hard time."

I say, "There is no way we can avoid this being hard. It is a hard time, it is going to be a hard time." I tell her now what I have not said directly—that I have come to realize I don't want to sacrifice my life for Dad. Neither of us does. But I also describe my impression of Dad at the moment: he is calm and content, even happy, sometimes extremely so. "Putting him in a nursing home may be the right decision for you and the right decision for me. But, even if he'd eventually get used to it, I don't think it is the right decision for Dad. Not yet . . . if ever."

She nods. "This is exactly what I was saying to Carole today. That's what makes this so terrible. He seems happier and more balanced than he's been in years." As if she recognizes she's just relaxed her guard, which she knows from experience is not a good idea, she adds, a little angrily, "But I just can't do it. I can't be there with him."

"Okay," I say. "I understand that. I just don't think we should rationalize this decision as being in Dad's best interest. It is in our best interest."

We sit for a while, not talking. "You sure you don't want any tea?" I ask. She agrees to have some. When I return from the counter, I ask if she has to move in with Sid right away, since it doesn't feel like the right thing at the moment.

"Well, I do want to."

"I thought you didn't."

"Well, I do, but with Dad—" Her voice trails off. That "juxtaposition."

She talks a little about Sid and the apartment, but for the most part he remains in the background. She is thinking, and feeling, about Dad. I have not seen her this way for months, maybe years. She is sad. Simply sad, overwhelmed with sadness. She does not fidget. Her hands—thin, wrinkled, and spotted but strong, the hands of a pianist—lie still on the table, as if in surrender. She is not avoiding, not denying, not hiding anything.

I'm not hiding anything either (except my longing for a lemon tart). We start to talk, guardedly, about how to tell Dad he is going to the Gardens. "I think we have to tell him the truth," I tell Mom. If he can't have autonomy, at least he can get a modicum of justice. Or, as the philosopher Harry R. Moody writes, "In thinking about the ethics of dementia, it is critical to understand why it is not autonomy but dignity or self-respect that should be the primary value."

She says, "He won't understand, or he won't remember."

"Then we can tell him the truth and he won't understand or remember. Much easier."

She takes another tack. "He won't go. If he understands, he'll just refuse. Just like he refused to talk to the nurse who came to do the PIA. That time Nilda rescued him."

"But no one will rescue him this time," I say, completing what I assume is her thought.

"Judy, he doesn't understand anything." Then, not quite logically, "Telling him will only exaggerate his anger."

"Look, Mom, he's going to be angry. Everybody's angry who gets put in a nursing home. Wouldn't you be?"

She's quiet. "If there's one thing I've learned in all this Alzheimer's stuff, it's that there are no right answers." She says we should talk to Kitty Henderson at the Gardens, who has experience with these things.

I agree that she has experience, but Kitty also has a conflict of interest. Her interest is to represent the nursing home as a good place, a good solution. For some families, who have no money and no decent home care, there may be no other solution. But the person with Alzheimer's—Dad—has his interests too. I tell Mom briefly about the disability rights literature I've been reading, and the contention that even the mentally "incompetent" have rights.

She doesn't defend herself. My mother believes in justice, I know this. She doesn't say what she leapt in to say last time I told her about my research: *you have to look at it from the caregiver's point of view.* She does speak up for the caregiver this time, but meekly. "Why can't we tell him that I am old too, and I can't take care of him anymore?" She is almost requesting my permission.

"That's the truth," I say.

"But there's no point in making him angry and upset."

"Those are his real feelings. They're very appropriate feelings."

"What about our feelings?" She doesn't say *my feelings.* Her face almost pleads. I know she feels guilty. She as much as told me so when she complained that the men in her support group don't. But now what I'm seeing in her eyes is grief.

"All I can say is this: it's his life. We still have our lives. We have our homes and our friends, we can walk around and do what we want. But he's going to be locked inside a building where he doesn't want to be. He has a right to be hurt and angry. And scared. The least we can do is respect him and let him have his feelings. And if it's hard for us, it's hard for us. We'll just have to deal with it being hard."

"Carole said that, often, the person adjusts just fine, and the people it's hardest for are the family, everyone else." Wishful thinking again, I say to myself, and not too persuasive coming from a woman who rarely dares to wish.

I don't quibble. "It's going to be hard for everyone."

She brings up her standard happy ending: the gay partner of the guy in her group who is in a gorgeous nursing home in the Berkshires and is perfectly happy. I bring up my friend Susan's father, who has been in a home for years, screaming to be taken back to his house, which was sold ages ago.

"You never know," she says. "There's no right way."

"But there might be an ethical way." This sounds pompous and I'm not sure how useful. Are ethics for the benefit of the practitioner or the person on whose behalf they are being practiced? Gloria Goldstein asked me once if I am "doing all this" (I wasn't sure if she meant writing about Dad or trying to make amends with him) so that I will "feel like a better person." Maybe I do want to feel like a better person. Or be one. But I don't have to prove I'm better than Mom to do that. I smile to myself as the previous night's dream flashes through my mind. In it, I am writing a piece on a prescription drug that makes you feel good about doing bad things. I decide to take it to see how it affects me. The drug is called Copaset.

Mom looks at her watch. She's got someplace to be. She pays the check and I walk her to Twenty-third and Ninth. We hug. "This is going to be a horrible time," I say. "Let's not make it more horrible by being against each other."

"No, let's not." She hugs me again and we both say truthfully that we love the other.

The phone rings at seven-thirty the next morning: Mom. "After our talk yesterday, I've been thinking a lot." She says she had a long talk with Sid, who, as usual, said he'd support any decision she makes. She has explored with Nilda her misgivings about the Gardens, unknown to me until now. What about the four-person rooms? Nilda said that all the nursing homes the people she's cared for have gone to had private rooms. What about a place for Dad's little things? Nilda is worried about his modesty and pride in his possessions. I have discussed these things with Nilda too, but not with Mom. I'm moved that Mom is thinking about them too.

Mom tells me that there really isn't a rush to take the next bed at the Gardens. It won't be the last. Kitty has told her—another fact she hasn't shared until now—that beds come open every three to six months.

"I've decided to put off Dad's going to the Gardens," she says, as if exhaling. "I feel much, much better about it. At least everything won't be happening at once." She says she is going to interview a friend of Jack's who may be able to work nights and weekends. I tell her Paul and I are willing to take on part of the management, which she politely declines. She says instead she will hire Doris Berman, who will oversee the staff and find replacements when necessary, keep abreast of developments at day care, and keep track of the money and the law. "As long as I don't have to live in the apartment," Mom says, "I can handle this."

"I understand," I say. "I understand completely." Then I say, "I'm really happy, Mom. I'm really glad you've made this decision. I think it's the right one. Thanks for doing this." It isn't until later that I realize she was also thanking me for our conversation.

```
Subj: caregiver update
Date: 2/24/02 12:32:00 PM Eastern Standard Time
Dear Friends,
     I just wanted to let everyone know that we have
found a lovely and experienced man named Ernesto
Cabrero to take on nighttime care of my father. He
was recommended to my mother by the Alzheimer's
```

Association, where she takes part in a support
group, and he had just completed a refresher course
in Alzheimer's care.

Enormous thanks to everyone who sent supportive
notes and spent time and thought in helping us. So
many of us are in the same boat, trying to patch
together care for elderly parents. And just as with
child care, it's every family for itself. The whole
experience only increases my rage at the official
indifference to human need in this ultra-wealthy
country. There is not even a rudimentary government
policy for long-term care, and now that all funds
are consecrated for war, none on the horizon.

Your communiqués reminded me how good it is to
have friends and community. And how necessary it is
for us to stick together and work for social change.
My warmest gratitude, Judith

I receive a number of responses, all of which bemoan the personal toll of this woeful political inaction and second my call to
action. The great sociologist C. Wright Mills talked about the
importance of understanding private troubles as public issues. In
other words, misery needs, and has a right to, company.

·   ·   ·

The main argument against a tax-funded long-term-care government entitlement is cost. So to fill in the budget gap, a tax-averse
government, spouting "family values," relies on what it deems a perpetually renewable resource: love. In the economic context, "family
values" is another way of saying privatization, paid or unpaid.
Almost every American caregiver adviser accepts this premise, which
lends their usually gritty counsel a surreal tone of denial when it
comes to money. "Stretching is supposed to be good exercise . . . I
stretch my abilities to meet ever-changing demands. I stretch the

finances to meet all our needs," reflects Lyn Roche in *Coping with Caring*. Nurse-adviser Eileen Driscoll's observation that "love is essential to successful caregiving" turns grimly literal. "As an effective caregiver, you will try to . . . anticipate, and find, great satisfaction in caring for your loved one. You see this satisfaction as a bonus you receive." Take that to the bank.

In reality, the economics of love are heartless. For an individual family—my family—they mean a bunch of bad options: Mom can find $100,000 a year (a lot more than most people have to start with) to remunerate Nilda, Ernesto, Jack, and the day care center for their professional love and use up Dad's money in three years; she can mortgage her own health and happiness to devote herself full-time to Dad's well-being; she can sign up for a Medicaid program that finances a minimal salary for a home caregiver in return for a "payback" of so much of Dad's pension that she can't afford the care the government is supposedly subsidizing; she can spousally refuse Dad and put him in an institution. Or she can leave the whole mess to her daughter, who then climbs down the staircase of lost income and depleted love.

But if it's deadly for the caregiver, the expectation of endless family love can deal an awful, subtle blow to the cared-for, too. At Tom Kitwood's Bradford Dementia Group in England, the staff "found that those [caregivers] who are well supported only very rarely suggest that their relative has acquired a different personality, or 'disappeared.' " In other words, if they had enough help—say, some excellent community-based day care—caregivers might not feel the need to obliterate the patient's personhood, with its incessant needs and desires.

If all this does not seem like a sustainable economy, I suspect it's not meant to be. The expectation behind America's health care system is autonomy, for every adult at every age. Disability may be a sorry circumstance, but it is considered an aberration, a temporary inconvenience. Dependency is an incidental cost, not an ongoing expense.

And this, say the politicized disabled, is the biggest denial of all. Disability rights activists call us sighted, hearing, mobile bipeds "the currently able." What they know, what the rest of us deny, is that the body is mortal, and autonomy, cornerstone of Western ethics and personhood, is a myth. Sooner or later we will all be in some way halt, in some way blind, and neither science nor the grace of God will prevent us from going there, where the currently disabled already are. In the meantime, we already are what they are—dependent. The only difference is that they are more so than the rest of us. They argue that the denial of the fact of universal interdependence has the effect of making the disabled more disabled. "The reason I can't get around Wellesley isn't that I'm blind," Adrienne remarks. "It's that there's no public transportation."

Paradoxically, our dependence may be more acute in this age of web-shopping, tax-resisting, SUV-driving, single-person-householding consumer-citizens than it was when we hunted in packs and dragged home a bison for the communal feast. Then, you didn't survive long without the help of others. Today, you need the help of others because you survive so long. Modern medicine has all but defeated premature death from acute illness; we stay healthy for more years. The irony of this accomplishment, notes historian Thomas R. Cole, is that we will be sicker later, and for longer. We can count on surviving seven, eight, even nine decades, but an American who reached the age of sixty-five in 1996 can expect an average of five and a third years of physical "dysfunction," probably from a chronic illness, before she dies. "Much of the peculiar pathos of aging in American culture," Cole comments, "derives from the denial of this new fate."

This new fate is the same old fate: we need care. Dementia, with its prospect of near-total incapacitation, can distract us from the fact that vulnerability is a chronic "premorbid condition," beginning in infancy and inescapable until the last breath. Dependence is the human condition, write Richard Martin and Stephen Post, and care is not an extraordinary need, but "part of the fabric of civilization." Or as the sociologist Jaber Gubrium tells me, "Failure is a natural part of life."

The pathetic thing is that if we fail—*when* we fail—the expectation, and exaltation, of autonomy makes us ashamed to be caught needing. We'd rather do anything but—including die. Ninety-four percent of candidates for physician-assisted suicide fear dependency more than physical pain. And those who cringe at reliance on others conceive of it as insupportable for everyone. Indeed, people with severe disabilities both physical and mental, who are used to pain and dependency, have recently become nervous about the mercies that may be dispensed in their best interests should physician-assisted suicide become legal. Demonstrating the autonomy that the able-bodied and quick-minded assume they're incapable of, they have converged on state capitals, propped up in their wheelchairs and trailing their oxygen tanks, chanting with raucous rage the name of their most radical organization: *Not Dead Yet*.

Many people in the Alzheimer's world are big supporters of assisted suicide. And when I first learn I might be genetically predisposed to dementia, I spend more than a little time contemplating how I'd accomplish my own demise and who might assist me. Shall I try drowning? What, and ruin a lifetime of swimming pleasure? Exposure in the snow? Too cold. I hit on insulin overdose, since Julius's diabetes keeps our supply constant. But since I don't want to end up like Sunny von Bülow, I mention to Paul that I'm counting on him to administer the final dose. He looks up from his computer and says, "Do I have to do everything around here?"

I decide that if I can depend on him to kill me, I might be able to depend on him, or someone else, while I'm still alive.

But I cannot help wondering, if we stopped denying the natural fact of failure and entitled each citizen to a comfortable old age and a meaningful death, how many would be hoarding barbiturates at the back of the medicine chest?

10. *Family*

February 14, 2002

All day, I am thinking about the Valentine's Day slogan, printed on sugar candies and Hallmark cards, "Be mine." It's a sentiment I have long abhorred and militantly avoided—love as possession, with its implication of unending security. Paul and I have never vowed before a justice of the peace to have and to hold until death us do part, and we don't plan to tie the knot officially. But as time goes by, the knot tightens on its own.

After dinner I sit on his lap and kiss him. "You know that thing, 'Be mine'?" I say. "I'm starting to think it's good for people to belong to each other."

He looks astonished. "You didn't always think that," he says, laughing at the obvious.

As Paul has noticed, we Levine women are phobic about dependency. Mom counseled me as a girl to earn my own money, and I was proud that she, unlike my friends' stay-at-home mothers, did not rely on a man for the roof over her head. Of course, Mom depended on her husband, as every married woman does. And Dad depended on his wife, as every married man does. Aside from the shared family chores and breadwinning of a two-career couple before its time, their mutual terror of abandonment bound them. Dependency was the beam that girded their marriage and the dry rot that undermined it.

As a teenager, I regarded this arrangement with haughty disapproval. My mother was a feminist, yet their marriage was so compromised, so—ugh!—conventional. Now, though, I'm rethinking the question of belonging. Mom's waning love for Dad has revived my childhood fear about the review to which we Levines are perpetually subject, of our fitness for membership in the family club. Dad is proof of what I've always dreaded: one can fail and be disqualified. It has occurred to me lately that unconditional love is an illusory good billed as a bonus of family life, something everyone else's family is alleged to provide. Too bad I didn't get it as a child, but isn't it time I got over that? In fact, the realist in me has made peace with a distrust of marriage and families by constructing a tribe of friends instead, much as my parents did in reaction to their own emotionally unreliable families. The rituals and gatherings, the shared faith, hope, charity, and neurosis of the Greater New York Jewish bourgeois communist clan, both assuaged my parents' intimate troubles and gave me the sense that whatever happened at home, I possessed a sturdy extended "family."

So perhaps I'm reacting to the dissipation of my own adult tribe (and American community in general) into stressed, self-sufficient, and self-protective family units, as much as I am to the disintegration of my parents' marriage along with my father's brain. But I find myself cherishing Paul's easygoing loyalty and valuing security—coupled security—in a way I would have disdained years ago.

Security comes at the cost of some freedom, of course, but I am willing to make the trade. After ten years together, I promise to be monogamous, which Paul has wanted and I have resisted. We agree to move back and forth between New York and Vermont together, rather than organize two sovereign, only partly reconciled, schedules. And we creep toward economic interdependence. When my car dies, Paul buys me a reliable used Honda. For the house in Vermont,

I pick up a table at one auction, a jelly cupboard and hooked rug at another. Now we make an appointment with an accountant to discuss putting our finances together. Since we share no children (unless you count Julius) and no property, both of us are self-employed, and neither earns much money or receives paid health benefits, the chief advantage of joining forces is that we will worry together instead of separately.

As for my parents' tribe, it too is showing signs of frailty. Half its members have moved to Florida. Those left in New York are either ailing or disinclined to spend time with those who are ailing in the manner Dad is. Where are the pledges these comrades made to each other? *An injury to one is an injury to all! Solidarity forever!* The Goldsteins and Levines can barely pull together a Thanksgiving dinner. If I am disturbed, Mom is desperate. She wants not only succor but someone to take care of business, of Dad, and of her.

Enter Sid, chief executive officer, bringer of tea. "Don't worry, Lillian," he says, something I don't remember Dad ever uttering except in annoyance. For Sid, the burden of Mom's anxiety is light because he's not its cause. I learn two weeks after the fact that on a visit to Brooklyn, Mom fell down a marble staircase. She got up, unbruised and unbowed, except for a bump on her head. She didn't call me. Sid looked after her.

Shortly after Valentine's Day Mom moves in with Sid on the Upper West Side, just two blocks from where she lived with Dad before they decamped for Ithaca. The piano arrives, the cook makes meals according to her dietary restrictions. She continues to pay for the apartment on Twenty-fourth Street and all of Dad's care. But Sid pays the mortgage and expenses uptown, buys her clothes, and picks up the restaurant tabs, gym membership, and travel bills. She won't throw in her whole financial lot with him; she is holding on to her nest egg just in case. But her heart is his, and now her lifestyle is too. She has said that at their age they don't have time to fool around with the preliminaries of courtship. It's all or nothing. My mother and I, phobias intact, are slouching toward dependency.

The move to Sid's wipes the last of the scowl from Mom's face and the dreary, weary note from her voice. She is radiant, buoyant.

"Did she tell you they're going to Paris and Venice?" I ask James on the phone, reporting another episode in the astounding transformation of our mother.

"Wow, is she bringing her food in a baggie?" Because of her Crohn's disease, even the thought of a long plane trip or the stomach-confounding cuisine of virtually any country has paralyzed Mom with anticipated misery. She and Dad went abroad only once, for a week in London.

When Paul hears about the European trip, he says, "More power to Sid. He's getting your mother to live!"

Before she packs for Venice, Mom packs her things on West Twenty-fourth Street. She does this a little at a time and removes items from "the apartment," as it is now called, when Dad is not home. Her papers and computer are still there, but she's got another one at Sid's. And as Nilda takes over the household and assumes the responsibility for purchasing Dad's prescriptions and keeping track of everything from new socks to doctors' appointments, Mom appears less. Having folded up her emotions and carried them, tiptoeing backwards, out of his life for months, she now hopes he won't hear the door shutting behind her.

But he notices. He resists the nighttime caregiver. One evening when I'm with Dad, Ernesto arrives, carrying a take-out container of Cuban-Chinese food. "So what brings you here?" Dad asks sarcastically, as Ernesto hangs up his coat and folds his *New York Post* on the living room table.

"You. You bring me here."

"You?"

"You, Stanley."

"SHE brought you here!" shouts Dad. I'm not sure if he means me, who is the only "she" in the room, or Mom. I herd them into the kitchen for tea, hoping to derail an argument. Dad is in Ernesto's face. "I don't know you. Who are you? Get out of my house."

"I'm Ernesto," says Ernesto in his Jamaican English.

"AIR-NEST?"

"Ernesto."

"Air-nest-toe?" The same thing he did with Nilda at first—mocked her accent. "You know everything? You know better of me?"

Ernesto just smiles and thanks me as I hand him a cup of ginger tea. He comments that it's good for the digestion.

On several occasions Dad hits Ernesto, whose strategy is to run into the bathroom and lock the door until he senses Dad has cooled off. Usually, it works. When he emerges, Dad may still be glowering, but he's contrite too. Ernesto isn't bothered. "Oh, I've been through much, much worse," he assures me. "In the hospitals I have been kicked, punched, thrown down to the floor. Many times." He shrugs and laughs. "It's part of my job." When I ask him if he's comfortable sleeping on the couch, he says he'd rather not be too comfortable. Staying awake to listen out for Dad is also part of his job. When I hear this, I silently applaud Mom's hiring skills.

The hitting disquiets her, of course. She tells me wearily that she will probably have to spend "all day Sunday" with Dad, and reduce the time he is alone with Ernesto. "I just realize it's going to be like this until one of us dies." I tell her that she suffers from pretraumatic stress disorder. It's a mark of her generally improved mood that she chuckles. Then I remind her that Dad hated Nilda at first and resists each new person who joins the day care group. She agrees we have to wait and see, though we both know that waiting and seeing is not her forte.

One afternoon when she is with him, Dad asks, "Where do you go?" She answers, "You know, you've been sick for eleven years and I've been taking care of you. I'm very tired and now I need help."

Deprived of his lifelong beloved foe, Dad distributes his hostility more broadly. Like Ernesto, the recipients are mostly male. With women Dad tries chivalry first, and when that doesn't bring approbation, resorts to groveling. It's what he has done throughout his life. With men, he also has a time-honored pattern. His one-upmanship begins with half-sarcastic charm, and when that doesn't bring the rival down, he moves on to undiluted sarcasm and "funny" humiliation. With no wit left at his disposal, the routine is simplified: escalating levels of mimicry, followed by shouting and, as a last resort, blows.

At the day care center he has two chief nemeses. One is Izzy, a man with a belly like a flour sack and a nose made of dough, whose remaining gifts are a vast repertoire of left-wing anthems, which he sings in four or five languages, switching among them from line to line, and a resonant belch that he can, and frequently does, call forth at will. The more threatening antagonist, though, is the center's part-time music therapist, Ralph, who is as irked by Dad as Dad is by him. Sick of the dustups, Ralph periodically suggests that Dad be expelled from the program, which sends Mom temporarily into a fit of pessimism. The other staffers, all female, stick up for Dad; they seem to regard conflict as part of a day's work. Nevertheless, after a scrape with Ralph turns violent, Dad's psychiatrist increases his dosage of Neurontin, an antiseizure medication also prescribed for "agitation" in demented patients. About a year later, hostilities will increase on all sides, and Dad will be kicked out of the group and transfer to another program uptown.

At this point, there is one casualty of Dad's growing belligerence: his relationship with Jack Smith, his caregiver of longest tenure. Dad took immediately to Jack, admiring his intelligence and humor, and the admiration was mutual. Jack treated Dad like a pal, not a patient, and Dad felt respected. Now, such egalitarian treatment has become too demanding for Dad. He responds to Jack's genial banter as if it were a salvo and flings insults at Jack in defense. When Jack is uninterested in fighting, Dad reads this as condescension. To even the score, Dad pats Jack on the head, sometimes hard, and calls him "little boy." Jack responds with more kindness, which only piques Dad to rage. When Dad jabs, Jack takes his hand; when Dad lunges, Jack pulls him into a hug. As Mom says, Dad won't take yes for an answer.

One Saturday when I've spent the morning with Dad, Jack arrives with concert tickets that Mom has given him for the two of them. Dad is eating the lunch I've prepared, a bowl of canned minestrone in which he has sunk a fleet of crackers. Jack sits at the table and rests his lean jaw between forefinger and thumb. Dad mimics him.

Jack says, "Soo, Stan, are ye riddy t' goo?"

"Myoo, myoo, mya mya mya mya mya goo?" says Dad.

"Let's git your coot on then."

Dad stands up—this much cooperation he will extend—but menacingly close to Jack, and twists the lithe ribbon of Jack's lilt until it is tight and mean: "Coot on NEN?"

I feel myself sliding back to our suburban house, listening to the endless, dirty fight between Dad and James, hating Dad. But Saint Jack jollies him out the door, tossing me a grin, like a posy.

The day goes downhill, and before it's over Dad has swung at Jack with an open can picked up from the sidewalk and clipped his ear with the ragged edge. When they get home, Dad punches himself in the mirror. Their meetings after that do not improve. When Ernesto is ensconced, Jack withdraws.

I talk to Jack a few months later about the end of what he calls their "friendship." He wants neither explanation nor revenge. "It's a pity. I'll miss old Stan," Jack says, cocking his head in a gesture that strikes me as typically Irish—accepting fate, but quizzically. "All things must pass, mustn't they?"

With Mom's move, everything reconfigures. It's hard to find my place in the new pattern.

I am still wedged between Mom and the caregivers. Nilda is consistently wonderful to Dad, but she continues to bring her grievances to me, and I continue to count on her for evidence of Mom's failings. If, at my urging, they make their way to Mom's ears, Nilda's complaints become little daggers of power poised over my mother, who worries that she will leave, and over me, who feels guilty for pricking Mom's anxiety by sympathizing with Nilda.

I'm wedged between Mom, the caregivers, and Dad.

"I told Ernesto you would come at one on Sunday," Mom says on the phone one Wednesday, when I return from a reporting trip.

"Well, I didn't plan to come at one. I spoke to Ernesto before I left and we agreed that I'd come sometime in the morning. I told you that. Remember?"

"It's okay. You can come at one."

"No, it's not okay, because I have an appointment at three." We tussle. Finally, I say, "If we arrange something, will you please not go and change it without asking me?"

"Well, Judy, you weren't here." She doesn't agree to my proposal.

Later, Paul the business manager intervenes. "Someone needs to oversee the whole thing, and that person is your mother," he tells me. "She's right. You're not there."

"But by messing around with the plans, she gets to reinforce this idea that I am unreliable." I've been smarting from that for weeks.

"Let her manage. Be reliable that way."

This turns out to be largely good advice. But her "management" makes her the gatekeeper of my relationship with Dad.

I tell her I am planning to pick him up at three on Wednesday, my usual day.

"Well, you can stay until seven, because that's when Ernesto comes."

Just two weeks after she almost wiped me off Dad's Sunday schedule, this miffs me anew. "Do you want me to spend time with Dad or not?"

"Yes, of course I do."

Over coffee in Brooklyn, I recount this exchange to Adrienne.

"Why do you have to leave when the guy gets there?" she asks. "You're his daughter, not his caregiver." Interesting way of putting it. Mom and I are competing for who cares more about Dad, she by being the better caregiver, me by being the better family member.

Mom's new life stretches the space between her and me.

"Will you be at my talk at Columbia?" I ask her. It's the first major presentation of a new book, an event to which she would have longed to be invited only a year ago, and which I've mentioned to her several times.

"Oh," she says, obviously having forgotten. "I—I can't." She has to play a piano piece at her performance-anxiety class that night.

I fret all evening, then decide to tell her how I feel, instead of accusing her. I call the next day. "Do with this what you will," I say, "but I wanted you to know that it hurt my feelings that you didn't think of changing the day you were playing at your class so you could come to my talk. Because it's important to me."

"I was thinking the same thing," she says. She comes to the talk with Paul, enjoys it, and has lots to say afterward, since it is about teen sex and she ran a birth control clinic that provided the first confidential teen services in America. And as always, she is proud of me.

I call to arrange a church music date for Easter Sunday. It's an outing she has initiated twice a year, at Christmas and Easter, for as long as I can remember and that has always included her, Dad, and me, with or without a current boyfriend. This Christmas, for the first time Dad had another companion, and Mom and Sid had so many theater and concert tickets that we skipped it. Neither of us had much energy to be together anyway, we were fighting so much. And Sid wasn't keen to spend time with his lover's torturer.

"Oh. Yeah. Oh . . . okay, that's a good idea. Is it Easter already?" she says. We agree to look in Friday's *Times* for a good chorus and get back to each other. Neither of us does.

Twice, she and I arrange to meet at political demonstrations. Both times, she fails to show up. After the first, she calls to tell me she marched with Elinor, Sid's daughter; the second time she and Sid decided at the last minute to go with another group. She does not apologize.

Mom is adopting Sid's family and it is adopting her. She frequently sees Elinor, who invites her and Sid to her parties and to the screenings and openings of her friends. I think of her as Mom's good daughter, who is thrilled about her father's relationship and whose complaints, compared to mine, are few and (since she has cancer) legitimate. Mom even loves Elinor's dog, precisely the kind of small, "yappy" canine she ordinarily detests, and kvells about him as if he were her grandson. I could be wrong, but it seems she has stopped inquiring quite so often about her real grandson, Julius.

Mom keeps up with her old friends, but if she is hurt that her own people are deserting her, Sid's tribe is large and generous enough to enfold her. She joins in the constant round of bar mitzvahs and weddings involving throngs of cousins and nieces and nephews, as well as the members of a Russian Jewish clan he sponsored years ago for immigration. Mom expresses no end of delight with these tiny, warm babushkas and their brilliant doctor-lawyer-scientist-musician offspring. And "the Russians" adore her. Along with Elinor, they are more "gratifying"—the word she often uses to describe a child—than her own kin have turned out to be.

After about a month of cohabitation, Mom calls to tell me that she and Sid are "making lists" of dinner guests. A few days later, Paul and I receive our first invitation. While Sid hangs our coats, Mom dances us into the spacious rooms (she loves giving house tours) and through the tiled kitchen, formal dining room with a river view and a table large enough to carve a hippo on, living room furnished with tightly upholstered parlor chairs and bright op art, and three bathrooms, one featuring the "pièce de résistance," the bidet. She and Sid both laugh about this. They have many private jokes.

As Mom and Dad did, Mom and Sid look like a couple. But where my parents favored old jeans and sturdy shoes, Mom and Sid are dressed with casual elegance, a phrase that once would have made her giggle. Still, she looks beautiful, and the chic duds are the least of it. Mom and Sid do not bicker. New lovers that they are, each finds everything the other says amusing and fascinating. As we sit on the couch, she relaxes, not fussing over the hors d'oeuvres or rushing us to the table. I feel a bit tense as I attempt to ruffle neither Mom nor Sid (nor drop herring on his white sofa), but I have to admit, it's a pleasure to be with her here.

Sid brings us our drinks and touches Mom on the shoulder, then goes to the kitchen to check on the food that the cook has prepared earlier and is now heating. I am oozing down warmly into my drink when he calls out to her.

"What, dear?" my mother calls back.

Dear? Dear is my father's name. I sit up straighter, soberer—vigilant.

It has always been my mother who chased me, wanting to talk, wanting me to confide in her, and I who have run. Now she has someone else to trust and rely on, and after decades of resisting her need and what felt like her intrusions, I find myself missing them—and her. She is furious that I did not embrace the new We, the new Dear, because they made her happy when she had been so unhappy. Why am I so angry that she should have a happy life? I am angry not that she is happy but that she is furious; angry that she will accept nothing less than grace and cheer as she withdraws her passions from our brittle, already underdevoted family.

But then my own passions contribute little to the Levines' elusive cohesion, either. Like an ardent, abusive lover, I court my mother, then punish her when she turns her attention to me.

Dad has a new family, too. Where Jack was a friend who visited, Ernesto is a younger brother who sleeps in the next room and who is smarter in school and better at sports than he. Ernesto is willing to take care of his big brother, and the nonchalant competence with which he assumes the task hurts Dad's pride.

After a while, though, Dad lets Ernesto in. His provocations gentle. Nilda helps. "Stan-ny, it's your friend Ernesto!" she announces each evening when the shift changes. "Say good-bye to your friend Ernesto," she coaxes again in the morning. Dad's nastiness toward Ernesto becomes the time-honored abuse of younger brothers, competitive but affectionate, even protective.

In the little stepfamily of the caregivers, I think of myself as the middle child, the mediator. The evening that Dad confronts Ernesto with the fact that this new acquaintance does not "know every-thing" or "know better of me," I encourage a little getting-to-know-you. "No, Dad," I say helpfully, "Ernesto doesn't know you. Why don't you tell him about yourself?"

Too complicated an idea, Dad ignores it and turns to—or on—me. "You have troubles?"

I laugh. "Yes, some troubles." Right now my troubles are these two boys inept at carrying on a conversation.

But it is Nilda who holds the family together. She has made of Dad's apartment a small, safe haven. *"Il ne touche plus rien"* —he doesn't touch anything anymore—she tells me proudly, because she has moved every temptingly breakable thing out of his reach. He doesn't forage for food between meals because she has put away the bread and crackers and gives him a hot snack when he gets home from his program. His meals are all homemade, not the take-out Chinese and rotisserie chicken to which Mom had resorted in the last few years. Nilda even prepares food for Ernesto and Dad to eat on the weekends.

Although the house is impeccable, Nilda is unruffled by Dad's messes emotional, domestic, or excretory. *"C'est mon métier"*—my craft, my calling—to deal with whatever comes along, she says, echoing Ernesto. Messes and misbehavior are dealt with both swiftly and firmly, but sweetly. Dad hardly raises his voice to her and, where he will continue to resist Ernesto's help in toileting, is lamblike when Nilda bathes or shaves him (later, he will submit to her cleaning him with a baby wipe after he defecates). When they sit side by side in the morris chairs watching television, he takes her hand. He lets her hold his plastic teacup to his lips or spoon food into his mouth. "Thank you, dear," he says. Dear is Nilda's name too.

"You are welcome, Stan-ny," Nilda answers.

Mom visits this household as a proprietary visitor. At first, she has things to do, papers to go through, appointments on the agenda directly afterward. Nilda mentions Mom's habitual hurry and Dad's resultant vexation. *Ta pauvre Maman,* Nilda always says, while also implying that she is better suited than his wife to care for my father (this may often be true, that a loving professional, free of old wounds and competing claims to justice, makes a superior caregiver than does a family member). Soon, Mom settles into doing her business at the apartment when Dad is at the day center and visiting him on Sundays.

The three of us no longer spend time as a family, so I doubt Dad associates me with Mom anymore. Sometimes I arrive with Paul, which only confuses things more. When James shows up, once or twice a year, he is a stranger to his father. People ask if Dad recognizes me. I don't know. He seems to recognize the woman in the kelly-green leather jacket who arrives once a week at the day program and walks with him to the river, laughs with him at the antics at the dog run, and discusses the boats docked at the piers. "Ah, you!" he exclaims when I pull up a folding chair beside him and tap him on the shoulder. Sometimes he calls me Shorty.

On Monday morning, I imagine my mother at the huge dining table, pouring coffee for the man who has arrived like a miracle in her life, while my father crowds into the narrow vestibule of his apartment to kiss his own miracle good morning. "I love you, I love you, I love you! My darling!" I think of him crooning. I have heard these declarations to Nilda (whom he sometimes calls "Lil"), recalling almost word for word the rapture he poured out onto onionskin fifty years ago to his new bride, the woman he believed would love him as his mother never did. Mom loved him, but she could not give him that.

Now Nilda gives him that, and the irony is, she would not be there if Mom hadn't fallen in love with Sid. Mom has said many times that had she been forced to keep living with Dad, she would have been unable; he'd be in a nursing home today. Sid rescued Dad from that fate. And with his wife's love siphoned out, another love has poured into my father's life.

Nilda answers Dad's every need without needs of her own, she loves him openly and without judgment, she neither competes with nor criticizes him, is always there, and (as far as he knows) will never leave him. She lavishes on my father the love he sought to no avail from every woman since his tight-hearted mother—his teachers, his friends, his wife, and his daughter.

"I was a little, little boy, all alone." With Nilda in his life, this plaint ceases. At the age of eighty-three, as the layers of his adult self curl away, Dad has finally been granted his infantile wish, the wish of the boy, the youth, and the man he became. Occasionally, Nilda calls him *mon bébé*. And besides Dear, Darling, and sometimes Lil, he has another name for her, which he calls out, almost without guile: "Ma-ma! Mmmaa-mmaah!" He is a little boy, but he is no longer alone. Finally, my father has a good mother.

.   .   .

April 2002

Mom is in the hospital with what looks like pneumonia. I am in *The New York Times*. My recently published book, a defense of children's sexuality, has attracted the ire of social conservatives from Dr. Laura to Tom DeLay, who are denouncing me as an advocate of pedophilia, homosexuality, promiscuity, and every other evil they can think of. This is attracting lots of media attention.

When I arrive at the hospital, Sid has gone home for a few hours. Mom is wan. She has tubes in her nostrils but can hardly breathe, and she hasn't slept. They've put her in a double room on the oncology ward, the only place a bed was available. The woman next to her, medicated for gallstones in the middle of cancer treatment, is hallucinating. Mom says she has been screaming and weeping all night.

The article about me is open on the windowsill. Whenever anyone calls, Mom waves for me to hand it to her, and she reads to her caller from the page, using up most of her scant breath. She reports briefly about her illness, then hangs up. I feel tender and worried, appreciative and appreciated. When I walked out of high school during the student strike over the U.S. invasion of Cambodia thirty years ago, my parents supported me. Now she's standing behind me again. I inscribe my book to her, "Thank you for teaching me right from wrong."

She has asked me to bring her health care proxy form from Dad's apartment. She wants to be sure he no longer has power of attorney. She amends it now, making me her legal surrogate and James my substitute, not Sid.

Nilda calls me to say Dad punched someone at the program after another contretemps with Ralph, and the staff asked us to explore upping his medication. I call the psychopharmacologist, who again increases the Neurontin. I ask if we aren't drugging him to deal with what is essentially a personal conflict with a possibly incompetent worker. "Are you asking whether we are medicating the patient to cure the doctor?" she asks. "That's a danger, which we need to watch out for." Unlike most everyone else, the doctor does not think of Dad as a puppet of his disordered brain, but rather a person with relationships to other persons, who might be the cause of his legitimate ire. Nevertheless, she generally encourages Mom to give Dad the latest drug (and Mom often declines), and today she reassures me that Dad's dosage is still comparatively minuscule. Nilda and I decide not to tell Mom about the incident or the new dosage until she's out of the hospital. Dad goes back to being content in the group and inexplicably (for a while, at least) becomes Ralph's biggest fan.

The protest over my book heats up. I'm on national TV, doing phone interviews twelve hours a day, being discussed on neo-Nazi websites. I receive a death threat in care of the publisher. Paul is with me in New York when the police call to inform me. I don't tell my parents.

I break away one afternoon for a walk in Brooklyn's Prospect Park. It is still cool, the trees still bare, the daffodils green but not yet blossoming. I run into my parents' old friend Sam Nemerov, Rila's husband, whom I frequently meet in the park or the public library.

"Isn't it a crazy world?" exclaims Sam, his face a mass of animated wrinkles.

Yes, I concur. It is indeed a crazy world. But did he have something specific in mind?

"Three of our friends, all in their eighties and nineties, are having *hot* romances!" He says *hot* with steam in it, like Jimmy Durante.

"So, who are the other two?" I ask and we both laugh.

He says his first cousin has just met "a young chick in her seventies," and his second cousin is enjoying himself with a new belle at the nursing home. "This cousin, not my first cousin, my second cousin, Milt, he's—what? He's eighty-nine!" He grasps my arm for emphasis. "He says to me, 'I may not be able to get it up anymore. But I still got *plenty of moxie!*' "

At the hospital that evening I repeat Sam's story to Mom and Sid. They love it. Of course, I'm a little embarrassed. Is this a thing to tell your mother—and your mother's lover?

In July Mom and Sid visit Elinor in a house she is renting in southern Vermont. When Mom returns to New York, she calls to say there has been "another incident." Dad went into the kitchen, opened the cabinet door under the sink, picked up the cover of the garbage can, and peed into it. "There was a mess all over the kitchen," she says. When I talk to Ernesto, who cleaned it up, he says it wasn't bad. But each time one of these "incidents" occurs, Mom considers the nursing home.

Since the trip to Vermont, she has also developed some flulike symptoms, and when they do not go away after several weeks, her doctor diagnoses Lyme disease. On a day she is feeling particularly weak, she goes to Twenty-fourth Street when Nilda is out and Dad is at his program and finds the lock isn't working. She has to wait around for an hour until the locksmith shows up. "I'm the only one taking care of anything," she says. The nursing home is now constantly in the wind.

She is waffling on the decision to hire a care manager. "Everyone who hires these people says they don't really do anything and you end up doing it yourself."

A third call. "It's very likely, Judy, that I'm going to have one thing or another, from now on." She pauses. "And I have to die of something."

I weakly reply that she might recover from Lyme disease. On the matter of dying of something, I offer no rebuttal.

"Judy, it's too much. I've done it for eleven years."

"Are you saying you want to put Dad in a nursing home?"

"I can't make that decision right now. I have to concentrate on getting better."

"That sounds like a good idea."

"You know, he's happy, he's taken care of. But no one cares if I'm happy."

"Would you be happy if he were in a nursing home?"

"Yes," she says plainly. Then, "If it weren't for Sid, I'd be on the rails."

"Do you think if you were sick and Sid weren't around, I'd let you lie in bed unable to take care of yourself and not take care of you?"

"Well. Okay."

"Do you think I would?"

Gruffly. "No. No, I don't." She says she has to get off the phone.

"Because I wouldn't," I say, as the phone clicks. "I would take care of you, Ma." The dial tone hears my vow.

September 17

Paul and I are poring over *The Cake Bible*, deciding between the White Velvet Butter Cake and the Golden Luxury Butter Cake for my fiftieth birthday, which is a few days away. The phone rings. It's Sid on the cell, with traffic noise in the background. "I'm putting your mother on the phone."

They are in the car on the way to Columbia Presbyterian. The so-called Lyme disease has not responded to antibiotics, and over the months Mom's dizziness and fatigue have been worsening. Mom tells me she consulted a neurologist, who prescribed an MRI, and the MRI, done yesterday, showed "hemorrhaging in the skull."

"What!?"

"Not in the brain," she says. "Just the skull."

"Oh, well, that's a big relief."

She says the doctors will evaluate, then either drain the blood by drilling two holes in her head ("which is no big deal," she says, oddly chipper. "It's minor surgery"). Or they will let it take care of itself, she's not sure how.

Is this hemorrhage the reason for her symptoms? I ask.

"Probably." Then, "Maybe not." The hemorrhage happened this week, she says. Or maybe it started before that, a while ago.

"Was it from that fall down the stairs?"

"Or—maybe. I don't know." Her voice is calm and rational; she isn't.

I call Dr. Horst, the neuro-otologist at Columbia Presbyterian who ordered the MRI. His nurse puts me on hold while she pages Dr. Grillo, Mom's new doctor, Sid's doctor. After a couple of hours and a bit of phone tag, I find out only a little more than what Mom told me. I could have called Mom and Sid back, but I feel I'd be bothering them, wanting to satisfy my need to know instead of Mom's need for peace and quiet, which is now provided by Sid and Sid alone.

I don't like giving up adult equality in return for his generosity to my mother, but since I'm not there to take care of her, I'm thankful that he is. With each emergency, though, I am also increasingly, and uncomfortably, aware that not only his love but his money and his apartment are keystones in the architecture of my father's care. Along with Mom, Paul and I, Nilda, Ernesto, and Dad have joined the wide circle of people in Sid's debt. I've lost a father, only to inherit a paterfamilias.

September 18

The surgery is tomorrow. I'm flying to New York. Out of guilt? Worry? Love? What I know is, getting a hole drilled in your head is not "minor surgery."

"You don't have to go," Paul says as I pack a small suitcase. "Sid is taking care of the practicalities."

"I want to be there, to give her emotional support."

"Then you should go."

I call her and say I'll be there at about two-thirty.

"I'm really glad you're coming, Judy."

"Me too."

By two, I'm in Mom's hospital room with her and Sid. It's a comfortable scene by now, our family life. Dr. McCourt, who looks and acts more like a high school track coach than the neurosurgeon he is, bounds in to explain that he will drill two "burr holes" into the skull, flush out as much of the clotted blood as possible, then cover the open holes with a dressing to let the rest of the fluid drain out, "just like a can of beer." It's minor surgery, he says, obviously the party line. "A routine operation."

"Trepanning," I say, recalling the word from the histories of medicine I've read. Routine indeed—they've been doing it since the Dark Ages, and it doesn't appear to have changed much since. Except they used to release demons from the holes along with the blood.

Mom lies, small in her bed, not smiling at the doctor's pleasantries. She's just passed on to me a helpful bit of information from Gloria Goldstein. Gloria told her this is the same condition and the same operation that Rhea Rosenberg had. Rhea is the woman who thought my Thanksgiving fight with Mom was a play.

September 19

Sid and I sit together in the "family waiting room" while Mom is under the knife. We're still awkward talking with each other, so we sit mostly in silence. Neither of us is able to read the newspapers we're carrying.

I find a pay phone and call one of the two or three numbers I have for Doris Berman, the care manager Mom has finally decided to engage. Within a week's time, Doris has interviewed Mom, spent time with Dad, visited the day center, and talked with Nilda and Ernesto. She knows Mom is in the hospital; Nilda has called her. She asks me to relay her best wishes.

"Dad is stable," Doris tells me in a tough, smart Brooklyn-girl manner. "Over the six years I've known him, I don't see any significant functional change. He was able to sense me as a new person coming in. From what I see, he's an early six. I'm hearing now that he's on the cusp of some incontinence. But he is relatively healthy. We could increase his walking, and I am not thrilled with the program he's in. It's very mediocre. He doesn't have much stimulation or much to bounce off of. I was impressed with both of the caregivers, and they are very used to Stan and he's used to them. Basically, " she concludes, "I don't want to fix what's not broken."

In our first conversations I find Doris incisive and knowledgeable, and as I get to know her, funny, sympathetic, and bullshit free. Now she says, "Eighty-five percent of Mom's stress is that Nilda will leave her high and dry." But Mom doesn't need to worry. "Nilda definitely wants the job and she needs the job, for at least another three years. And she wants to live in five days a week."

"Wow," I say. "That's great." I'd begun to think that Nilda's complaints were a way to prepare us for an imminent exit.

Doris will set up two positions: Nilda will work twenty-four hours a day, five days a week, and Ernesto will come in and take over on the weekends. They will be paid by the shift rather than the hour, which is a substantial pay cut for Ernesto. She'll help him find another job for the rest of the time if he needs one. She tells me how she will explain the changes to Nilda and Ernesto. "The family wants to keep Stan at home as long as possible. That means they need a viable financial plan." She is in favor of keeping Dad at home as long as possible, too. "If he goes into a nursing home, he could decompensate quickly." There's that word again. I picture parts of Dad spinning in entropy off his body. I tell Doris that Paul and I are willing to become the first responders to an emergency.

When she proposes all this—the new shifts, the money, even Paul's and my role—everyone accepts the plan. Including, amazingly, Mom.

Doris is the final member of our cockamamy family. She's our social worker, our probation officer, and our guardian angel, keeping our dysfunctional relations functioning, making sure we spend our money wisely and don't fight too much. She will communicate regularly with Nilda and Ernesto, and I will communicate with her, not Mom, about the caregivers. Doris also talks to each of us separately about Dad, which prevents the worst fights between Mom and me. Eventually it will release enough tension to allow us to talk to each other about Dad and even—another surprise—to agree on many aspects of his care. Doris tells me now that she tries to avoid "triangulation." She says, "When I ask caregivers what's their biggest problem, they never say 'the patient.' It's always 'the other family members.' " At the end of our conversation she reports, "Mom has realized she is not irreplaceable." Apparently, this is a good thing.

About an hour after I return to the waiting room, Dr. McCourt sprints in wearing his green scrubs and kente-cloth head scarf and reports that everything went well. They have drilled the holes, spritzed in some fluid, and gotten out about three quarters of the clot. They had hoped the brain would "spring back" once the pressure was relieved, but since it's an "old brain" it was not so "resilient" and remained somewhat squished to the left. Still, they expect that as the gunk drains out and is carried away by fresh cells, the brain will puff back up and shift into its proper spot, at the center of the skull. Once Mom is past the effects of the surgery, her symptoms should abate.

Will it happen again? I ask, still unnerved by the image of my mother's brain smashed like a sponge in a jar against the inside of her skull. He says it could. As the brain shrinks with age, he explains, the blood vessels between it and the outer layer of the meninges, the tissue between the brain and the skull, stretch and become fragile. Even a small concussion can cause a tear, and then a leak or a burst. If the break had been inside the brain, Mom could have had a stroke.

"So it's an old-brain problem," I say.

"Yup, you could say that." Dr. McCourt tells me my mother will have to be careful not to "jostle or bump" her head, lest she start another hemorrhage or worse.

September 20

Mom is on the mend, so I will return to Vermont for the birthday party that Paul has tentatively planned. When I stop by the hospital in the morning, Sid has brought a sweet roll from a French patisserie in their neighborhood. He presents it ceremoniously on a paper napkin and they sing "Happy Birthday."

"Thanks for surviving," I tell Mom, who directs only her smile in my direction. She's not allowed to sit up or move her head.

Sid goes out and Mom and I spend a companionable hour. I fetch her ice water and find a nurse to give me permission to raise the back of the bed a little. We make sick sickness jokes. She has staples in her head, which will have to be taken out in a week or so. Why can't they use Scotch tape? Or how about this stuff (the oatmeal-like substance on the breakfast tray)? Much easier to remove! We discuss the proscription against jostling or bumping her head. "Stay out of the mosh pit, Mom," I advise. It's nice to take care of her, I think, remembering our emergency-room conspiracies at NYU three years ago.

Soon it's time to catch the plane. Sid is in the hall, talking to a nurse, providing the same cushion between Mom and the harsh hospital bureaucracy that he provides between her and her often harsh daughter. Trying not to let her notice, I inspect the pad of sterile gauze protecting her brain from a world of eager toxic invaders, to make sure it's stuck securely all around. Then I kiss her good-bye on the lips. I am careful not to jostle or bump her, my irreplaceable mother.

October 16

Belated birthday card from Mom:

Darling Judy

My hopes and expectations for you from the moment the doctor placed you on my belly in Kew Gardens Hospital have been fulfilled beyond all my dreams.

I am so proud of you: for your steadfastness to what you believe and your courage, strength, and brilliance in standing up to fight for those beliefs.

The recent past has been difficult for both of us. My hope and expectation, and my birthday wish for both of us, for whatever years I will be here, is that our relationship will be close and loving and that we will find the ways to end all bitterness and anger.

Know that, as always, I love you dearly.

Ma

November 7, Mom's eighty-third birthday

The accountant Paul and I are consulting about joining our finances is just down the block from Sid and Mom's apartment, so after our appointment, we drop in to bring her a birthday present. We finesse our reason for being in the neighborhood (either I don't want to discuss our private decisions with her, or I don't want to give her the satisfaction that we are contemplating anything resembling marriage), and she is delighted by the unannounced visit.

Offering us wine, she sits down to unwrap the gift, *The White,* a novel about a European settler who is captured by Native Americans and ends up marrying one. "It got a great review," I tell her.

"Oh, yes, I remember." Mom is a cover-to-cover reader of the Sunday book review. "Mmm, looks good," she says, dipping into the first page like a child unable to keep her finger out of the icing on the uncut cake. When I was a teenager, whenever she'd see me beginning a classic—*Middlemarch* or *Sense and Sensibility*—she'd say, "Oh, you are so lucky you haven't read that yet!" Fatalism notwithstanding, my mother loves the anticipation of pleasure.

Sid is napping when the doorman buzzes us up. A mass has been found in his thyroid, and he's spent the afternoon at the hospital having tests. Mom is pleased to see us, and it's nice to see her in her pilling old blue sweater, her hair mussed and her dental bridge on the bathroom sink. The fashionably clad and coiffed Lillian is lovely, but to me right now, my mother looks like herself.

Sid emerges from the bedroom, spiffy in cords and a sport jacket, and offers us wine (unlike my father's collection of Gallo half-gallons, Sid's *cave* is excellent). He deflects sympathy about his thyroid—"The doctor said it's probably nothing"—and talks angrily about some corporation that has been secretly paying mercenaries in the Middle East. He sounds more political than usual—Mom's influence?—and warmer. Maybe he's touched that we came uptown to see Mom.

I flip through the *New Yorker* on the coffee table to find a William Hamilton cartoon of two conservatively dressed, balding, more-than-middle-aged men dining at their club. Says one: "Lately, I've begun to understand—and forgive—my parents."

"D'ya see this one?" I ask Mom, and she squints through her glasses and nods. She looks at me through narrowed eyes. Then we both laugh knowingly.

That night, Paul and I go over the notes we've taken at the accountant's and decide to keep our separate mortgages and checking accounts. We can transfer a fair amount of cash and in-kind support back and forth without paying taxes on it and we're in each other's wills, so for the moment the conversion is more trouble than it's worth. Still, we confirm that we will help each other in a pinch. "I won't let you go under," is how Paul puts it. That's already happening, and not only with the purchase of my car. When we talk about Dad's care, Paul does not say "you." He says "we."

I take a shower and Paul brushes his teeth. As often happens when we're both in the bathroom, Julius meows at the door to be let in. He sniffs at the shower curtain, then rubs against Paul's leg. "The whole family is together," Paul announces with saccharine tenderness as he surveys the scene. But it's true, we *are* a family.

November 17

I pick Dad up not at the little cinderblock room on Twenty-sixth Street where his program is usually held, but at the housing co-op's main senior center on Ninth Avenue. This afternoon, the memory-loss group has joined other habitués of the center to hear a concert of aging lounge lizards performing thirties and forties pop standards on a squealing sound system. It is Mom and Dad's sixtieth wedding anniversary, not exactly the music he'd pick, but a nice, inadvertent celebration anyway.

Dad is scatting louder than the singers, but because Sonja, from his group, knows all the lyrics and is singing equally loud, she is invited to join the singer onstage. "Seymour! Seymour!" Dad calls out, to divert attention from his sometime rival. The more with-it members of the audience look on in exaggerated puzzlement, as if to shield themselves from the contagion of dementia. I listen as long as I can bear to the man with a helmet of slicked-back silver hair and a carapace of gold jewelry covering the front of his white turtleneck. As "Luck, Be a Lady" winds down, I gesture to Dad to leave with me.

"LUCK la-la-la-la!" Dad belts out, shimmying up the aisle, flinging his arms dangerously close to the faces of those seated next to it.

In the hallway, he goofs around with the armholes of his jacket, pretending he can't get his hands in. It's a trick that usually irks me, but today I laugh and role my eyes at Dahlia, who has accompanied us into the hallway to say good-bye. I zip him up and wait through his ceremonious bowing and patting and hand-kissing.

"It couldn't be better!" he shouts to her.

"It couldn't be better," she replies, smiling at me.

Outside, he takes my hand and laces his fingers between mine. It's the first time we've held hands since I was a child.

"Are you all right, dear, dear?" he asks.

"I'm fine," I say. "Are you all right?"

"Hmm."

We walk in silence for a half a block, I a half pace ahead, guiding him forward. "How's your group?" I ask.

"What?" A mile from reason now, he resorts to his "joke," the shrug, the arched eyebrow, the sardonic smile that says, *I know it's fucked up, but it's funny,* the underlying sentiment of most Jewish humor. I laugh with him. He holds my hand all the way back to the apartment.

Nilda greets us at the door. "Ah, you!" Dad says happily.

"Hello, Stan-ny, my friend," Nilda says, kissing him on the cheek and helping him off with his coat. She reaches up to unlatch the lock she's added at the top of the closet door, since Dad peed once behind the door, then developed a new habit of pulling her things out and tossing them around the living room.

Nilda has made the place subtly her own—and his. His newly pressed shirts hang alongside her house dresses, also pressed, from the shower curtain pole. In the corner of the living room where the sofa used to be is one twin bed, with a stuffed pug on it. Sometimes Dad likes to sleep with the pug or nap on Nilda's bed. The sofa is where the piano was, the piano against the wall where the round table stood with its leaves dropped. The rugs Dad used to trip on have been taken up. In the hallway, the photographs he used to knock off the wall have been removed, and the remaining ones brightened with orange construction paper mats. Nilda likes orange; Mom doesn't.

Now the round table is open at the center of the living room, where Dad, the seigneur, can draw or eat and oversee his domain. When he catches his reflection in the mirror, he may babble at the guest or rail at the intruder, "Get out! Get!"

Nilda serves us tea at the table, with her homemade, dry, and lemony-sweet Argentine semolina pound cake. Mine is on a tray, with a spoon and fork, the milk in a small pitcher. She ties a dish-towel around Dad's neck like a bib, directs his attention to the piece of cake in her hand, then puts it in his mouth. "Thank you, dear," he says.

When the dishes are cleared, Dad and I do a puzzle of a pudgy propeller plane. The puzzle is made for children ages three to five, with about a dozen pieces in a flat, spongy form. Dad cannot figure out which goes where, and within months he won't remember how a puzzle works at all. But now I lay a piece in place, and he presses it down.

I put a Thanksgiving turkey color-in contest sheet that Nilda has picked up from D'Agostino's, the supermarket, in front of him. "You have to put your name here," I say.

"Stanley?"

"Right." I am happy to hear he knows his name. I guide his hand to the line. "Stanley," I prompt. "You write Stanley on this line." He writes an S and a T and then a trail of letters and letterlike forms to the edge of the page.

He picks up the page and "reads" the instructions on the back, singing the words. "The think and the from from and the from and the one and the twenty-five and the twenty-five and the dollars and cy, and cy and cy and the return and the gotta get them to talk about it. Take your D and there and there and here and here. The time and you take it and in dess in here. And the D'ag, ag ag dag dag. Get twenty-four. Not bad, not bad and two here. And two here." I turn the page over to the turkey and hand him a crayon. He presses each end on the table as if it were opening a ballpoint pen. "And it's going and it is have it, you know, and you have to accept," he tells me. His plain gold wedding ring glints under the light. "Kola keela kela ko, ko," he sings along with the Muzak version of "Penny Lane" on the television. "Da da dee DA!"

Once he is absorbed in his task, Nilda and I chat. Occasionally he watches us, a little suspiciously, and inserts himself into the conversation, even though it is in French. "They accept it and anyway, they have to work it ouk," he tells me, putting on his professional face. "Have to get it into place. Well, we'll put it through and see what they have. We'll have to come it in." Like many not-quite-fluent speakers, his conversational English is better than his reading comprehension. As he recites, he punctuates the sentences with little snatches of singing: "Da da da dee."

"Show it to Nilda," I say, admiring his artwork and guiding him over to her.

"Lil, Lil, you see?"

"Very nice, Stanley," she says, touching his hand.

"It's rather nice. Rather bood," he says, the approving critic. "Seymour! Mma-mmma!" When he sits back down I hand him another color and direct his hand back to the page, though he is as happy to "color" with a piece of plastic from the basket of crayons. He leans industriously into the task. "I'm doing this wine, they're luck that. Have to clean this up. You have to gotta build it us and it's going pretty well." He scratches at the color with his fingernail to "erase" it. "All pretty well and all of us and here it's a hello and to get it off. But I'll eat it on. You know, way to way, I don't know it I'll make it. But it's rather good."

I could call this logorrhea (aka diarrhea of the mouth) a symptom. Or I could see it as Dad's liberation into another lifelong fantasy. At last he is the World's Foremost Authority, blathering on endlessly without interruption or argument.

As he works, I look around the apartment, taking inventory of the few remaining knickknacks. The three graduated pitchers in delicate blue and white porcelain, bought in a junk shop in Maine, are on a high shelf. The Mexican painted fish, wooden and indestructible, are within reach. I ask Nilda where she has stored Bee's blue glass Mexican jar. "You know the one, shaped like this?"

She watches my hands trace the contours of the only heirloom I love, square on the bottom with a squat, round neck. *"Ah, chérie,"* she says ruefully. *"Ton papa, il l'a brisé."* He shattered it. His mother's beautiful vase, purchased on a trip away from her pesky, unwanted child. I don't delude myself that he remembered this affront and broke the piece on purpose.

As if to cheer me up, Nilda tells me a story. A few days ago when she met Dad at the program, a new aide asked him who she was. "Is this your sister?" she teased. "Your grandma?"

"Him?" Dad said, stalling until a word bubbled up from the marsh of his memory. "Oh, him?" He patted Nilda companionably. "That's my sergeant."

When I get home, I call Mom. I'm not sure if she wants to be wished a happy anniversary, so I don't mention it.

Instead we talk about Thanksgiving, a subject neither of us has touched since last year's debacle. "Did you tell me Paul and you weren't coming to Thanksgiving?" she asks.

"Uh, no," I answer.

"Oh, I thought you did." Pause.

"Why do you ask?"

Longer pause. I'm ready to feel hurt. "Well, Elinor invited Sid and me to come to one of her friend's."

"Yeah. And?"

"Um, what do you think I should do?"

"I think you should come to our Thanksgiving," I say a little tartly. Then I soften. "I mean, I'd *like* you to come to our Thanksgiving."

"Well, okay," she says uncertainly. "I'll talk to Sid."

After a few days she calls back. She's decided to come to the Levine-Goldstein dinner, then have dessert at Elinor's friend's, where Sid will dine. Dad won't come. We concur that he won't know what the celebration means and the large crowd will rattle him. I have considered speaking up to let him come, but reconsidered. Why would I be doing that? To show that I love him? To challenge Mom? To create some long-past fantasy version of our family? I call Nilda and tell her that Paul and I will come by after dinner and bring some leftovers. Like Mom, we'll have another little family celebration, but ours will consist of two un-thankful American vegetarians, one Argentine who hates turkey, and a seriously wandering Jew.

On Thanksgiving, Mom arrives exactly on time at the big loft of the Goldsteins' son and daughter-in-law, Alfie and Lisa. She is wearing the heavy silver and pewter necklace Sid gave her for Christmas and a simple, slate-gray silk suit. She looks elegant but for the uneven coverage of lipstick, which also creeps into the creases around her mouth. She and I don't talk much; the group is big and we are minding our manners. I'm looking forward to the food this year, and the wine, brought by Lisa's father, which is excellent.

When we sit down around the huge square table, I eat until I'm stuffed. But I feel unsated. Where is our family? Most of the guests are Lisa's relatives, whom Mom, Paul, and I do not know. Jill's son Tony has left to have dinner at a restaurant with his father, David, who is now divorced from Jill. Leo is dead. And of course, Dad is gone.

After supper, I find Mom alone on the couch. "So how's it going?" I ask.

She tells me that last week she had gone to the apartment to see Dad and celebrate their sixtieth anniversary. Her voice puts *celebrate* in quotes. Her description of the visit is stripped down, as no doubt the visit was. She and Dad listened to the Bach Coffee Cantata. He danced. They looked at photographs from Maine. "I refer to myself as Lillian in the pictures and him as Stanley. Of course, he doesn't recognize anyone, including himself. He just repeats his litany, 'There he is, there they are.' But he seems to enjoy it."

Our conversation is interrupted. Alfie and Lisa's daughter, Annabel, and her second cousin Milo are playing a piano-violin duet. As the banging and sawing get louder, Milo's mother winces sympathetically in our direction. When they finish, Mom applauds loudly, a mixed message.

"So how was that for you?" I ask Mom, when the concert is safely over. "I mean, the anniversary."

"Maybe it was a little masochistic," she begins. She was supposed to go with Sid to a memorial service for someone in their Alzheimer's support group but decided to visit Dad instead. "Because it was very painful to see him, so completely innocent and vulnerable like that. It's always so poignant. So painful." I feel my heart lie down and relax, as if caressed, when she reveals her sympathy for Dad so plainly. She takes a breath. "It's just very sad that Dad got sick."

"Yeah."

She mentions that Shirley Miller, a lifelong friend, advised her to discard all the photographs she has of Dad. "Just wipe my life clean of him," says Mom. "She doesn't understand one single thing." Her voice breaks. "So many of my friends—" She sits up, her tone brightens. I shouldn't get the wrong impression. "It's a miracle, what has happened with Sid. But needless to say, I never expected my life to turn out this way."

"No," I say, to say something. "You never know what's going to happen."

"And I was thinking, when I was there in the apartment, looking around at the things we bought together when we were young, the pine chairs and the Brueghel"—a framed print of a big, busy winter scene that I loved as a child—"I was thinking that if he hadn't gotten sick, we probably would have stayed together until we died."

"You probably would have."

"And it would have been okay. It wouldn't have been great, but it would have been okay." She would not have left him. And she is damned if she'll discard those photographs—keepsakes, kept for the sake of keeping. Maybe because I've stopped demanding that she love Dad, she can admit that she used to love him. Not only will she take care of him, she will care about him. And she does not intend to forget him.

Just before eight, Mom gets her coat from the bedroom. "Have fun. Say hi to Sid and Elinor," I tell her. We embrace—her forceful, meaningful clench. In her trim little black jacket and beret, with soft, gray curls framing her forehead, she looks like a Parisian girl from the 1920s, but wrinkled—a beautiful old girl. She is not "aging gracefully," that languidly aristocratic process, but scrambling headlong into the last adventure of her life.

I wander into the kitchen and help Paul and Lisa clean up. Then I call Nilda and find out that Dad is already in bed. "*C'est pas grave, chérie,*" she says, forgiving as always. I pour a cup of coffee and carry it to the table, where Jill is nursing a glass of wine and a piece of cake.

"It feels strange," I say, "without the fathers."

She says she always misses Leo at this time of year.

"Not only your father and mine," I say. "Even David is gone." She nods ambivalently. Alfie walks by and we shake our heads and giggle. Even at forty-seven, with a serious art career, a wife, a ten-year-old daughter, and a middle-aged gut, it's hard to count Alfie among the fathers. He will always be the goofy little brother, eating a "hambugger" with ketchup dripping down his chin.

I raise my coffee cup in a toast. "To our fathers."

She raises her wineglass: "Our fathers."

11. *Himself*

ON NEW YEAR'S DAY 2003, Dad and I stop by to see Captain Bob at his tropical drinking establishment on Pier 63. To chase the frigid wind off the Hudson, Bob is burning an old wooden beam over a rusty oil barrel, into which the embers drop. It feels cozy and funky as the pier itself, a last vestige of Manhattan's pre-gentrified waterfront, and it's probably illegal.

But it seems anyone who might object, including a passing cop, is in bed recovering on this afternoon after, and our barkeep, as usual lounging in a deck chair with tanned varicose legs in khaki shorts stretched out across another chair, is nursing his own hair o' the dog. His orange-dyed gray hair is disheveled under his cap, and as he rises to welcome us, his legs are a bit less landworthy than usual. "I've got my secret-recipe banana eggnog today," he offers.

I decline.

"How about one of my six famous beers?"

"No thanks." Since Dad has been taking psychotropic drugs, he's off alcohol. Bob waves graciously toward a few sooty plastic chairs, and I get Dad settled in for a chat.

Bob raises his own glass for one more try. "Manhattan?" He takes a swig, as if to endorse its tonic powers.

I zip and button Dad's parka to the top against the wind, and the captain segues into his sailing days in the Southern Hemisphere and his several circumnavigations, one of them solo.

"My father used to be a sailor," I say, as I always do, reminding him as well as Dad of his seagoing days. "Owned Hereshoffs, first a Bullseye, then a Marlin."

Captain Bob is, as always, impressed. "Ah yes," he says, hoisting his drink in salute to Dad. "Lovely boats. The loveliest."

"That was in Maine," I say, again, for the benefit of both of them. "Penobscot and Blue Hill Bays. Right, Dad? You sailed in Maine?" Dad has gotten interested in a beer bottle cap on the ground.

"Ah," says Bob. "Lovely waters."

Dad looks up, and from one of us to the other, not sure if he's being left out, but Bob's smile seems to put him at ease. He warms. "But you see, I'm not entirely canter that there is, to, you know, in here and here there," he says. He waves vaguely maybe at the Hudson. "It can be a cursty. You have to in and in, and binning out."

"It's true," says Bob. "The sailing can be tricky on a river like this." Dad peers at him. "But weather doesn't bother me," Bob continues. "I don't consider any weather 'inclement.' I don't even own a pair of long pants!" He points to his legs, which are approximately the same color as his hair; both more or less match the Manhattan.

"But they won't kick you up, you see," says Dad, nodding his head sagely. "I'm not quite sure what to do abouk."

"That's the beauty of sailing," answers Bob. "You take it as it comes."

"And you never know what's coming," I, the landlubber, contribute.

With an inebriate at the helm and a half-wit as first mate, the conversation tacks back and forth between sense and nonsense. Dad is enjoying it. "And I'm saying, 'Jesus Christ!' I mean, *they* don't." He chuckles. What he's saying may have no relation whatsoever to sailing. But in some sense, he is connecting. He has his boat.

"No, no. Of course not," says the captain. He gets up from his chair, slips behind the bar, and starts sponging, while Dad and I keep our chairs, huddling against the wind. We look down the Hudson River to New York Harbor, beyond the Statue of Liberty to Staten Island to southern New Jersey and Philadelphia, and after that, to the world. "Hey, what do you think?" Bob suggests in our direction, still his only customers. "You sure you don't want to try some of that eggnog?"

"Can you make it without alcohol?" I ask him. Then, to Dad, "Do you want some eggnog?"

"What?" asks Dad, stalling for sense.

"Eggnog." Near-comprehension flickers across his features, then flees. "Some eggnog," I say again. I laugh to defuse his incipient frustration-fed anger and touch his arm. He pretends to fall sideways out of his chair, makes a face of goofy terror.

"We're high on the real thing," I tell the captain. Then, not to derogate his own means of mood elevation, I add, "It's a bit early in the day for us."

"I understand. I understand completely," says Bob, mixing himself another drink and nodding respectfully toward Dad. "A sailor's got to keep his legs."

.   .   .

The chapters of the standard Alzheimer's story can be read in the titles of accounts of the disease. The narrative begins with the loss of memory and language: Thomas DeBaggio's book about the beginning of his own forgetting is called *Losing My Mind*. Then, along with rational capacity goes identity: *He Used to Be Somebody* is by a caregiver about her husband. After that comes the fundamental loss: *Losing the Self*. The coda to the story, informed by the Cartesian values that equate salvation with the reasoning mind, tells us the de-mented are also de-souled, banished not just from the world of persons, but from the company of angels, as well. It might be called *Paradise Lost*.

The protagonist of this narrative is an individual: the self. The self interacts with people and the environment, but it is autonomous by nature, protected by the boundary of the skin and protective of its privacy, its authenticity. This sovereign self is familiar to us; its existence seems evident. It is the reliable narrator of the nineteenth-century novel, the Freudian artifact excavated from the sediment of neurosis and forgetting. It is the Inner Child crouching like a homunculus next to the heart, awaiting restoration, fresh and whole.

This self fits comfortably in the biomedical model of Alzheimer's disease. As long as the individual brain thrives, the self thrives with it; when that brain goes, so goes the self. Because the corrosion is an internal organic process, the preservation of selves is assigned to nutritionists and biologists, physicians and pharmacologists cooking up anticorrosive agents in their labs. Ironically, this method of preserving the self's wholeness is accomplished by reducing the person to his constituent parts: his organs, neurons, chromosomes. It is a model that recommends the kind of relationship Martin Buber called "I-It," between the cognitively intact individual and the person with Alzheimer's: the "I," or subject, is the person with an intact brain; the "it" is the diseased brain of the demented other, who himself becomes an object, an "it." Even most of our nonmedical Alzheimer's preventatives and treatments enact a kind of I-It relationship between the demented person and his own body: eat blueberries and salmon, do crossword puzzles. These tactics are not social and certainly not societal. Each is personal, private—self-help for the self.

But the autonomous self is a myth. From the microscopic to the global, there are no inner narratives without outer narratives. The body is porous: each cell constantly absorbs what is outside it and excretes what is inside it. No organism can exist without a congenial environment, and no environment is unchanged by the organisms in it.

There is no "me" without "you." The psychologist D. W. Winnicott saw the birth of the self in relationship: the baby knows itself as a reflection in its mother's eyes. "No self is an island," said the post-modernist philosopher Jean-François Lyotard. Far from autonomous, "each exists in a fabric of relations."

This is as true for the demented as it is for the able-minded. "Selves are joint productions," write the psychologist Steven Sabat and the philosopher Rom Harré, and without collaboration they founder. "It is possible for the [Alzheimer's disease] sufferer to attempt to construct a particular self with another person, but if the latter refuses to cooperate in the constructive process, that self will not come into existence. This has a profound effect upon the AD sufferer's 'position' in the social situation." Shooting the breeze with Captain Bob may not recall to Dad's mind a fifteen-knot westerly across Penobscot Bay on a particular afternoon in August of 1971. But for a moment, Bob helps restore Dad to himself, or one of his selves, the old salt. That self is reborn not only in Bob's recognition of Dad, but in the two men's mutual recognition, their half-dotty skipper talk. Theirs exemplifies Buber's I-Thou relationship, what he calls a "meeting" of selves.

We don't need special training or talent to create that meeting (I have the feeling that in many respects, the orange-haired, orange-legged captain is only marginally more seaworthy than Dad). But if one of the people has lost his ability to communicate in language, it might not just happen; it must be *enabled*. This means a profound transformation of the way we conceive of the demented and of selves and persons in general. "Keeping the sufferer's personhood in being," write Kitwood and Kathleen Bredin of the primary task of dementia care, "requires us to see personhood in social rather than individual terms."

•   •   •

As time goes by, Dad is less and less the protagonist of a nineteenth-century novel and more the ever-transmuting character of an avant-garde film. The film is full of flashbacks and fast-forwards, real people interacting with animated figures, natural scenery melting into special effects, fact into fiction into fact. Each frame begins the story anew.

In true postmodern fashion, this multifarious character, my father, borrows bits of history to construct himself. In 1996, in a writing workshop for people with early-stage Alzheimer's, he writes about his first kiss. He reveals an encounter with an older cousin, "Archie by name." The encounter sounds like a molestation, with Dad as the victim. At the end he writes, "Enough, Enough—My mother never knew of this, and I was just a sweet child with a small penus." A slash of the pen, then, "I really don't want to talk of this— And here I am—how well I remember this."

This event, like Dad's college tennis exploits, is plausible enough. Still, it is the first anyone, including Mom, has heard of it. People with brain lesions sometimes "confabulate." Is this recollection true? If not, where did it come from? Beneath Dad's memory runs a current of menace that flooded the media during the early 1990s, the first years of his decline. With rumors of widespread child abuse prolifer- ating, molestation narratives were giving coherent and dramatic explanations to people who could not locate the source of their inex- plicable sadness, loneliness, or anxiety. Did Dad, a sad, lonely, and anxious child, adopt molestation as his metaphor? Telling the story this time, the hapless protagonist can conjure himself the victimized child in the news: fretted over, rescued, comforted, and vindicated.

Appropriating history, meeting himself through others, Dad cre- ates "now-selves" that feed the hungers of his "then-selves." His social inhibitions in tatters, with Jack Smith or the day center's music ther- apist Dad can be the swaggering Herman Schullenklopper of Tremont Avenue, who steals a pickle and doesn't care who knows it. Minutes later, with Nilda or Dahlia, he is the violin-playing mama's boy Seymour Lipschitz, contrite and worried about displeasing the grownups. For a while, even Alzheimer's provided a useful now-self. The same year he told me he was facing a "tall, black wall" he threw himself into the role of the early-stage "victim." He joined groups and spoke at conferences. He even employed his condition as a conversation starter. "I have this memory loss," I heard him say to a squirming guest at a party. "You see, Alzheimer came to me." I pictured Dr. Alzheimer arriving at the door with a black bag, offering what appeared to the floundering Stan to be a new, socially potent, and fascinating identity.

Dad borrows and bends culture, and like Zelig he inserts himself into it. Walking with Nilda on Twenty-third Street, he wanders into a synagogue. As it happens, the rabbi needs a minyan for a service. He asks if Dad is Jewish, Nilda says he is. So he hands Dad a skullcap, which Nilda puts on his head. Dad speaks no Hebrew, he knows no prayers (he may have attended three services in his life, including his own wedding, and every one was endured under protest and in silent, repentant supplication to the dictatorship of the proletariat). In the synagogue he looks around at the men bowing and mumbling in syllables hardly more mysterious than the ones he hears in English and starts to *daven*. Nilda holds back her giggles, but Dad takes it seriously. He is a member of the group, and a necessary member at that.

And although he cannot remember history, Dad is vulnerable to its forces. One day we arrive at Pier 63 to find Captain Bob's bar—and Bob himself—gone. I read in the paper some weeks later that the city is spiffing up the pier as part of its "renewal" of the waterfront. Bob is a victim of gentrification, and Dad, losing this last living link to his skipper self, is a victim of Bob's victimization. At home, Dad continues to array his old piloting and seamanship guides on his bed and turn and touch their pages with pride and an attenuated interest. A year later, he starts tearing the leaves out, and Nilda asks if she should put them away. It hurts me to see these sturdy and appealingly artless books destroyed, but I tell her no; they belong to my father.

.   .   .

Every premodern culture recognizes the social nature of the self. Some don't even conceive of a "self" as such. *Cogito ergo sum* could not be uttered in many languages, comments the humanities scholar Michael Bérubé, because those languages lack a first person singular. Amina Mama, a Nigerian writer and the director of the African Gender Institute at the University of Cape Town, South Africa, notices that "there is no word for 'identity' in any of the African languages with which I can claim any degree of familiarity. Perhaps there is a good reason for this. In English the word 'identity' implies a singular, individual subject with clear ego boundaries. In Africa, if I were to generalize, ask a person who he or she is, a name will quickly be followed by a qualifier, a communal term that will indicate ethnic or clan origins."

Living with the Akaramas of Peru, the anthropologist Tobias Schneebaum ate, hunted, played, slept, and engaged in sexual bacchanalia with the tribesmen in their small, same-sex groups. But, he found, only the group existed. The tribal culture admitted of no individuals. A person who went away was not mentioned, including the dead.

Schneebaum's Western ego couldn't take it, and he left. I'd leave too. After all, the modern self is not just familiar and evident, it is compelling. I am fond of mine, and of the political institutions and cultural practices—from the Bill of Rights to psychotherapy (and the personal memoir!)—that protect and nurture it. So I am not invoking some preindustrial Utopia where the individual self is abolished. For better or worse, we Western moderns are where we are in history, and even those "selfless" cultures may be moving in our direction. Amina Mama, while respecting Africans' historic affiliations, also proposes that a more personally complex concept of identity is crucial to people and political movements in a post-colonial, globalized world. We don't have to choose, she suggests. We can treasure our idiosyncratic selves and recognize that they are, in every fiber, social.

In an essay called "Sharing One Skin," a Native American who signs her name "Jeannette Armstrong—Okanagan Nation" limns a self that embraces both a Western "inner-ness" and an expansive social connection. Both ancient and extraordinarily postmodern, the Okanagan self stretches beyond the human lifespan, beyond family and circumscribed culture to the infinite time and space of the natural order. "Our word for people, for humanity, for human beings, is difficult to say without talking about connection to the land," writes Armstrong, having begun her piece describing her birthplace, the weather and geography, and the ancestors who inhabited it. "When we say the Okanagan word for ourselves, we are actually saying 'the ones who are dream and land together.' "

Contained in the word *Okanagan* is a multifaceted conception of the self. The portion translated as *dream* more accurately means "the unseen part of our existence as human beings," including mind and spirit, memory and imagination. Emotion is essential to being fully human, but this emotion is the antonym of the Western self's private experience and of its struggle for expression against the strictures of family and society. Rather, "in [the Okanagan] language, the emotional self is that which connects to other parts of our larger selves around us," to other people, tribe, history, and nature, writes Armstrong. The part of the word referring to that connection means the twining of strands, as in a basket.

In world views that posit a socially created self, the disabled self signals a social failure. In Banaras, India, University of California/ Berkeley anthropologist Lawrence Cohen found that dementia is conceived as corporeal, as it is in the West, though to the Indians it is the condition of a "cool," normally aging, body that develops an abnormally "hot" brain, the angry, foolish brain of the young. The Indians don't locate the origins of this disorder in biology, however. Hot brains "point to bad families, those who do not offer adequate sevā (devoted service) to their parents," writes Cohen.

If the Indians of Banaras view dementia as a familial ailment, the Okanagan see mental "dis-ease" not as the disintegration of a body or a person but of the world in which that individual dwells. Looking down on a crowded, traffic-loud valley from a hillside wild-flower field, Armstrong's grandmother comments, "The people down there are dangerous, they are all insane." Her father agrees. "It's because they are wild and scatter anywhere." Social dislocation is the worst malady.

Social dislocation is the worst malady for all of us—our epidemic, the disease of our century, says Jesse Ballenger, the historian who brought to light the work of David Rothschild, that early social constructionist of dementia. And Alzheimer's is its perfect metaphor. "Why have we come to fear AD more than any other thing now?" Ballenger asks. "After all, they were talking about the aging population and the ticking time bomb [of illness, dependency, and health care costs] in the 1920s and '30s. Why is it such a problem now?" My father isn't the only one who is coming unglued from history and relationship, says Ballenger. Postmodernity is shaking us all loose.

The postmodern potential for reinvention is thrilling, the historian explains, but the instability that comes with it is mightily discomfiting. We are literally unsettled: we are not born in one place, grow up, marry, work, and die there. We live at twenty addresses in a lifetime, and at each address our lives are everywhere. Of course, transience is nothing new to Americans. De Tocqueville observed that Americans planted an orchard and did not stick around to harvest the fruit. But modern technology exacerbates rootlessness. Our desires are manufactured on Madison Avenue and in Hollywood, our anxieties flash in orange terrorism alerts from Washington, our guilt floats over the Internet from Somalia or Iraq. Airline travel, immigration, exile, psychotropic drugs, genetic engineering, class mobility, sex reassignment surgery—all these and more can transform any of us at any time, by choice or by circumstance, into someone else. As a thing to count on, says Lyotard, "a *self* does not amount to much."

With all this cultural forgetting and redefining, a disease of personal, literal forgetting assumes outsized symbolism, Ballenger says. Alzheimer's emerges as the apotheotic apocalyptic affliction. "As selfhood itself has become more problematic in the late twentieth century and it has become more difficult to create and maintain a self, the symptoms that rob people of the ability to tell a coherent self narrative become much more frightening."

This is the fear that Jeannette Armstrong's Okanagan relatives smell in the polluted air rising from the city. "Communities used to hold people in place and define who people were," Ballenger tells me. "There were a lot of bad things about that in terms of hierarchies and lack of freedom. Still, there were good things, too. When you talk about the self-made man in the nineteenth century, the community is not going to determine who that man is, but it is not going to support him either. The social and political developments [that led to the fracturing of communities] are connected to why selfhood is such a problem now. When an autonomous self becomes the ideal, it leaves no room for meaningful dependence, and no commitment to the public sphere." And that means people who can't fend for themselves are not just extraneous, they become a burden, even a threat.

"There are people who are happy about postmodernity and see it as liberation. They see the possibilities that are opened up by the destruction of grand governing narratives of social class, race, and gender," Ballenger goes on. "And then there are others who are asking, how do we have a meaningful life in spite of postmodernity?" Ballenger puts himself in the second group. And I am a member of both: I celebrate the liberation of postmodernity. And I worry about how we can have a meaningful life within it.

How do we have not just a meaningful life, but a secure one? Premodern cultures suggest alternative ways of thinking, but they don't necessarily offer solutions. "Don't romanticize other cultures," cautions Lawrence Cohen as we drink tea in a café on the seedy edge of San Francisco's Castro district. "In the U.S. we see only the medical [in dementia]. In India, they see only the familial. Both are socially constructed and both have their problems." Right. Would I rather have my "bad family" blamed for Dad's dementia? Or do I prefer to be condemned the American way, which holds the disease responsible for his condition and then charges our family with total responsibility for his fate, unaided by the community or the state? In the end, says Cohen, "the important question is, what are the stakes of any given analysis?" One thing that is not at stake in India, he notes, is "whether the demented person is a person or not."

We cherish the self. But nothing binds us to cherishing *only* the individual self, or predicating that self's existence only on a working brain, or entrusting that brain or that self to the expensive engineers of medicine. We do not have to accept a political ideology or an economic system that conjures us each self-made and requires us each to be self-sufficient. In a postmodern world we may acknowledge that our selves are protean and discontinuous, bound to history and unstuck from it. But we don't have to abandon hope of "meeting," in Martin Buber's sense. In fact, we must cultivate connection among our battered, rattling selves; we must demand mutual commitment. We can opt out of social Darwinism and behave instead according to the rule of the civilized human jungle (and of the European social democracies): people survive collectively, not alone. That means never to relegate the disabled, either by compassionate pity or hard-hearted budgetary policy, to a status of diminished personhood.

·   ·   ·

Pursuing a meaningful life, Dad and I take the bus to the Metropolitan Museum of Art to see an exhibition of Netherlander Renaissance paintings.

Most of the pictures are religious, large diptychs and triptychs busy with action and narrative. A few pictures into the exhibit, as I steer Dad through the crowd, I realize he might not remember the dramatis personae, Jesus Christ, Mary, and the rest. So I start telling him the stories. "This is the angel, who comes to tell Mary that she is pregnant with the son of God, even though she's a virgin."

"Um-hmm," says Dad equably. Once a vigorous railer against all superstition, he has become catholic in his acceptance of world-views, all of which are credible to him.

"The guy with the wings—that's the Angel Gabriel. He's God's messenger."

He looks more or less in the direction of the angel, burgherlike and earthbound under his ponderous feathers.

I guide Dad to another triptych, this one depicting the story of a saint who stole food from her well-to-do parents. "When she gave it to the poor, the angels replenished it. See, over here there's no food, and in this next part, there's food. I think those are her parents over there."

He's concentrating on a whippet and a peacock in the bottom left corner of a painting. He seems very interested in them.

"The townspeople thought she was a witch, so they strangled her," I tell Dad, privately enjoying the demented logic of religion. "Over here, at the end, they're realizing she was a saint all along. All this stuff floating around her? Those are her miracles."

"Hello, little fellow," Dad says, stroking the painted dog with a fingertip.

"Dad, don't touch!" He flashes me a look. Then he presses up close to the plaque describing the painting, drawing his brows together in a convincing imitation of comprehension. He looks back up at the picture. "It's a nice," he says.

I've read that "representational thinking," understanding that a drawing stands for a real thing, can deteriorate in AD. But I can't help thinking that the form of the painting is a good representation of Dad's mind and his transmuting self. As in other paintings of the period, the story unfolds in a succession of scenes undivided by frames wooden or painted. The saint is tortured, buried, resurrected, and beatified; the girl appears beside the woman, the torture victim beside the crowned saint. She is a multitude, a Renaissance version of the postmodern procession of metamorphosing "performances," the then-self and the now-self, continuous and fractured.

The picture could also be read as an illustration of what Buddhists call not-self—*anatta*—the mind as a moment-to-moment lapping of phenomena, rising and falling away, impermanent, free of regret and craving, free of reliving the past and fantasizing the future.

.   .   .

I have practiced Buddhist meditation. I've tried to be "mindful," living with full awareness and involvement in every instant, tried to let go of attachment, of craving and regret. I have puzzled for years over what not-self could be. My drifting, mindless father is a lesson in a kind of mindfulness: he lives in the moment. But if I have learned anything from him, it is that the self, rather than bow out gracefully, holds on by its fingernails to the end. Dad may be almost down to his final, here-and-now "core self." But watching him, I have come to think that the self is inalienable.

Dad and I no longer go places like the Metropolitan Museum of Art. The bus ride is too long—way too many rising and falling moments. A crowd unnerves him and he unnerves members of it. Now an outing is the three-block walk to the river. I hold his hand, trying to move him without noticeable coercion in one direction, dissuading him from picking up used straws and lottery tickets from the sidewalk, distracting him from staging dangerous revolts at the street corners, exclaiming about the daffodils in spring, the dogs in winter. Sometimes we don't make it all the way to the river, but stop and sit on the bench in a toddlers' playground, where he pipes at the oblivious babies, "I see you! I see you!" I measure his diminishment in our shortening walks.

Will he erode to corelessness? Is there such a person as in Robert Musil's eery title, a "man without qualities"? I ask Damasio, "Is there a level below which a person is no longer a person?"

"This is a very important question," he answers in his softly Portuguese-inflected English. "I think there is a point in which I would give up, for instance, if you have a person in coma or vegetative state, like Sunny von Bülow. With her I have deep doubts that anything is going on. The machinery that would allow her to have any kind of thought or feeling is gone. There I think, especially if there are relatives involved, and if keeping the person alive would prolong their suffering, I would say, give up. But with Alzheimer's disease, I wouldn't. My feeling is that we should err on the side of thinking the person is there."

"It can't hurt," I say.

"And it can hurt if you err on the wrong side."

I get the same message from Ajahn Pasanno, a revered teacher and administrator of the American branch of the Thai "forest tradition" of Theravada Buddhism. Some years ago, the sect's master, Ajahn Chah, began losing his memory. At sixty-three, he underwent brain surgery, and not long after that his speech and ability to move were gone. He remained bedridden at his monastery for nine years, in a state somewhere between Dad's and Sunny von Bülow's. One of the monks who was at his bedside was Ajahn Pasanno.

Who is the person for whom mindfulness is life when he no longer has a mind? I ask Ajahn Pasanno, speaking by phone from his California monastery. I am thinking of Dad, for whom thinking was everything. Evidently, Ajahn Chah found this an interesting question, too. "After his operation, one time we were chatting," says Pasanno. "He was saying, 'You know, people talk about not-self, *anatta*. Sometimes they get an inkling of the not-self of the body, but they do not see the not-self of the mind.'"

I don't understand. "What does this mean, 'the not-self of the mind'?"

"It is a non-attachment. We impute so much to this—that if I am thinking intelligently, cleverly, rationally, then I am a good, useful being. If I'm unable to connect my thoughts, my being is diminished, my value or my work is diminished. That is the judgment coming from a place of self that is always measuring. When we need to create the causes for clarity and composure, we need mindfulness and awareness. When the physical element of the body and the mind is unable to perform its function, what the mind relies on is its inner tranquility or purity, [and] that is something separate from the physical. It's a real radical letting-go. Of everything." He goes on: "I remember an elder monk who came to visit Ajahn Chah. He was quite well known for his psychic power, and he spent some time sort of checking in, meditatively reflecting on Ajahn Chah's state of mind. He said, 'Yeah, Ajahn Chah's mind is just really pure and bright. He's not suffering.' "

I picture Ajahn Chah's mind as looking something like the disembodied souls of Renaissance paintings: white-blue, translucent. Dad's mind, on the other hand, might resemble a storm drain after a heavy rain. A radical letting-go? It is hard to apply this wisdom to my father, who felt he never had enough and thus hoarded whatever he got. I recall a lecture by another Buddhist scholar, Andrew Olendzki. It's hard for many of us to get to *anatta*, Olendzki said, because of our insecurity and neurosis, which is our *dukkha*, or suffering, which, somewhat tautologically, is caused by our inability to let go. "Before you can be no one," he noted, "you have to be someone."

I sometimes think that what will finally do Dad in will not be the loss of himself, as the Alzheimer's Association predicts, but his self's obdurate survival. The guy who gets kicked out of the day center or locked in the nursing home will be the same old insatiable, irascible Stan Levine, the man who can't take yes for an answer, because he so desperately needs another yes.

And yet Dad is letting go of attachment—not because he wants to, but because he can't help it. He is unable to dwell in regret or anticipation, because his mind doesn't recognize time. His craving seems almost sated, because after a moment it is forgotten. My father is closer to *anatta* than he's ever been, and if the Buddhists are right, it may account for his newfound happiness.

I ask Ajahn Pasanno how the Thais think about dementia. "In Thailand, a rural, agrarian culture, if someone has their faculties until old age, that's seen as a good thing. But if they lose their faculties, it's not a big deal. It's not hush-hush; everything is openly talked about. Thais don't like to take things too seriously—nothing is sacred in that sense. They make jokes about themselves or others," he says, and laughs.

This good-natured self-teasing, he implies, is related to the acceptance of mortality. "When you drive into the monastery I lived at, the first thing you see is a crematorium"—two sets of stairs with a space for the pyre in between. "Before it was a monastery, that forest was a cremation ground. So whenever anyone dies in the village, that's where they bring them. Old people come up and children come up. Having had the teachings since childhood, it's not terrifying." Ajahn Chah once articulated those teachings this way: "Whatever thing is born, that thing must change and grow old as a natural condition and eventually it must die."

Perhaps the Buddhist not-self is like the protean postmodern self. Neither is solid; both melt into air. Both inspire exhilaration and also vertigo. The difference is that the former accepts change, whereas the latter is driven to it and thus driven by it. If death is the ultimate change, how does the modern self age and die? If the world is moving relentlessly away from that pre-technological agrarian society, can it also divorce itself from the inevitable fate of the plants and creatures, the other things that are born?

"Reason, or sense, is the only thing that makes us men and distinguishes us from the beasts," wrote Descartes. One fruit of our reason is technology, which is helping us to live longer and someday may let us live forever. Will the ultimate gift of reason be our radical separation from all other living things, which will die while we will not? The zealots of genetic engineering and stem-cell therapy ecstatically say yes. They preach a secular religion of eternal life without the sting of death. These people call themselves true optimists. Sometimes I wonder, is my stance against "curing" aging just a version of my parents' fatalism?

I have tried to explain the human costs of viewing old age as a

biological engineering problem to be fixed and to plead for a different kind of fixing and a new concept of what is, or ain't, broke. In
the end, though, this atheist Jewish skeptic comes down to what can
only be described as a principle of faith: *accepting death is not the same
as giving up on life.* I once heard the Buddhist scholar Robert
Thurman say that procrastination is a denial of mortality. If your
days are limitless, anything can be put off until tomorrow. If they're
finite, you have to get down to business now. To accept death is to
value every moment of life. The bioengineers prophesy the day when
we will all be perfect. But even if by some miracle everyone in the
world will become rich enough to buy the perfecting technologies,
we aren't perfect now. Our imperfection is the living sign of our
mortality. Just as we can accept death and love life, we can embrace
imperfection as the thing that unites us as humans and also try to
be better. All along, to paraphrase the twelve-steppers, we need the
humility to know when to leave well enough alone.

Ajahn Chah's forest-dwelling brotherhood did not reject
modern medicine. When the master became ill, he underwent
surgery. Later, he refused medical treatments. How did the monks
know the right thing to do? Ajahn Chah's cognitive faculties were
"unraveling," Pasanno tells me. The queen of Thailand was inviting
the great man south to receive treatments. The decisions were
finally "very practical. If something works and is helpful to preserve
a quality of life, then it's useful. If it's not, then pack it in. It was not
idealistic or dogmatic."

Soon, there was not much to do, medically. Ajahn Chah was old
and he was moving on. But as long as the master's body was alive,
the monks assumed his mind was, too. Both required the same
meticulous care. During nine years in bed, he never had a bedsore.
And, says Pasanno, "part of the duties of looking after him was to be
very mindful of speech. One didn't want to be either frivolously
speaking or speaking with conflict"—speaking "unskillfully," the
Buddhists call it. "Everybody felt that Ajahn Chah knew what was
being said." He was there.

. . .

As he loses language, my father sings the world. Car alarm, tea kettle, crow: he matches the pitch, taps out the rhythm. Like John Cage, he makes no distinction between music and sound, between sound and noise. Although he cannot truly converse, he responds to a question with the falling intonation of an answer. His voice climbs half a scale to a question, and his eyebrows follow. In assent or dissent, curiosity, certainty, or mockery, he retains the music and dance of the English language. And when he sings, his pitch is more precise than in the past, when it mattered less to him, when he considered himself Middle C, the man with "the point."

Paul calls Dad's random singing his "dah-dah-dah" and says he uses it to insert or assert himself when ignored. *Present!* says his dah-dah-dah. *Account for me!* The way I look at it, Dad deploys sound as a bat does, to situate himself among things, among people.

"He was a pretty good musician," comments his old clarinet teacher, Peter Pane ("Peter Pan by name," Dad described him in the early, flowery Alzheimer's days, though the name is pronounced *pane,* like the window glass). Peter liked my father and was intrigued by the challenge of teaching someone who could barely assemble the instrument or read the music or even remember what the teacher said an hour earlier. He is a kind man, Peter, a jazzman, used to listening and improvising and playing modestly while somebody else riffs. He met with Dad to "play" long after Dad could play.

When Dad can no longer place his fingers on the keys, the clarinet is packed away. Dad leafs through his music at home and carries a score or two to the day care center in his knapsack. After a while, Nilda gives him an insulated lunch tote, and the pack is discarded and the music "filed" away with the other miscellany on his windowsill. From Dad's consciousness Peter Pane flies to Never Never Land. But I put a clarinet sonata on the CD player, and Dad sings his dah-dah-dah to a melody he knows as well as his heartbeat. He points to the sound coming from the speaker and says, "I was this."

"He was a pretty good musician, but mostly he liked sitting in the clarinet section," says Peter. "He liked being in the band." *I was this, like them. With them.*

Who is my father?

My dad's a dement, victim of the Disease of the Century, the very model of a modern mortal monstrosity. His brain is chewed and his tongue is tangled. His thumbs can't find the holes in his mittens and he pisses in the closet. He's an unfunny funnyman, expelling a gurgling fart in the elevator, then bowing at his appalled fellow passengers as he steps from the car. He's a practiced seducer who has forgotten how to beguile, an egotist who doesn't know his own face in the mirror.

But as I sit beside my father at the round wooden table in the middle of his living room, in the middle of his hometown, in the middle of his loving little makeshift family, I hear the man who sings the world. In this demented moment of history, in his own vague and vivid here and now, Dad bellows *Dah-dah-dah!*

My father is singing the song of himself.

Reading List

Any source quoted or paraphrased directly in *Do You Remember Me?* is cited in the text and repeated below. But the following is not an exhaustive bibliography (it does not include most daily newspaper articles on developing science, for instance). The categories are for convenience; many overlap.

The Brain, the Mind, and Consciousness

Block, Ned, Owen Flanagan, and Güzeldere Güven, eds. *The Nature of Consciousness: Philosophical Debates* (Cambridge, MA: MIT Press, 1998). An excellent anthology for both the beginner and the more sophisticated philosopher of mind.

Damasio, Antonio R. *Descartes' Error: Emotion, Reason, and the Human Brain* (New York: Putnam, 1994).

——*The Feeling of What Happens: Body and Emotion in the Making of Consciousness* (New York: Harcourt, 1999).

Dennett, Daniel C. *Consciousness Explained* (Boston: Little, Brown, 1991).

Descartes, René. *Discourse on the Method of Conducting One's Reason Well and of Seeking the Truth in the Sciences.* George Heffernan, trans. (Notre Dame: University of Notre Dame Press, 1994). This bilingual edition offers a useful introduction and a clear, true translation of the text, which was originally written in 1637.

Epstein, Mark. *Thoughts Without a Thinker: Psychotherapy from a Buddhist Perspective* (New York: Basic Books, 1995).

James, William. *Principles of Psychology* (New York: Dover Publications Reprint Edition, 1955). James's description of consciousness is still widely influential and even consistent with new neurological discoveries.

Luria, A. R. *The Mind of a Mnemonist: A Little Book About a Vast Memory*. Lynn Solataroff, trans. (Cambridge: Harvard University Press, 1968).

Proust, Marcel. *À La Recherche du Temps Perdu* (Paris: Editions Gallimard/ Folio Classique, 1988). After reading Proust, it is almost impossible to imagine a modern self without reference to his writing.

Sacks, Oliver W. *The Man Who Mistook His Wife for a Hat* (New York: Summit, 1985).

———*An Anthropologist on Mars* (New York: Knopf, 1995). Only two books in a fascinating oeuvre.

Varela, Francisco, Evan Thompson, and Eleanor Rosch. *The Embodied Mind: Cognitive Science and Human Experience* (Cambridge, MA: MIT Press, 1993). Both a primer of and a generous critique of cognitive science.

Aging, Dementia, and the Self

Barker, Judith C. "Between Humans and Ghosts: The Decrepit Elderly in a Polynesian Society," in *The Cultural Context of Aging: Worldwide Perspectives*, Jay Sokolovsky, ed. (Westport, CT: Bergin and Garvey, 1997): 407–24. This article, like the other anthropological citations below, opens a reader to the possibilities of conceiving dementia differently from the ways we do in the United States.

Cohen, Lawrence. "Toward an Anthropology of Senility: Anger, Weakness, and Alzheimer's in Banaras, India," *Medical Anthropology Quarterly* 9(3), (1995): 314–33.

Freud, Sigmund. *On Aphasia* (New York: International Universities Press, 1891/1953).

Gubrium, Jaber F. *Oldtimers and Alzheimer's: The Descriptive Organization of Senility* (Greenwich, CT: Jai Press, 1986). A crucial text.

Harding, Nancy, and Colin Palfrey. *The Social Construction of Dementia: Confused Professionals?* (London: Jessica Kingsley, 1997).

Herskovits, Elizabeth. "Struggling over Subjectivity: Debates about the 'Self' and Alzheimer's Disease," *Medical Anthropology Quarterly* 9(2), (1995): 146–64.

Holstein, James A., and Jaber F. Gubrium. *The Self We Live By: Narrative Identity in a Postmodern World* (New York: Oxford University Press, 2000).

Ikels, Charlotte. "Long-Term Care and the Disabled Elderly in Urban China," in Sokolovsky, *The Cultural Context of Aging*, 452–71.

Kitwood, Tom. *Dementia Reconsidered: The Person Comes First* (Bucking-ham: Open University Press, 1997). Another seminal book on de-mentia, personhood, and care.

Mama, Amina. "Gender, Power, and Identity in African Contexts," *Wellesley Centers for Women Research and Action Report* (Spring/Sum-mer, 2002): 7–15.

Post, Stephen G. "The Concept of Alzheimer Disease in a Hypercogni-tive Society," in Peter Whitehouse, Konrad Maurer, and Jesse F. Bal-lenger, *Concepts of Alzheimer Disease: Biological, Clinical, and Cultural Perspectives* (Baltimore: Johns Hopkins, 2000): 245–56.

Sabat, Steven R. *The Experience of Alzheimer's: Life Through a Tangled Veil* (Blackwell: Oxford University Press, 2001).

———, and Harré Rom. "The Construction and Deconstruction of Self in Alzheimer's Disease," *Ageing and Society* 12 (1992): 442–61.

Schneebaum, Tobias. *Keep the River on Your Right* (New York: Grove, 1969).

Shenk, David. *The Forgetting: Alzheimer's: Portrait of an Epidemic* (New York: Doubleday, 2001). Beautifully told, with a surprising conclu-sion about the value of forgetting, the book recounts the medical-ized story of Alzheimer's.

Smith, David H. "Seeing and Knowing Dementia," in Robert H. Bin-stock, Stephen G. Post, and Peter J. Whitehouse, *Dementia and Aging: Ethics, Values, and Policy Choices* (Baltimore: Johns Hopkins University Press, 1992): 44–54.

Snowdon, David. *Aging with Grace: What the Nun Study Teaches Us About Leading Longer, Healthier, and More Meaningful Lives* (New York: Ban-tam, 2001).

Taylor, Charles. *Sources of the Self: The Making of the Modern Identity* (Cam-bridge: Harvard University Press, 1989).

Traphagan, John H. "Localizing senility: Illness and agency among older Japanese," *Journal of Cross-Cultural Gerontology* 13(1), (1998): 81–98.

Žižek, Slavoj. "The Cartesian Subject Without the Cartesian Theatre," in Kareen Ror Malone, and Stephen R. Friedlander, editors, *The Subject of Lacan: A Lacanian Reader for Psychologists* (Albany: State Uni-versity of New York Press, 2000): 23–40.

In addition, one cannot understand the modern concept of the self and its relationship to other people and to memory and language without reading the great psychologists Sigmund Freud, Jacques Lacan, and D. W. Winnicott. A lesser-known but provocative investigation of the postmodern self and the unconscious can be found in the work of the British psychoanalyst Christopher Bollas.

Disability, the Medicalization of Aging, and Death

"The Age Boom." Special issue of *The New York Times Magazine* (March 9, 1997).

Bérubé, Michael. *Life As We Know It: A Father, A Family, and an Exceptional Child* (New York: Pantheon, 1996). A loving and intelligent book on the experience and politics of disability.

Conrad, Peter, and Joseph W. Schneider. *Deviance and Medicalization: From Badness to Sickness* (Philadelphia: Temple University Press, 1992). Practically canonical in this field.

DeBaggio, Thomas. *Losing My Mind: An Intimate Look at Life with Alzheimer's* (New York: Free Press, 2002).

Death with Dignity Alliance. *How to Ensure Yourself or a Loved One the Right to Die with Dignity* (Washington: Death with Dignity Alliance, undated).

Estes, Carroll L., and Elizabeth A. Binney. "The Biomedicalization of Aging: Dangers and Dilemmas," *The Gerontologist* 29 (5) (1989): 587–96.

Ferry, Carol Bernstein. "A Good Death," *The Nation* (Sept. 17/24, 2001): 8.

Foley, Joseph M. "The Experience of Being Demented," in Binstock, Post, and Whitehouse, *Dementia and Aging,* 30–43.

Frank, Arthur W. *At the Will of the Body: Reflections on Illness* (Boston: Houghton Mifflin, 1991). The patient speaks, eloquently.

Kaufman, Sharon R. "Senescence, Decline, and the Quest for a Good Death: Contemporary Dilemmas and Historical Antecedents," *Journal of Aging Studies* 14:1 (2000): 1–23.

Lewis, C. S. *A Grief Observed* (New York: HarperCollins, 1994).

Morris, David B. "How to Speak Postmodern: Medicine, Illness, and Cultural Change," *Hastings Center Report* (November–December 2000): 7–16.

Rothschild, David. "The Practical Value of Research in the Psychoses of Later Life," *Diseases of the Nervous System* 8 (1947): 125–28.

——, and M. L. Sharp. "The Origin of Senile Psychoses: Neuropathologic Factors and Factors of a More Personal Nature," *Diseases of the Nervous System* 2 (1941): 49–54.

The History and Politics of Aging and Alzheimer's

Ballenger, Jesse F. "Beyond the Characteristic Plaques and Tangles: Mid-Twentieth-Century U.S. Psychiatry and the Fight Against Senility," in Whitehouse, Maurer, and Ballenger, *Alzheimer Disease*, 83–103.

Butler, Robert N. *Why Survive? Being Old in America* (New York: Harper & Row, 1975).

Cole, Thomas R. *The Journey of Life: A Cultural History of Aging in America* (Cambridge: Cambridge University Press, 1992).

Dillmann, Rob J. M. "Alzheimer Disease: Epistemological Lessons from History?" in Whitehouse, Maurer, and Ballenger, 129–57.

Fox, Patrick J. "The Role of the Concept of Alzheimer Disease in the Development of the Alzheimer Association of the United States," in Whitehouse, Maurer, and Ballenger, 209–34.

Katzman, Robert, and Katherine L. Bick. "The Rediscovery of Alzheimer Disease During the 1960s and 1970s," in Whitehouse, Maurer, and Ballenger, 104–14.

Maurer, Konrad, Stephan Volk, and Hector Gerbaldo. "Auguste D: The History of Alois Alzheimer's First Case," in Whitehouse, Maurer, and Ballenger, 5–29.

Möller, Hans-Jurgen, and Manuel B. Graeber. "Johann F: The Historical Relevance of the Case for the Concept of Alzheimer Disease," in Whitehouse, Maurer, and Ballenger, 30–46.

On the Politics and Ethics of Care and Duty

Benedict, Elizabeth. "When Baby Boomers Grow Old," *The American Prospect* (May 21, 2001): 21–5.

Callahan, Daniel. "Terminating Life-Sustaining Treatment of the Demented," *Hastings Center Report* (November–December, 1995): 25–31.

Dresser, Rebecca. "Autonomy Revisited: The Limits of Anticipatory Choices," in Binstock, Post, and Whitehouse, *Dementia and Aging*, 71–85.

——. "Dworkin on Dementia: Elegant Theory, Questionable Policy," *Hastings Center Report* (November-December, 1995): 32–38.

——, and Peter J. Whitehouse. "The Incompetent Patient on the Slippery Slope," *Hastings Center Report* (July–August, 1994): 6–12.

Fitzgerald, Joan. "Better-Paid Caregivers, Better Care," *The American Prospect* (May 21, 2001): 30–32.

Francis, Leslie Pickering. "Decisionmaking at the End of Life: Patients with Alzheimer's or Other Dementias," *Georgia Law Review* 35(2) (2001): 539-92.

Fraser, Nancy, and Linda Gordon. "A Genealogy of Dependency: Tracing a Keyword of the U.S. Welfare State," *Signs: Journal of Women and Culture* 19 (Winter 1994): 309–36.

Hughes, Kathryn. *George Eliot: The Last Victorian* (London: Fourth Estate, 1998).

Kittay, Eva Feder. *Love's Labor: Essays on Women, Equality, and Dependency* (New York: Routledge, 1999).

Kuttner, Robert. "Budget with Care," *The American Prospect* (May 21, 2001): 4.

Martin, Richard J., and Stephen G. Post. "Human Dignity, Dementia, and the Moral Basis of Caregiving," in Binstock, Post, and Whitehouse, *Dementia and Aging*, 55–68.

Moody, Harry R. "A Critical View of Ethical Dilemmas in Dementia," in Binstock, Post, and Whitehouse, 86–100.

Noddings, Nel. *Caring: a Feminine Approach to Ethics and Moral Education* (Berkeley: University of California Press, 1984).

Ozick, Cynthia. "The Buried Life," *The New Yorker* (October 2, 2000): 116–27.

Ruddick, Sara. *Maternal Thinking: Toward a Politics of Peace* (New York: Ballantine, 1989).

Trilling, Lionel. "Mansfield Park," *Partisan Review* 21 (1954): 492-511.

Although I have not cited any of her articles, my conversations with Adrienne Asch over the years have been invaluable in understanding the experience and politics of disability.

Caregivers' Advice

Driscoll, Eileen H. *Alzheimer's: A Handbook for the Caretaker* (Boston: Branden Books, 1994).

Mace, Nancy L., and Peter V. Rabins. *The 36–Hour Day* (New York: Warner Books, 1992).

Roche, Lyn. *Coping with Caring: Daily Reflections for Alzheimer's Caregivers* (Forest Knolls, CA: Elder Books, 1996).

For caregivers' testimony and ongoing information on caregivers' support, scientific developments and clinical trials, and the political developments around Alzheimer's and aging, I have referred over the years to the Alzheimer's Association website and the newsletters of the New York and Vermont chapters of the Alzheimer's Association, as well as those of the AARP.

Acknowledgments

MANY THANKS to Ann Snitow, Deborah Stead, and Paul Cillo, who read the manuscript with generosity and ruthlessness; to Joy Harris, for constancy in an inconstant time; and to my mother, for stepping aside and letting me write this book.

About the Author

OVER THE PAST TWENTY-FIVE YEARS, Judith Levine has written about the ways in which culture, politics, and history are enacted in people's intimate lives. Her articles and essays have appeared in dozens of national publications, including *Harper's*, *The New York Times*, and *salon.com*. Her other books include *My Enemy, My Love: Women, Masculinity, and the Dilemmas of Gender* and *Harmful to Minors: The Perils of Protecting Children from Sex*, which was awarded the *Los Angeles Times* Book Prize in 2002. Levine lives in Brooklyn, New York, and Hardwick, Vermont.